# Stayir

CW00428940

# Play......

## and other amusing diversions from the primary classroom

# David Critchley

The author has spent all his working life in the field of education. Twenty-eight years as a primary school practitioner were followed by several more as Senior University Lecturer attempting to pass on a knowledge & understanding of the profession to the next generation of teachers. The experiences from across this time form the basis of this first instalment of tales from the classroom, as David chronicles the tribulations facing a newly qualified teacher in the 1970s.

Any similarity between the characters within this book, including the names used, and any actual person, is entirely coincidental.

First published Summer 2013

Then the whining school-boy, with his satchel,
And shining morning face, creeping like snail
Unwillingly to school. – *As You Like It Act II sc. VII.*

## Chapter One – We Three Kings.

It was definitely Christmas that much was clearly obvious, even to the untrained eye. Over in the far corner of the school hall, a twisted spiral of bright tinfoil, fashioned by eager little fingers into what had been ambitiously billed as: *a festive garland,* had become detached from the piece of dusty sellotape still clinging to the flex above the light fitting. The garland now trailed behind the wall bars and had come to rest across the tower of well-thumbed hymnbooks, piled ready and waiting for tomorrow morning's assembly. No, wait a minute, wait a minute, what am I thinking of? Tomorrow's Wednesday, when assembly is always replaced by hymn practice and of course at this time of year carols will obviously take the place of hymns, and, if I'm not mistaken – tomorrow is indeed my turn to lead that joyous mid-week-whole-school-singalong extravaganza. A glance at my watch also reminded me that this event was now scheduled to commence in around fifteen hours' time.

It was pitch black outside – nothing unusual there, it being 6pm in mid-December – I was knackered, the caretaker was mutinous and to be honest, we'd both rather have been elsewhere as it had been a very long day for the pair of us. Still, Nativity backcloths don't paint themselves you know. Perched on the corner of the stage blocks, surrounded by a dozen jam jars of steadily congealing paint in a range of colours, I stood back with pride to survey the masterpiece now nearing completion. It was - even if I do say so myself – pretty damned impressive. I mean if you screwed your eyes up a bit, switched off the fairy lights, shut out the sound of the rogue Honda 50 currently revving noisily across the school field with three teenagers on board, and instead replaced all this with a gentle desert breeze, I'll swear you really could *actually be* on the plains around Bethlehem.

Advent had seen me repeatedly experiment with several different mixes of paint for this mammoth task. Get it too gloopy and you needed a trowel to apply it, whereas too runny meant it would cascade down your arm in waves to ruin a perfectly good shirt. No, they don't teach you stuff like that at Training College, however I did begin to understand the wisdom of what my Education tutor had been banging on about for three years: "Never forget David, it is essential to ensure an appropriate consistency when working in school."

Many indoor games had now been completely prohibited in the hall until further notice in order to avoid the heartache of a wayward bean bag taking out the guiding star as it twinkled above the door to the sports cupboard or punching a hole in the 'No Vacancies' sign on the door of the Inn. Mind you to be honest, PE lessons were pretty much off limits anyway during the whole of the festive season as most afternoons would see the hall floor littered with an assortment of restless shepherds pulling hideous faces and making rude gestures at members of the Deputy Head's elite percussion group as they sat, relentlessly coshing chime bars into a state of submission.

Through the open door to my left I could see the approaching caretaker, wistfully pushing a mop in front of him as he trudged the quarry tiles of the junior corridor, extinguishing classroom lights as he passed by each doorway. He wasn't happy, that much I could tell even from this distance. A song was never far from Bill's lips when things were going well. More often than not his ballad of choice was: *Knock Three Times on the Ceiling* although for the past fortnight this had been replaced by Mud's: *Lonely this Christmas,* the ballad hotly tipped to be this year's Festive No. 1. Right now though the corridor was quiet as the grave and any moment it would be my turn to be put in the dark.

For the last hour I had been frantically multitasking, dividing my time between inking in the midnight sky of Judea (please God don't let anyone need any blue powder paint between now and next Spring) and marking Standard Two's writing books. The clock was definitely against me if I was to finish

5

the final one before Bill arrived, and looking down, I noticed this last book belonged to the new girl, only arrived in school this morning after moving from Leeds. She'd cried pretty much non-stop since being pushed in through the classroom door by her mum at 9:30 and in a bid to appease her, I'd dangled the reward of an uninterrupted half-hour with the Lego box should she manage to complete a short piece of writing describing something / anything she'd done recently in her spare time.

Call it intuition if you will, or possibly *Probationer Teacher's premonition*, but looking at it now in the twilight, there was definitely something about that book's front cover that failed to instill a sense of confidence regarding the quality of what might actually lie within. Maybe it was the child's fairly sketchy familiarity with the use of capital letters that did it, or possibly her aborted attempt at completing her own surname, I can't be certain. Or perhaps I'm just being picky and judgmental, I mean who knows, that could very well be how *Angela* is spelled over in Yorkshire, so hey, let's give the kid a chance for Heaven's sake, I mean it's Christmas after all. So, having purged my mind free of all unfounded presumption, I picked up my marking pen and turned to the opening page:

we orl went to my granse too lok at ur tre and I ad sevn minge pisers and afftur I wus sik

The hall lights went out with a resounding 'click' and I could read no further.

- - o O o - -

Actually there was no more to read, as that was it, the sum total of her morning's work. Obviously, given her age and standing within the school community, it was not exactly a major literary triumph, but we all have different talents and boy, could she work that Lego. I was studying the book once

6

again in an attempt to fully decipher its content, this time by the light of a reading lamp whilst sitting up in bed at home. Fuelled by exhaustion, bizarre images of wartime Britain played games with what remained of my consciousness – now for example I was actually tucked up in a Bletchley Park attic, frantically wrestling with the Enigma Code as bombs fell in the distance onto The East End, before I fell too, into the very deepest pit of sleep.

The long, long school day that had begun with my sharing a staffroom pot of tea with Bill around 7:30 a.m. had ended with us come together once again to share refreshment, this time in the tap room of the local pub as I waited for my bus home. The status quo had again been restored, evidenced by the few bars of *Mary's Boy Child* being hummed by Bill in between grateful sips at his pint of Mild.

It had taken only a matter of weeks into my first term of teaching to understand the real pecking order in terms of staff importance – yes, yes Headteacher, Deputy Head, Scale III teachers etc all had their part to play of course blah, blah, but other key movers and shakers within school were undoubtedly the Caretaker and his gallant band of cleaners. I had soon learned to keep on the right side of these good folks and so I viewed the odd pint or two of the local brewery's best efforts to be a sound investment. It's essential also of course, not to overlook the infantry troops either, and so I'd remembered to slip a tinsel-topped bottle of *Charlie* by Revlon into the pocket of Ada's overalls as she bent to sweep pencil shavings from my classroom floor at the close of the day.

I was actually quite incredulous to realise it was Christmas to be honest. The wonder and amazement lay not so much in the fact that Christmas was here in December you understand, but more that December and its attendant celebration had arrived quite so quickly. My first term of teaching was pretty much at an end already – another hundred and twenty or so of the same and I'd be almost eligible for retirement with any luck – where does the time go to?

- - o O o - -

Probably to the same place that three years at Training College had recently disappeared to I guess. It seemed but a fortnight ago surely since I'd arrived at Christ's College Liverpool, pony-tailed, pimply of face, loon-panted and full of trepidation as I prepared to face the rigour of deeper academic engagement.

Ahh those gloriously heady days of 1971. The blazer and satchel had only recently been abandoned and uncertainty lay ahead during a time of monumental change on the world stage. We had new currency to cope with for example. Indeed with a pint of Whitbread Trophy costing just eleven of our new pence, the opening weeks of Higher Education remain to this very day but a gentle haze. Actually I only frequented the College Social Club in order to escape the strains of Leonard Cohen's *Songs of Love & Hate* wafting incessantly along the top corridor of Sherwin Hall, played at maximum decibels by the manic depressive occupying the end room. Those of us with a penchant for more lively offerings by the likes of Rod Stewart, Roxy Music or even *Kraftwerk* ... had rechristened all Leonard's efforts: "Music for Slashing Your Wrists To."

Ted Heath was in number 10, *Love Story* played nightly to sobbing couples at the Odeon, Apollo 14 was off to the moon, Arsenal won the double, Swiss women finally got the right to vote, Jim Morrison had been found dead in his bath and China was allowed into the United Nations. Closer to home however, there was also a good deal of celebration to greet the momentous news that Christ's College had finally secured *Mixed Visiting Rights.*

It was most definitely a different world back then in everyone's favourite Catholic College of Education. Yes,

8

there were male and female students on campus but they were fiercely segregated in terms of their accommodation. Following tense discussions between representatives of the Student's Union and the College Fathers, the unthinkable news broke to widespread acclaim that henceforth, the twain *shall* indeed meet after all. Women were to be allowed to visit the chaps in their rooms and indeed vice-versa – an unbelievable display of liberal mindedness at the start of a new decade – however there were several strings attached to this undeniable largesse, including for example:

Rule 1: Any mixed visiting could only take place between the hours of 1pm and 7:30 pm daily.

Rule 2: Visitors to rooms must only be seated using the *mixed visiting stool* provided and must not sit on bed or easy chair.

Rule 3: Alcohol is forbidden in any hall of residence room at such times.

It's a well-known adage however that rules are made to be broken and so a favourite late-night activity was to set off the fire alarm in order to play *count the nighties* standing shivering at the assembly point on the car park.

*(A lifetime later when I myself assumed the role of Senior Lecturer at Christ's College - aka Liverpool Hope University – I watched with some sadness as the old Halls of Residence were demolished. Just before the demise of our wonderful places of residence, when Newman, Andrew & Sherwin Halls would be turned into piles of rubble and hardcore, I sneaked a peek into one of the ground floor rooms. In accommodation terms little had changed during the intervening thirty-odd years. A bed, bookshelf, armchair, desk, along with a potentially lethal anglepoise-effect lamp remained still, whilst centre-stage was the ultimate challenge for students of both genders and site of many an afternoon /*

*early evening acrobatically amorous encounter – the mixed visiting stool.)*

For the most part I enjoyed my time at Christ's College. The work got done on time (mostly) and my time on Teaching Practice (TP) was pretty joyous, with one exception. As my course was designated *Primary / Secondary Teaching*, I had the opportunity to sample school life in both phases. During second year I was allocated to a boys' secondary school in a district of Liverpool undergoing a demolition and re-housing programme, meaning many of the formerly vibrant streets surrounding the school were now just piles of rubble. On the plus side, this resulted in small class sizes, but the kids in there, many of whom were returning to deserted streets and neighbouring properties with bricked-up windows and corrugated iron roofs each evening, were absolutely hard as nails.

As a student of English, I was expected to light the fire of literary appreciation amongst the set of 11-14 year olds in my charge and was at a bit of a loss as to which books might be well-received to be honest. I turned to my Head of Department for assistance in choosing something appropriate and indeed it was at this early stage of my career that I learned the essential lesson which has stayed with me ever since, namely: 'if ever you think you may not like the answer, don't ask the question in the first place.'

I can remember sitting in his room surrounded by shelves groaning under the weight of leather-bound masterpieces and blinking in total disbelief as he smiled at me over the top of his heavy-framed glasses before announcing with absolute conviction:

"Why David, my dear boy, you simply **must** build your programme of work around Chaucer's Canterbury Tales."

"Really?" was the best I could manage in terms of a coherent reply as I tried to picture *Koogie*, the gold-medal-winning 13 year old middleweight darling head-case of the North Liverpool & District Boxing fraternity, grappling with the challenge of 14<sup>th</sup> Century literature.

"Why of course – it's simply too, too perfect. How they'll love reading extracts written in the original middle-English, making comparisons with the language we use today. Take *The Knight's Tale* for example – filled as it is with duels, bravery, imprisonment, castles – all the very stuff to fire a young man's imagination. Then there's *The Wife of Bath's Tale* of course, enabling consideration of the changing role of women in society – but do be careful David to avoid the er, how shall I put it – the more *saucy* aspects of the story."

Actually I thought, *saucy* might be more up Koogie's street than armoured sword fights and tales of derring-do. But my tutor wasn't finished yet - oh no.

"Creative writing – that's what we need more of in our schools, colourful outpourings onto the page from our legions of oft-misunderstood youth. Remember David, today's adolescents are tomorrow's writers, and sitting before you in those classes each day could very well be a fledgling Dickens, a Conrad, a Melville or a Hardy."

I did have serious doubts about this as a notion but nodded in mute recognition of his sentiments as his enthusiasm for this project gathered momentum.

"Oh my boy I can see it now," he went on, rather I thought in the manner of an unsupervised steam-roller careering along a busy street towards certain disaster. "After learning the basic structure of the Tales themselves they will go on to construct their very own modern-day, urban versions, chronicling in narrative form, the frustrations, the desires and the *angst* they themselves are experiencing on a daily basis. Through this you will learn so much about those young men both as individuals and – for want of a better term – as a *species*."

As the room fell silent once more, I ventured a comment:

"Are you really sure about this, I mean…"

"Absolutely certain," he interrupted with an upraised palm of reassurance, "trust me!"

And like a fool I did.

Squadrons of heavyweight butterflies charged around my intestines on the Sunday evening before my first day in the school, despite a fairly extensive procedure of preparation. The C&A suit was pressed, the shoes were polished, and my tie was draped casually across the door handle. I'd even gone as far as having my hair trimmed, the normally exuberant locks teased instead into a much softer look, giving me I mused, turning first this way and then that, in front of the mirror, more than a hint of the *David Cassidy.*

Despite turning in for an uncharacteristically early night, Leonard Cohen was as nocturnally active as ever, so with sleep difficult to come by, 9pm saw me returned to the Social Club for a nightcap instead. Of course as was usual, one thing led to another, meaning the planned *quiet pint* soon morphed instead into an impromptu darts tournament followed by a fiercely contested game of fizz-buzz and ensured a fairly bleary demeanour at breakfast in the refectory next day.

- - o O o - -

Stepping down from the bus that Monday morning in 1972, I picked my way through the deserted streets of inner city Liverpool and in through the peeling paintwork of the school front door. Even though I'd noticed not a soul around on the short walk, I removed my mac in the staffroom to discover a *green gozzer* of quite considerable proportions had been yocked with unerring accuracy between my shoulder blades where it now sat, congealing nicely and taking the edge off my otherwise faultless sartorial elegance. Ah well, it was a welcome of sorts I suppose.

My five weeks at the school became a daily white-knuckle survival ride and battle of wills with the campaign-hardened troops lounging before me. Whilst the majority of the boys could never be described as natural or regular readers, they turned out nonetheless to be quite enthusiastic literary critics, unafraid to voice an opinion on the quality and content of what was laid before them. My initial fears were soon realised - there was indeed but scant regard for the efforts of Sir Geoffrey Chaucer - one memorable comment summing up the whole experience for this challenging group of youngsters as I distributed duplicated sheets of his master work one rainy morning:

"Oh Christ, not more of this shite?"

Sticking to my guns I persevered as best I could, eventually reaching the point at the start of my last week, the culmination of my literary programme at which the class were set to work writing their own *tales*. After outlining the task in great detail, I fully expected to receive a mutinous chorus of catcalls and steadfast refusal to participate willingly… but amazingly, I was proved wrong. As usual, to a man, (and I'm ashamed to say I do include myself in this) every face in the room turned towards Koogie in order to check his reaction as he was the man to provide a clear lead with regard to the future success – or otherwise - of the lesson. On this occasion his face was impassive and expressionless for a few moments beneath that monumental afro-cut until, with a barely perceptible shrug of the shoulders, he picked up a biro and began to write, leaving his disciples with little option but meekly to follow his cue.

Thinking that I had finally managed to successfully engage with their collective creative nerve, I dropped my guard and relaxed at a table to the rear of the class, there to revel in the unusual sight of my group gainfully and sedately employed. The euphoria of my *Mr. Chips* moment continued for the next twenty minutes or so until, whilst wary of possibly breaking the spell, I thought that I'd better go and do the rounds to assess their efforts. Where better to start thought I, than with the great man himself, there to take the opportunity of heaping him with praise for his achievements thus far.

Approaching Koogie's table with the assured manner of one who has faced adversity and found himself up to the task, I crouched beside that exuberant mop of hair before enquiring with misplaced confidence:

"So Koogie," (surely the moment had arrived in our relationship when I could relax into such informality) "and so what's your tale about then?"

After calmly placing a well-chewed biro into the groove at the top of his desk, he stretched his long legs out in front before clasping his hands together behind his head and relaxing into story-teller mode. All around the room a dozen pens fell similarly idle as the class tuned into our conversation with obvious relish.

"Right den,'" he began, "dis is called De Docker's Tale."

"Oh excellent," was my supportive comment, "just summarise the plot for me briefly please."

"Well, it's about when dis fair-haired student teacher is standing at de bus stop one night after school on his way back to College - and *incidentally*", he went on, "we know just where dat college is..."

*Incidentally?*... he used *'incidentally.'* I was absolutely thrilled, the boy was including adverbs in his language.

"...any road, when de docker and his mates come round de corner and see him standing dere with his briefcase..."

"Go on, go on," I encouraged.

"Well to be honest, that's pretty much it," went on Koogie in his matter-of-fact manner, "dey just walk over and give the poor sod a bloody good kickin'!"

This was the point at which I realised that maybe High School antics weren't really my cup of tea and acknowledged with some relief that I may be much better suited to the Primary sector.

- - o O o - -

In a flash the whole three-year party was over and the remainder of my higher education journey evaporated pretty much before my eyes. There was no graduation ball, no tasteless, overblown prom night to mark its passing, no photographs to return to and treasure in the years to come. Neither was there a ceremonial exchange of e-mail addresses / social network details to enable a continuation of contact when we had all passed into the great beyond - even the arrival of the very first, breeze-block-sized mobile phones was some dozen or so years away yet. This was 1974, when communication was limited to either snail mail or no mail.

After spending my final morning re-sitting the Catholic Teacher's Certificate exam for the third time, I met up with the rest of my small but select group of chums in the Blue Common Room as we prepared to spend our final hours together. This is where we'd spent a good deal of our leisure time, engrossed nightly in one or other of the games and innocent pursuits on offer. There, beside the door to the Students Union office, was the jukebox, which at that moment was belting out *Homely Girl* by the Chi-lites. As it played, surely every red-blooded male within earshot was taken back to that hallowed Thursday evening some weeks before when, clustered in an unseemly scrummage around the communal TV for Top of the Pops, we delighted at the sight of *Pan's People* cavorting to this very song, clad only in matching fur-trimmed baby doll nighties – a memorable moment in our College lives for sure.

For old times' sake we engaged now in a three-cornered competition in our favoured disciplines for the last time, opening with a four-handed game of table football – 'it's all in the wrist action' – before moving across to the pool table. This afternoon though it would have to be the straight version of the game, and not the *strip snooker* alternative which had often provided so much hilarity for both players and spectators alike in the wee small hours.

The climax of the sporting action centred of course around everyone's favourite video game: *PONG!* by Atari. Opposing players rotated a silver control wheel, which moved an electronic ping pong *bat* up and down vertically to strike the *ball* – all in glorious black & white of course – these were simpler, happier days surely - pass me another can of *Top-deck Shandy* and let's get going.

From there it was back up to our rooms to prepare for the next leg of our valedictory tour. Switching on the elderly Dansette that had seen me through so many late-evening sessions in number 65 Sherwin Halll I scanned my collection of LPs, now carefully boxed for the journey home, in search of something appropriate. I was feeling in melancholy mood, (but dear God no more Leonard Cohen please) and so went for a particular favourite from sixth-form days, allowing Neil Young's *After the Goldrush* to become the soundtrack to this momentous occasion. As the crackles and hisses of the run-in were replaced by that reedy voice and the opening strains of *Tell me Why* filled the room, I stood before my open wardrobe and considered the options.

Twenty minutes later, it was surely nothing less than a fashion demi-god that was heading back out through the door once more. A pair of bottle green needlecord flares, (courtesy of *Way-in,* Kendal's, Manchester) was teamed with my beloved black & white Budgie jacket - purchased on the back of a not inconsiderable National Westminster Bank overdraft - from *Harry Fenton* in town. Accessories included faux-crocodile platform shoes, a lilac, floral print shirt with penny collar, and the obligatory palmful of *Hai Karate* applied liberally to all parts of the ensemble. Preened to perfection, I was ready to meet my public.

We were off into town. Specifically we were off to visit our personalised back catalogue of Liverpool monuments in order to say our goodbyes. The Anglican Cathedral would feature in this list obviously, along with the naked man outside Lewis's. The Walker Art Gallery would be there too, noted for its glorious, technicolour images in front of which we'd passed many a rainy afternoon, and how could we forget *The Jacey Cinema* on Clayton Square, also with its glorious, technicolour images in front of which we'd passed many a rainy afternoon, (grubby overcoat not absolutely essential for this one but such a garment did enable clients to blend in more easily.) Tonight though we were focused instead on several other destinations that we'd come to know rather more intimately.

Transport down into town came courtesy of a black cab, flagged down on Woolton Road and as the four of us piled into the back, the driver issued his usual warning:

"Now you're not gonna throw up are you lads, 'cos any mess in the back'll cost you ten pound awright?"

No worries, it would be most unusual for the outward leg of the trip to cause any such problems, so instead we stated our destination with the confidence that familiarity brings:

"Tuebrook please – The Painted Wagon."
Situated in the old Carlton Cinema beside the roundabout, I'll never really be able to explain the appeal of this place. Sure, there were western saloon type swing doors and a few tacky plastic cowboy artefacts but the beer was lousy, the music awful and the soles of your shoes would always stick to the

carpet. Somehow though, "The Wagon" as we affectionately referred to it had a special place in our hearts and had been the location for many a lunchtime pint. Time to supp up now though and move on.

Another cab journey, another trip down memory lane or, to be precise, down Hardman Street instead. Here we mounted the steps and in through the pseudo-classical arch of *O'Connor's Tavern* (or simply *O'C's* to we in the know) where we once saw Adrian Henri after a Scouse Poets recital at the Philharmonic. Only time for a half in there tonight though, (so many sights, so little time) before a lung-busting gallop back up the hill and along Hope Street to The Augustus John (The A.J.) and a pint of Cain's.

As we were now getting in the party mood, there was bound to be some difference of opinion concerning the remaining venues. Common sense prevailed however during the debate, as we all recognised that visiting Yates's Wine Lodge would mean several glasses of *Aussie White* which would then be certain to bring the evening to a premature close as it had done on numerous occasions past. We were in agreement then – time for food instead.

Arriving at the Pier Head, the weather took a definite turn for the worse and drapes of rain coming off the river pebble-dashed our faces as we battled towards our all-time favourite eatery. We'd been visiting *The River Rooms* Berni Inn overlooking the Mersey on a twice-termly basis for three years, and so simply had to make this the venue for tonight's last supper. With heads bowed down against the elements, we were unable to take in the full majesty of the building, completed as it was in an early lavatorial / monstrous carbuncle architectural style. Whoever sanctioned the siting of this planning monstrosity within spitting distance of the waterfront's Three Graces, obviously had an active sense of humour.

What it lacked in aesthetic appeal however, it most certainly made up for in terms of the dishes on offer and as we strolled towards our waiting table, we just felt so sophisticated. The menu never changed, meaning diners there could always feel comfortable with the fare on offer, unless that is you were in search of *balsamic crushed potatoes* or *lentil crusted Queen scallops with a morel coulis*. This was the 1974 version of haute cuisine remember, there were still some years to wait yet for example before man would discover The Rocket Salad.

We all had our own favourite three courses, (there were *always* three courses) meaning we could actually dispense with the menus altogether and just order from memory – told you we were sophisticated. For me it would have to be a prawn cocktail for openers, how I loved those clammy little grey crustaceans perched on a bed of shredded lettuce in a sundae dish topped off with a generous gob of sickly sweet Marie-Rose sauce – pure magic. Main course would be sirloin steak, *well done* of course, and accompanied by chips, garden peas, fried tomato and…(roll on the drums and head lowered in reverence)…battered onion rings. Dessert - as if you needed to ask – was a hefty wedge of Black Forest Gateau.

My saliva glands were positively aglow as I sat back to await the arrival of this culinary extravaganza and so decided to treat myself to a little aperitif:

"Could you bring us a pint of brown & bitter please love?"

- - o O o - -

Two bottles of Mateus Rose and one of Blue Nun ensured there was an atmosphere of mellow satisfaction around the table after the clearing of the crockery. The quality of the food had been, we agreed, simply first-class and as for the skills of the team serving us – truly unbelievable.

To illustrate their capabilities, Paul hoisted the glass containing his Irish coffee and indicated the top layer of cream, floating there as it did, spirit-level-steady with no trace drifting down into the darkness of the coffee below.

"Now that's *class* that is," he ventured, " that, might I say, is the mark of an expert, these guys are true professionals."

With his eyes closed in anticipation, he raised the glass to his lips - murmured a little prayer of thanks – sipped and spluttered – before exclaiming:

"Ahh - she didn't put sugar in!"

The evening was well advanced as we turned back out into a Mersey monsoon, but at least taxis were plentiful as we headed back up towards town once again, and whilst I'd dearly love to give details concerning the antics associated with the final leg of our farewell celebration, this simply isn't possible. I can remember getting out of the cab on Dale Street, I can remember legging it into the *Pez Espada* nightclub out of the rain, I remember too buying the first round of drinks – four Tia Maria & Cokes, what else? – I can even remember the song that was playing as we stood by the bar – *Billy Don't be a Hero* by Paper Lace – but beyond that? Nothing, not even the faintest inkling surrounding the return cab journey back up to Taggart Avenue and a bed surrounded by packing cases.

## CHAPTER TWO – Offside Ref!

It was a great surprise then, after all that alcohol, to wake up free from a monumental hangover, but, following a glance at the alarm clock beside me and the familiar surroundings of my old bedroom at home, the realisation soon dawned that I had in fact just been re-living previous times throughout the night – that was *then* and indeed this was *now*, so to speak. There was just time for a quick shower and a breakfast prepared by mum before heading off for the bus into work.

Ahh the bus - the good old bright red, Lancashire United Transport double-decker. Sitting there, I began reliving memories of similar trips made daily to one school or another since the age of seven and here I was once more, relying on its services for the next chapter of my continuing educational odyssey.

This seat, I mused to myself, as I watched condensation trickle in growing rivulets down the inside of the windows, could be the very self-same seat that I sat in one grey Monday morning just nine short years ago on my way to Grammar School, clutching the Physics notebook that contained only blank pages where my completed homework about concave mirrors and focal length should have been, and predicting that I would be sorely battered for this heinous misdemeanour at some point later in the day... turned out I was indeed correct in this assumption.

Despite the bleak, drizzle-heavy wind bumbling down the elderly terraced streets of this Northern industrial town, there was a pleasantly buoyant feeling as I skimmed along the wet pavements and in through the gates of Morton Street County Primary School. Science homework and drunken Liverpool nights were all behind me now - this was a new dawn and I was loving every minute of it. As the corridor lights struggled to overcome the early morning December gloom, the only real signs of life were the strains of 'I saw Mommy kissing

Santa Claus' wafting along from the direction of the Standard 4 classroom:

With that trademark tremulous lingering on the final phrase, the singing could only belong to one person. Either Bill was in mightily good spirits this morning or he was serenading Ada from beside her mop bucket – now there was an image to conjure with. How I loved these starts to the day, when I pretty much had the place entirely to myself – wonderful times indeed.

"Morning Bill," I called through the empty school, "everything OK?"

"Morning David," came the reply from a distance, "no, not really, some little sod threw a brick through your classroom window last night, so there's glass everywhere, I'll be down to fix it in a bit."

Even that news failed to dampen my spirits, as for the time being at least, God was in his Heaven and all was right with the world. Stepping onto the freshly polished parquet of the hall, I stood to admire the now almost-completed Bethlehem backdrop and congratulated myself once more on just how well it had turned out.

"Wait 'til the children see that this morning," I announced smugly, before continuing in the direction of my classroom, my kingdom, my empire and as it turned out this morning, my scene of carnage.

As the children filed into class later the questions came thick and fast.

"What's 'appened to' window?"

"Well it's broken I'm afraid."

"Did you do it Mr. Critchley?"

"No Sean I didn't do it."

"Who broke 'window?"

"We don't know who broke it Lesley."

"I know who did it."

"Do you really Gary? Well perhaps you & I can have a little chat later on."

"Who done it Gaz? Go on tell us, tell us, was it Bozzer? I bet it wus – it wus Bozzer wun't it?"

"Class 2, I think we'd all better get to our places and settle down," mine the voice of reason.

"Will we be sent home early?"

"Angela, that's what they call *wishful thinking* I'm afraid sunshine, now get out your Christmas books and finish colouring in the Magi presenting their gifts, then cut it out and paste it in carefully whilst I call the register. Stuart, hand out the scissors please."

"Can we use felt tips Mr. Critchley?"

"Yes you can use felt tips - just this once," I sighed, a concession I have to say made against my better judgement but the silence that this simple statement engendered was sheer bliss.

True to his word Bill arrived bearing chisel, putty and a new pane of glass shortly after register was called and so we all adjourned into the hall, and left him to his hammering. Hymn practice had been brought forward and I stood at the front, ever-watchful as the other classes filed in semi-silently whilst a very scratchy rendition of Berlioz' *The Shepherd's Farewell* played on the school gramophone. Rain hammered at the high windows now but I remained in good spirits, nodding at the formidable figure of the Deputy Head as she settled at the piano and prepared to launch her traditional early morning assault of the keys.

News of the broken window had spread like wildfire and snatches of illicit conversations could be heard whispered amongst the seated children:

…"police are coming…Bozzer done it… they've stole all 'dinner money… he's gunna gerr' arrested" and then the triumphant "… **we've** used felt tips!" before I called the assembled throng to order.

Another nod, this time to the music monitors standing gossiping at the back of the hall and Berlioz was cut off in his prime with a screech of distressed vinyl.

"Good morning everyone."

I dreaded the response to this, delivered without fail every day at an inane, monotonous snail's pace, laboured and sleepy to the point of tedium:

"Good….mor-ning….Mis…ter      Critch-erley….good….mor-ning….everybody."

Without further preamble, the piano keys were thumped by way of brutal introduction and we were straight off into *We Three Kings*, everyone's favourite, cheerful little festive offering. Try as I might to suggest more lively alternatives, several key members of staff, possibly being somewhat set in their ways shall we say, insisted on persevering instead with the carols that had been ringing through this venerable establishment for the past sixty-odd years.

Funnily enough it was only now at this my first Christmas in school, that I'd realised there are actually ten verses to this song, my undoubted favourite of these coming in at number seven:

> *Myrrh is mine, its bitter perfume*
> *Breathes of life, of gathering gloom,*
> *Sorrowing, sighing, bleeding, dying*
> *Sealed in the stone-cold tomb.*

I was always tempted at the end of this bit to call out with a smile and a cheery wave of the hand: " and a Merry Christmas to you one and all, ho-ho-ho!"

The Deputy Head's one concession to festive gaiety was to end this tortuous weekly session, (go on, you try sitting cross-legged and bolt upright to "let the sound out properly," on a wooden floor for half an hour) with *Deck the Halls*, encouraging the massed choir with a shout of:

"Gaily children, **GAILY** NOW!"

before each alternate line of "Tra la la la la, la la la la."

Oh what fun!

There was just time for a prayer before leaving and following this I asked the school to remain with their hands joined and heads bowed to focus individually on something they really wanted to achieve during the day. Apart from rain still clattering at the windows, at that moment you could have heard a pin drop... until that is, someone let rip the most outrageously spectacular fart, running on as it did for several seconds and reverberating across the parquet. Suddenly, dozens of faces turned to puce with the agony of holding in laughter whilst all around, countless fists were pressed hard into their owners' mouths. I nodded again to the giggling girls at the rear and Hector Berlioz came to the rescue, those soaring notes masking the fake choking sounds of hysterical Standard 4 boys as they clawed at their throats and pretended to be gassed. Ah yes, you can't beat bodily functions for bringing the house down with ease. Subtle it may not be, but you can be assured you're always onto an audience pleaser in any Primary School setting with a good old dose of flatulence.

Bill had finished his glazing job when we returned to class, just a few wood shavings and an all-pervading smell of putty to show for his labours. As the class filed in again to sit down and make a grab for the felt tips, I was somewhat perplexed to see the Head Teacher Mr. Antrobus, (*Ray* to his friends) tagging along behind. Balding and in his early fifties I would guess, Mr. Antrobus never seemed entirely at ease in the company of children. He would make occasional visits to classes from time to time, but truth is, he always seemed much happier shut away up in his office drinking tea and shuffling papers.

"A word if I may Mr. Critchley?"

I followed him out into the corridor, curious as to what had prompted this early morning visitation.

"Just had a phone call David," he informed me, "Mr. Lawrence is coming into school to see you this afternoon."

My puzzled / blank expression was his cue to provide further info on this one.

"Lawrence? PE adviser? Scottish chap? Ah, not come across him as yet then? Part of your probationary year requires you to be observed by some of the Local Education Authority advisers from time to time – nothing to worry about, it's just a formality really – I know your worth in the school and how hard you've been working, so it will take a great deal to overturn my opinion. He'll be here to watch your afternoon PE session at 1:30."

"But the hall will be filled with shepherds this afternoon," I pointed out, "as it has been most days since the Harvest Festival elves moved out."

"Ah, of course, hadn't thought about that," the boss went on, "maybe I should have put him off, mind you, Lawrence isn't really the most *put-offable* sort of fellow to tell the truth. Oh well, there's nothing for it David, you'll have to take them out onto the field for the lesson instead."

I looked past his shoulder towards the window, down which rain continued to cascade in strengthening rivulets.

"Yes it is a tad inclement," was his understated response, "fingers crossed it bucks up a bit eh?"

And then he was gone, only to stick his head back in through the door moments later, before I'd even got as far as my desk.

"Oh, by the by, er... probably not a good idea admitting to Lawrence that PE has been an unfortunate festive casualty as of late eh? These guys can sometimes be a bit *precious* about that kind of thing you know. Anyway, good luck with it all."

Despite the Head's encouraging words, this news shook me to the core. Indeed I could feel the confidence, which had accrued following over one hundred incident-free days at the chalk face, draining away by the moment and there was a reason for this. There was but one aspect of the curriculum about which I felt decidedly flaky due to never having really seen it being taught properly, nor having attended any classes related to its delivery as part of my training programme and that subject was? Got it in one – Physical Education.

My mind was a-buzz as I envisaged what sort of nightmare just might lie ahead at the start of afternoon classes, but this had to go on a back burner in the short term, as the start of the morning's English lesson was already well overdue.

The books which I'd marked on the stage during last night's painting session were doled out to the class and I asked the children to turn to their last efforts and read the comments I'd made about their work, along with instruction to re-visit the stories themselves and check if there was anything they might like to improve upon before finishing them off. The main focus of the lesson had been to write using a range of describing words in order to bring the stories rather more to life and I was pleased to note that several class members had really got to grips with this, one or two children busily scattering adjectives quite liberally throughout their work. A case in point being one of my real star pupils who was soon beside my desk seeking clarification with regard to what I'd written in her book.

"Mr. Critchley," she began, before coming straight to the point, "I don't really understand what you mean here," and she laid the open pages before me.

I was slightly embarrassed to note a smudge of blue paint in her margin, but tried instead to focus on the comment in red ink that I'd written beneath the story:

*Stephanie this is a really good effort, but I think it would sound even better still with a few less adjectives, don't you?*

"Well you see," I began, "er… let's take one of your sentences eh, maybe… this one here where you describe the dragon. Would you like to read it out for me and see how it sounds?"

After pulling the book closer towards herself in order to better see the text, she did just as I'd asked:

"The huge, scarlet, scaly, fierce, noisy, fiery dragon raised his menacing, wicked, pointed, terrifying, muscular tail high above his big, enormous, gigantic, massive, scary head and roared at me."

"Now Steph, d'you see what I mean?"

Her puzzled expression and the head tilted questioningly to one side, suggested that actually no, she didn't see much at all wrong with what she'd written.

"Well it's just that when using adjectives – and you've done that beautifully Steph I have to say, don't get me wrong – it's not always a good idea to use too many all at one go, maybe just two or three in each sentence is plenty – see?"

Her expression changed to one of bemused bewilderment and I could half imagine her thinking to herself: just what in God's name does this man want? "Use more adjectives," he told us and now I've done what he said and he's still not happy.

Glumly picking up her book she trudged back to the desk she shared with the new girl from Leeds and then glanced over at what I'd written beneath her neighbour Angela's rather less extensive literary efforts:

*Fantastic work Angela, I'm really pleased with what you've achieved on your first day, very well done.*

And I'd even applied a small silver foil star to the page, a gesture of encouragement, which in hindsight, was possibly rather extravagantly generous. Angela smiled blankly before turning the page fully towards Stephanie and enquiring:

"What's it say Steph?"

I wasn't quite able to hear Stephanie's disconsolate reply to her new classmate, but it might very well have been something to the order of:

"It says - *there's no bloody justice in this world Angela love!*"

The rain continued to bash the windows as the sky outside grew yet darker still and I took this to be an omen. In a bid to banish thoughts of the afternoon's forthcoming physical education pantomime, I thought I'd check on Angela's reading standard, especially important I felt, as no reports or records concerning the child's abilities had thus far found their way here across The Pennines. Selecting a range of *Ladybird Readers* from the bookshelf, I tried to predict which level would be most appropriate for the child. To be honest, I found this entire set of books to be quite mind-numbingly dull. I mean, a Reading Scheme is surely designed to fire a love of the written word in the hearts of young people, and in my opinion, the antics of Peter & Jane in these rather stilted little volumes fell some considerable way short of such a worthy goal.

A wry smile crossed my face as I flicked through the books and marvelled once again at the hilariously sugar-sweet, middle-class vision of home life as portrayed so vividly via the illustrations. There was Peter for example, playing placidly with an extensive train set laid out on the toy room floor, whilst daddy looked on benignly from behind his newspaper. Over the page Jane clapped her hands gleefully at the sight of the trayful of rosy toffee apples she'd successfully created beside mummy in their spotless kitchen. In other volumes, the children were on holiday – striding away through litter-free woodland, cheerfully tossing a stick for *Pat*, their faithful and improbably named Irish Setter – blessed as he was with a well-groomed, auburn coat glossy enough to see your own reflection in, or they were instead to be seen skimming across crystal clear coastal waters in a speedboat whilst flying a home-made kite from the stern.

Meanwhile back in the real world, ie the one located right outside the school gates, the one which seemed completely drained of the technicolour lifestyle so taken for granted by

Jane and brother Peter, things were very, very different. It was a tough area we were in, mostly of social housing estates, the odd corner shop and the pubs in which an evening's entertainment revolved around several pints of mild and a game of dominoes. Whole rows of adjacent terraced houses were earmarked for demolition and those that didn't have the doorways bricked up, made ideal playgrounds - ripe for after school exploration away from the guiding hand of *mummy & daddy*. Mind you, scrambling around in the fibreglass-filled loft space of deserted former homes or prising copper pipes out of the walls to sell on to the scrapman was surely preferable to the alternative. Spending leisure hours on the pavements bordering the busy road running beside the school railings had resulted in the untimely demise of several pupils over the years, poor souls fallen victim to the passing traffic which always hurtled by – terribly sad. Unemployment may have been high and money was always certainly scarce for the majority, but these children it has to be said were an absolute delight to spend time with.

So which book should I try and tempt Angela with this morning I wondered? Well *12b – Mountain Adventure* was pretty much *top of the shop* stuff, even Stephanie hadn't reached such dizzy heights as yet. In this one, Jane and Peter had become independent adolescents now, albeit with pearly teeth and faultless complexions, busily cooking breakfast outside their tent on the hillside before coming to the aid of a sheep that had fallen into a crevasse, finally managing to hoist the creature up to safety using a rope from Peter's haversack. Jane's backpack meanwhile would no doubt have been filled with pamphlets on wild flowers, sachets of home made pot-pourri, knitting patterns and possibly an abandoned kitten.

No, let's not push the child too fast eh? I decided to start instead at the other end of the scale and opened up book *1a – Play With Us.* After calling Angela out to my desk, the book was opened at random and we jumped straight in. She struggled with the simple, printed text on the page however, and, whether through shyness or a profound lack of ability, was unable to read it through aloud.

*"Consider the use of context and picture cues to help the reluctant reader decode text..."* the voice of my college education tutor came winging back through the mist, and I decided to put this theory to the test now.

"So Angela, what can you see happening in the picture?" I asked.

"She's on 'swing,'" was the simple reply.

No argument there. Jane was indeed *on 'swing*, clad in a spotless white dress teamed with bright yellow cardie, her blonde hair blowing in the breeze, she laughed gaily beneath a cloudless, blue sky. Peter meanwhile stood dutifully to the rear, also grinning broadly as he joined in the fun to push his sister.

"So what might they be saying do you think Angela?"

My question was met with a puzzled look as she turned this one over in her mind and I tried again:

"Do *you* have a brother Angela?"

"Yiss," she replied, "our Frank."

"And do you and Frank ever go to the park?"

'We do sometimes when we stop at gran's."

"Well let's pretend this is you and your brother in the park, d'you like being on the swings?"

'Yeah," this time she was almost animated in her response, "I can go dead high me."

"Can you now?" I encouraged, "so if you were there, swinging really high, what d'you think your Frank might be saying to you?"
She thought really hard about this one, before starting to speak then stopping again.

"Go on, go on," mine the voice of encouragement once more, "what would your Frank say to you?"

Finally, plucking up the courage to speak, she blurted out a response which to be honest, I really hadn't seen coming:

"Frank 'ud say – *gerroff that bloody swing, it's **my** go now!*"

- - o O o - -

Just before breaktime there was a knock at the door and one of the girls from top class popped in to announce that it would be an indoor playtime due to the weather and also to enquire waitress-like if I'd like tea or coffee, milk and sugar etc. The rain, if anything, was now falling even harder than ever and my mood suddenly began to brighten. With the hall out of action, it would surely be complete madness to take a class of children out for PE in a monsoon wouldn't it? Yes that's certainly the way forward in any difficult situation I thought – bank on an afternoon cloudburst – job done. Looking through the window I smiled broadly at the ponds and mini-lakes pooling on the playground and even managed a cheery thumbs-up to Bill who had the hood up on his oilskins as he busied himself with a set of drain rods and an open manhole.

After collecting in the scissors from this morning's lesson and ensuring these were put out of harm's way in the cupboard, (I'd learned earlier in the year that given half a chance when unsupervised, several of the girls would be only too ready to reinvent themselves as trainee hair stylists at the drop of a hat) I stepped out into the corridor to chat to colleagues and was just in time to see the Standard 4 tea monitor girls wobbling down the flight of stairs from the staffroom carrying trays of tea, coffee and biscuits for us all.

"Ah a visit from the *Lovely Lawrence* in prospect eh?" was the cheery comment passed by the *other David* from the class next door as he dunked his second custard cream. Four years my senior and therefore much more worldly-wise than little old rookie me, I'd come to appreciate the snippets of advice he often proffered and our friendship had blossomed over the months. Now he leaned in close to share yet more nuggets of wisdom:

"Don't you fret about that sour-faced Scotsman DC, the man's full of his own self-importance, a complete berk – just relax - all the time he's speaking to you, just close your eyes and picture Jimmy Krankie. And anyway," he went on," look on the bright side – the sun's coming out!"

And indeed it was – what a bugger.

What with trying to teach the rudiments of angle measuring using a giant wooden blackboard protractor with no handle, glowering angrily at the sun which was now merrily shredding the December clouds, keeping an eye on the galloping clock above the door and at the same time frantically thinking about the content of the forthcoming games lesson, the rest of the morning session passed by pretty much in the blink of an eye. The midday bell released an excited class into the unexpected lunchtime warmth and I was left alone to take stock. Finally the decision was made - *football* I thought, you can't beat a good game of football, so that's what we'll go for.

The improved weather may have come as a huge disappointment, (spring sunshine in Advent eh – what were the chances?) but sadly there was worse to come. Standing before the open cupboard in the corner of the room, I gazed in dismay at the empty space on the second shelf where my tracksuit and training shoes would normally have been had they not been taken home at the start of the week for washing. The sight of my whistle hanging lonely by its cord from a cup hook inside the door provided but scant comfort.

Suddenly I was distracted from further doom-laden visions as a banshee-like wailing out in the corridor announced the arrival of a distraught, red-eyed, Angela, shoulders hunched up to her ears as she nursed the throbbing fingers of one hand. Her speech came in strange little bursts between the sobs.

"Mi...his...his...ter...her...Cri...hi...hi...cher...lee...hee...hee"

"Why Angela what on Earth's the matter?" it was reassuring to note that even now in this time of great personal discomfort I was still able to slip readily into my well-practised, appropriately sympathetic tone of voice.

It took several valuable minutes to finally unravel the circumstances leading to the poor child's present state of distress - tears, snot and a heavy Leeds accent all playing their part in making this deciphering process such a difficult task. It turned out that Angela had been the victim of a particularly disturbing *Clackers incident* shortly after arriving on the playground. To be honest I'd seen something like this coming now for a while. Like being surrounded by a flock of demented woodpeckers, the irritating sound of several dozen pairs of plastic *Clackers'* balls rhythmically hammering together on the ends of their cords had provided the soundtrack to break times for some weeks and now it would appear we had our first injury courtesy of these devilish devices.

They'd be banned from now on, sure to be – just as conkers had been in the autumn. Initially it had been pleasing to see knots of children standing around to join in this age-old, low-tech game of skill. Unfortunately however, it only took a few days for the boys to discover a more engaging use for stringed horse-chestnuts as they charged round the yard, rather in the manner of armoured knights of old, swinging maces at the end of a chain, to *donk* the heads of unsuspecting bystanders.

Angela meanwhile had learned a lesson the hard way concerning the hazards of being blessed with a curious nature and I was willing to bet it would be quite some time before she would once again feel tempted to poke her fingers - or indeed any other body part - between the arcs of a pair of expertly operated Clackers in full spate.

- - o O o - -

My friend David was suitably supportive as lunchtime came to an end – that is to say he managed to avoid wetting himself with laughter at my sorry appearance, however as I'd been unwise enough to catch a glimpse of myself in the staffroom mirror, I was only too well aware of the reality. At any moment I was due to be paraded in front of an expert and ask to be accorded serious consideration as someone fit to further the physical education of a group of primary children. I held but slender expectation of success.

True, I had the whistle, but beyond that it wasn't a good look truth be told. Having removed my tie, (well I mean you can't wear a tie whilst teaching games can you?) I left the top shirt button fastened as protection against the stiff breeze, which had sprung up suddenly without warning. The three buttons of my C&A suit jacket were also securely done-up, but it was the waist-down bit that provided greatest cause for concern. In order to facilitate some freedom of movement, I'd tucked my suit pants into my socks, but as these were only of the short M&S variety, they provided only the most tenuous grasp on the turn-ups of my flares. Meanwhile, being blessed with rather slender ankles - a cross I've always had to bear - my lower legs slipped quite easily into the capacious zip-up platform-soled boots I'd chosen as today's footwear. Let's put it this way, I don't think Norman Hunter would have been overly concerned as, ball at my feet, I carved through the Leeds United midfield towards him. After giving a speculative toot on my whistle I was ready for action.

It was gratifying to note only minimal sniggering as I arrived back in class to call the register, and I had suspicions that much of this actually came from Noreen, the grey-haired midday supervisor who had the class all ready and seated in their places, before spluttering off to join her workmates in the corridor.

With all the appearance of an injured faun, Angela stood beside my desk still clutching her bruised fingers as she played the: *I'm not really well enough to do PE* card. No skin off my nose love, I thought and sent her off to run a fresh piece of cotton wool under the cold tap.

"Hold that on your fingers and it will help take the sting away," I advised.

I was a great believer in wet cotton wool I have to say, setting great store by that universal playground cure-all for ailments ranging from acute gravel rash through to a burst nose – magic stuff. Indeed should cotton wool be in short supply, I had heard that a well-soaked paper towel was every bit as effective in cases of extreme need.

At the command: "right everyone, start getting changed please," the class wasted absolutely no time in transforming the room into the jumble sale I'd come to know and love on a twice-weekly basis, and in the midst of this melee, the door opened and The Boss arrived to usher in my tormentor, before making a hasty exit once more. *Dismay* was an emotion I'd come to know well in recent hours and it raised its head again now that Mr. Lawrence had put in an appearance. Short in stature, shaven-headed, bull-necked and with a thistle tattoo on the wrist of his right hand, he had surely stepped straight out of Central Casting's pool of archetypal Glaswegian villains. His commanding presence benefitted it must be said, from a well-fitting tracksuit in the shade of purple that I believe is referred to as *African Violet*, which showed off a rippling, muscular physique to good effect. Faded, stripey football socks, obvious veterans of several hard-fought seasons, well-polished black training shoes, a clipboard and a no-nonsense, north-of-the border-frown completed the ensemble.

This expression turned to one of incredulity as he looked me up and down at length and I'm sure I even detected a faint shake of the head at one point. Uncertain of the correct protocol for greeting personalities of his magnitude, I prayed for some sort of distraction and this was immediately forthcoming from the back of the class. Maureen Pickavance was a complete busybody of a child, never really happy unless tittle-tattling about one or other of her colleagues and it was her indignant, wheedling little voice that sliced like a chainsaw through the chatter of the room.

"Mr. Critchley," (oh my she did sound hard-done-by.)

"Yes Maureen, what is it?" There was a palpable sense of relief on my part to be rescued in this way, but this was to be short-lived as she carried on her protest:

"Sean Bickerstaffe said he'd show me his willy if I wanted."

Cue great ribaldry and hearty guffaws from the class as a whole. Alas, 'tis true, reference to intimate body parts might even out strip flatulence in terms of its ability to render a class of primary school children totally helpless with mirth. It was time for a statesman-like intervention:

"Children, I really hope I don't have to get out my *big voice* today but I do feel that we've had quite enough silliness now, particularly as we have our Special Visitor come to join us."

At this, every face turned towards Lawrence who busied himself removing an imaginary stray fibre from his tracksuit trousers.

"Now then, let me see a lovely straight line at the door and we can go outside to start the lesson."

The whole thing was a total shambles from start to finish. True, I had expected nothing more, and so maybe I should have taken at least some small consolation from the fact there were no surprises waiting. Jogging out to the centre-spot on the field for example, my left shoe immediately fell victim to the vice-like grip of a mudhole by the touchline and I inadvertently ran on several paces with one stockinged foot. Recovering my composure, a long blast on my trusty *Acme Thunderer* at kick-off sounded professional enough I supposed, but it was also the signal for the start of unutterable chaos. The stiff breeze had escalated to a howling gale, which made the accuracy of clearance kicks from the edge of the penalty area something of a lottery and also caused my oversized suit lapels to batter both sides of my face with such vigour that at one point I thought I may lose an eye.

As the class charged around aimlessly under my direction, falling over with the relentless, depressing monotony of reluctant participants in The Battle of the Somme, I risked a surreptitious glance across at our Special Visitor standing on the sidelines. Even from this distance and through eyes blurred by wind-induced tears, I could see that he wasn't exactly enjoying the spectacle all that much as he clung grimly to his clipboard and scribbled away furiously.

The players weren't too impressed either, this I knew as a fact. The engagement quotient of Primary children is measured in direct proportion to how often they ask to be excused to the toilet. Give them felt tips, crisps, a TV programme, jelly or something else they really enjoy, and you're unlikely to see a single hand waved in the air. When something doesn't appeal to them however, there's a continuing mass exodus, seemingly in desperate need of the porcelain, and that was certainly the case here. Ever since a particularly memorable incident of incontinence in early September, I've made it a firm principle never to deny any child free and open access to the lavatory whenever requested, and that rule most certainly held firm today. Consequently there was a relentless procession from the field and across into the main body of the school throughout the lesson. Had I been paying proper attention however, I would have noticed that at one point I had in fact released six members of the same team to the toilets simultaneously, thereby causing considerable imbalance to the original numbers of fourteen-a-side. This resulted in a goal fest free-for-all in the opposition's favour, meaning the score stood at 7 : 1 as I blew the final whistle to bring down the curtain on this sorry spectacle.

In no time at all the children had changed back into assorted items of clothing plucked at random from the Junior two jumble sale piles and headed off to afternoon playtime as, in a considerably mud-spattered state, I stood in class awaiting the verdict.

Lawrence began his feedback quite calmly, rolling his *r's* in a distinctive Scottish burr, which, although not entirely unpleasant to the ear, did on occasion make it somewhat difficult to decipher exactly what was being said. I needn't have worried however, as despite this, I was left in no doubt about the underlying message. Indeed, had I been successful in following the advice DT had offered earlier, even Little Jimmy Krankie would have been forced to admit that the lesson *'wisnae exactly fan-dabi-dozi.'* Lawrence was direct and to the point:

"I came here today, fully expecting to see a games lesson being taught, and instead, I spent forty minutes standing on a field watching a really quite inept display of football refereeing."

A silent nod was my only reply as he continued.

"Wholly unacceptable Mr. Critchley, *wholly* unacceptable I have to say."

More nodding from yours truly.

"What you were doing out there," he continued, "was … well, it was like taking this pen," and at this point he held up his biro, the self-same clipboard biro that had been so frantically busy for over half an hour, "and asking the children to share it between themselves – quite ridiculous!"

To this day I don't know what on Earth came over me or prompted me to make such an ill-judged reply to the man. Maybe it was nerves, or perhaps I was attempting to lighten the mood a little, or possibly I'd just had enough for one day, I really can't tell. Anyway, for whatever reason, I said it, and the words were out of my mouth before I'd really had time to consider how they might be received:

"S'funny that Mr. Lawrence, because when I was at school, handwriting wasn't considered a team sport."

I watched amazed as his complexion underwent a miraculous and immediate change - within seconds it became almost impossible for me to see where his face ended and his tracksuit began. No more was said as he turned on his heel and exited the room, leaving me with the distinct impression that from now on I may well be a marked man.

- - o O o - -

"Didn't go well then David?" Mr. Antrobus suggested sympathetically after school.

"You could say that," I replied glumly, "what did he have to say to you if you don't mind my asking?"

"Oh not a great deal, he didn't stay more than a minute or two. He just asked me to point out to you that he's running some after school Physical Education courses next term and he fully expects to see your name at the top of the applicants' list."

Oh yes I thought, definitely a marked man.

The boss was in agreement that it had been an absolute sod of a day and so suggested that I get an early night for a change. No further encouragement was needed and so snatching up my briefcase I legged it down to the main road and managed to catch an early bus home. Less than an hour later I was sitting in an armchair, hugging a cup of tea to watch Lesley Judd light the third candle on the Blue Peter advent crown and thinking – it's amazing what you can knock together from a handful of wire coat hangers and a load of old tinsel.

## CHAPTER THREE – Jesus, Mary & Joseph.

Standing in the staff room early next morning I felt considerably better about myself and had indeed successfully managed to sweep my mind free of any remaining debris from the previous day. This may have had something to do with getting a really good night's sleep, or possibly it was instead down to my having just consumed an alarming quantity of duplicating fluid.

First session was maths and we would be continuing with our topic on measuring angles. Today the children would (in theory) be using their own protractors to calculate the angles I was now busy drawing out for them prior to copying a class set. Using special duplicating sheets with a piece of carbon paper underneath, I drew a range of these for their consideration later and even had the bright idea of using different coloured carbon undersheets in order to differentiate the complexity of the task. eg red ones for the top group, blue for the middling guys (biggest group) and green for the more academically challenged. My, was I proud of that.

The trouble with being first to use the Banda spirit duplicating machine each day was that setting the thing up to print could be a peculiarly hazardous operation. There were no default, wireless, laser / inkjet, offset, colour separated print buttons to push here oh dear me no, this was stone-age low-tech mass reproduction at its very finest. The Banda machine was fitted with a reservoir of toxic, powerfully smelling spirit, which was actually the medium that would enable the copies to be made. As the tube connecting this reservoir to the foam pads on the printing drum had perished several years ago, the only way to prime the damn thing now was to coax the fluid through by hand, or, to be more accurate, by mouth. The first you knew of your success in this process, was when the stuff suddenly hit the back of your throat without warning, an experience not unlike gargling with a particularly pungent, potentially noxious brand of aftershave.

Today I'd needed three attempts at this before decent copies started to appear off the press, and then the thing flooded, meaning all the printed sheets were absolutely sodden with spirit and I had them set out around the room to dry like a neighbourhood laundry. However as I collapsed into an armchair with a woozy head and a blinding pain behind my eyes, I was still able to admire my colour-coordinated handiwork.

The door opened and Bill entered.

"Bloody hell David it smells like a tart's boudoir in here. You been at the spirit again?"

"'Fraid so Bill," was my feeble reply.

"Well you just sit there quiet till the spots before your eyes go away and I'll make you a nice cup of tea eh? Let's get these windows open an' all - phew."


It was a bright morning and the class seemed in good spirits (well they soon would be when I gave these sheets out) as they filed into class and sat down to get out their reading books and wait for the register to be called. Moving onto the dinner register I gently reminded one or two class members that they were still in arrears with regard to the week's payment. Michelle was a persistent offender and she sidled up to my desk before sheepishly passing a scrap of paper across to me, which read:

*Mr. Critly I will send in dinner money on friday, am sorry for being late again with this. Money is tight this week, please could you lend our michelle 30p so I can buy some rusks for the baby and I will pay back on friday too.*

*yours ,*
*Mrs constantine*

I couldn't begin to imagine what Michelle's home situation must really be like but I knew for sure that the term *dysfunctional* wouldn't really come close to describing the day-to-day struggle that must go on. I felt so sorry for the child, and sadder still to think that a misplaced sense of pride on her mother's part, forbade her from taking up the option of the free school meals to which she was actually fully entitled.

"Thanks for this Michelle, I'll have a word with your mum at home time tonight. You can go back to your seat now sweetheart."

"Now then class," I went on, "It's the Christmas party next week remember" – (cue cheering and general merriment) – "now has anyone brought in their refreshments slip today?"

A couple of weeks ago they all took home a letter with end of term dates etc and this also included a return slip on which parents were asked to indicate by means of a multiple choice tick list, just what type of party food they would be sending in to supply this, the social event of the season. Devised by the Deputy Head who obviously moved in more aspirational circles than most of us mere mortals, I did express doubts about including the term *petit fours* as one of the options. As predicted this had caused widespread confusion and panic until I got the class to cross it out in pencil and change it to *little cakes* instead. The returned slips sat on the windowsill, dutifully sorted into separate piles by my trusty band of Christmas coordinators, a casual glance at this paperwork suggesting we should not really expect a balanced diet to be forthcoming.

"Well it looks as if we'll be fine for crisps next week," I pointed out to their smiling faces, " I just hope the potato farmers will be able to cope with the demand. Jelly's doing really well too – now tell me," I teased, "does anyone here really *like* jelly?"

The uproar, which greeted this question, was enormous and I smiled broadly to myself – ah bless 'em, they're like Pavlov's dogs.

"We're low on sandwiches though children, and sausage rolls aren't doing too well either so see what you can do eh?"

A hand shot into the air before we could turn our thoughts elsewhere.

"Yes Barry, what is it?"

Barry's freckled face looked most perplexed beneath his unruly shock of ginger hair – "Please Mr. Critchley, my mum says she's forgot what she said she'll send in, so please could you remind me?"

This was of course the signal for a chorus of similar requests from all corners:

"was mine sausages on sticks?..can't remember how many jellies I said…did I say beef paste or salmon?.. my mum said let her know what we're short of…" and so on and so on.

"OK, OK everyone, it's mathematics time now, we'll check through the festive menus again after break this afternoon, but this time you really must try and remember what you're told."

As expected, after handing out the angle sheets, these were pounced upon by the children and held up close to their noses, the better to savour the flowery aroma that still clung to the copies. They would do this every time without fail and I was beginning to wonder whether there was any link between their lack of success at certain tasks and their falling victims to a spirit-induced high each morning. Today's lesson went ok, even though success using the 'tractors was a bit mixed to be honest. There was also a bit of confusion as the different tasks had been outlined at the start of the lesson:

"Now then red group you're doing green sheets today with yellow and green groups both doing blue ones while the blue folks will be working on red – is that clear everybody?"

As mud; and I made a note to self that next year I really had to be more creative with regard to naming my class groups rather than just lumping them into colours. One of my colleagues for example had named hers after wild animals – plenty of opportunity for creativity there I thought in a moment of distraction as the work was being handed in. I could just picture it:

"Lemmings, please come down from the top of the wallbars - CAREFULLY if you wouldn't mind and as for you Hyenas, I'm not sure what it is you're finding so hilarious, but just calm yourselves down. Horses, come on now Horses, cheer up eh, no need for the long faces, and that group over in the corner... well...please don't do that Deer. " The possibilities were indeed endless.

I took the opportunity of a quiet moment during break to mark the children's efforts. First off the pile was Samantha's work. She was one of the less able children (Sloths group perhaps?) It was initially heartening to see that she had identified each of the angles measuring 90 degrees and had labelled these accordingly. For all the rest however, she had passed on the opportunity to actually measure them, and had instead simply written beside each: "wrong angle." Ah yes, I see where she's coming from with that one. Well there's plenty there to get my teeth into at least during the coming weeks I thought.

My friend David from next door passed en route to the staffroom and stuck his head in briefly:

"Can we get together at lunchtime DC, I've got a little project to run past you?"

How intriguing I thought, before agreeing to meet up later.

The rest of the morning session passed off fairly uneventfully as the children honed their English skills using a box of medieval torture known as *SRA*. This ghastly device was actually an ordinary-looking cardboard box housing several hundred progressively difficult, illustrated cards which the children were required to work their way through to the point of tedium. It was the very worst example of something broadly labelled *comprehension* exercises, a pastime involving the reading of an extensive passage before being confronted by endless pointless questions related to this, which then had to be answered using a complete written sentence. In its favour the thing was fairly low maintenance as the children also took out an answer card on completion of each and marked their own responses themselves.

The cards were graded and organised into different colour bands and the most exciting part of the whole performance was taking one appropriately hued pencil from the full range contained within the box, in order to colour in an individual progress record. As careless management of these often meant they'd became subsumed into the general mass of coloured pencils dispersed around the class, there was often regular consternation and cries of:

"Who's got the autumn russet pencil?" or maybe, "anybody seen citrus lime anywhere?"

The mere appearance of this dreaded box of tricks would immediately prompt groans from several quarters of the room, alongside the forlorn cry: " oh no, is it nearly playtime?" voiced despairingly from several corners of the room.

Great fun. Some children actually loved the whole thing, usually those with good reading skills anyway and a fiercely competitive nature, whilst others loathed it and referred to this weekly hour as "**S**oddin' **R**ubbish **A**ctivity" There was yet another group that passed no opinion whatsoever but, having developed sufficient sleight of hand to dip into the box and collect the answer card at the same time as the passage & questions, they made enormous progress through the whole process due to getting 100% success every single time.

Hey ho.

Being Thursday, there was a kind of unwritten rule that staff would meet together in the canteen for a shared lunch. As school was blessed with a really good cook who produced splendid meals, this was never considered a chore. David and I (DT & DC as we were known, to avoid confusion) opted for a plate of chicken and dressed salad with a side helping of what I mistakenly referred to as *home made crisps* as we were sitting down. Immediately the Deputy Head and her equally plummy sidekick paused in mid-forkful to share a knowing smile before putting me straight on that one.

"Actually David, I think you'll find that these are usually referred to as *game chips*," she purred, "Isn't that so Dorothy?"

"Indeed Eleanor," came the smiling reply, "they're normally served with any example of game fowl, hence the name you see, but are equally acceptable as accompaniment to chicken too I find."

"Well slap my thigh and call me a milkmaid's offspring," hovered briefly on the tip of my tongue at that moment, however as it was only yesterday that I learned the potential cost of sarcasm, I managed to bite my lip. Instead I made do with a thankful smile of acknowledgement and a grateful tug of my forelock as I marvelled – and not for the first time – at just how on Earth these two beings from afar had beamed down and ended up teaching in this area of the town. Who knows though, it mightn't be long before children are arriving to announce that they'll bring along seventeen packets of cheese 'n onion *game chips* to the party.

"So go on DT," I began, "what did you want to talk about then?"

"Oh yes," he replied, "I've been thinking about organising a school holiday for the top class in the summer term, but obviously I'll need some help with this, would you be interested?"

Before I'd even had time to consider a reply, Eleanor had dived in again.

"Oh David I really do feel that you should, it will be *awfully* good experience."

Alarm bells immediately began to ring, as *"it will be good experience,"* was a phrase I'd learned to be wary of for some time now. It had apparently been *really good experience* for me to singlehandedly supervise the whole school watching a travelling theatre group perform Sleeping Beauty in the hall a few weeks ago. As said Theatre Group were actually just two in number, the children were soon very confused...and mutinous. Despite rapid changes of costume and wigs, an observant and critical audience was having none of it.

"That's not 'princess, that's 'wicked witch wi' different 'air!" was an angry comment hurled accusingly from the front row by an extremely vocal tiny tot with a runny nose. Similar outrage became apparent when the realisation dawned on some that only a stick-on moustache separated the identities of Prince Charming and the grief-stricken father of Sleeping Beauty. The whole thing could have so easily got out of hand as I was forced to divide my time between reprimanding the outraged and comforting the distressed as the hall descended swiftly into anarchy & chaos.

I was confident that DT wouldn't let me down however and so agreed to be part of this adventure from the start and gave him the answer he wanted.

"Sounds good so count me in, where are we off to by the way?"

The reply was admittedly a little vague, but hey it was all a long way off as yet:
"North Wales…Youth Hostel…it'll be fab DC, trust me."

So I did.

The afternoon passed away pleasantly enough amidst a warm, festive glow. I'd brought in my cassette player from home, along with two of Mum & Dad's favourite December offerings. A quiet appreciation greeted *Herb Alpert's Tijuana Christmas* (my, how the children loved the muted brass on Little Drummer Boy) and this was followed by *A Ray Conniff Christmas*, a festive selection that surely proved to his critics once and for all that he was more than just the man responsible for *Somewhere My Love*, written to the haunting melody of *Lara's Theme* from Dr. Zhivago. To this soundtrack the children completed work on their Christmas cards, contentedly exploring just how much assorted glitter can be pasted to a folded piece of sugar paper before it is no longer capable of standing upright.

Muted conversations centred around one single topic – what they were each fully expecting to find in their Christmas stockings this year. Tuning into this I was strangely reassured to find that old favourites still enjoyed some currency in 1974, - so bikes, Lego, train sets and Barbie bits 'n bobs would have their place as ever, but there were new additions also to Santa's list. Anything *Womble* was seemingly extremely popular and there was also a place for assorted Dr. Who paraphernalia – Jon Pertwee proving to be strangely memorable in this role. Sean spoke excitedly to his group about a magic set he was hoping for, and for a moment I had a deeply disturbing vision of what exactly he might be whipping out of a hat on Boxing Day to astound his audience with. There was also talk in hushed and awed tones about a new-fangled device called a *Magna Doodle*.

A group in the corner continued putting the finishing touches to our crib figures. Construction of these had been a labour of love over what seemed like several months now, but finally it was looking as if Mary, Joseph and baby Jesus would indeed be ready to face their public before the festive period came to a close. Each figure had been created using a chicken wire frame onto which we had draped numerous layers of something called *Mod-Roc*, a sort of bandage impregnated with plaster of Paris, which after being soaked in water, sets rock hard when dry. There had been some teething problems with this medium I have to report, not the least of these being the plumbing catastrophe caused by some obsessively tidy little soul pouring a bowlful of creamy plaster down the plughole of the classroom sink at home time one Friday evening.

To be honest I would be glad to see the back of these creations really, as on numerous occasions over recent weeks, I'd innocently entered the early morning classroom only to be almost startled into an early grave by the spectre-like family group apparently lying in wait for me over by the bookshelves. The class loved them though, and the children now adding the paint and features to really bring the group to life, worked on proudly and in reverential silence. True, the Christ-child had been given rather a high facial colour, meaning he had the appearance of having to cope with a particularly nasty bout of colic, but his dad too wasn't without his own problems to manage. Poor Joseph had no neck apparently, his broad, carpenter's shoulders instead tapering rapidly into a rather pointed head with no ears. Frowning eyebrows and a sinister smile made for a peculiarly disturbing scene as The Saviour's Earthly Father leered down at the infant swaddled in an empty crisp box before him. Suddenly a plea was made by one of the little artists:

"Mr. Critchley, we've only got Mary's cape to do now but we've run out of blue paint, can we get some more from the stock room please?"

"Ah Susan," I replied hesitantly, "blue paint eh? There could be a problem there I'm afraid. What other colours do you have instead?"

"Well," she began hesitantly…"there's a shed-load o' bright orange."

Well why not I thought? I mean it would be very *70s* after all. Yes, you go for it Susan love, I'm pretty sure that a psychedelic Virgin won't be considered disrespectful or blasphemous in any way.

Before home time, we checked through the mass catering party slips for the umpteenth and final time before the class trotted off happily into the corridor, several of them having already forgotten what they'd been told only moments before. I decided to turn a deaf ear to some of the comments overheard as they reached for the coat hooks.

"Oh bugger, what was it he said again Sandra? – jellies & little cakes or sausage rolls & banana butties?" being an example of this confusion.

"Michelle," I called out over the exiting throng, "remember to ask your mum to pop in and see me for a minute."

The child nodded in embarrassed assent before pulling the hood up on her faded anorak and heading out into the yard. Meanwhile I returned to try and referee the afternoon cloakroom scrummage.

Great hilarity had broken out beside the openwork wire pigeonholes housing several pairs of ancient, sweat-stiffened and evil-smelling PE shoes and as usual, Sean was at the centre of the action. Having stuffed his pump bag up inside his duffle coat, hands placed now in the small of his back, he was doing a passable impression of someone preparing to enter the early stages of labour.

"Look, look, I'm Mary an' any minute now am gonna 'ave the baby Jesus!"

An appreciative audience guffawed with great mirth before being silenced by one of my *am-I-impressed*, raised-eyebrow stares. Still sniggering, the group scampered rapidly off up the corridor; almost colliding with Mrs. Constantine as she towed a reluctant Michelle in my direction.

"Ah, Mrs. Constantine, thanks for..." I began, but was immediately interrupted.

"Am really sorry about sending that note in this morning Mr. Critchley, I just don't know what came over me at all."

"No problem at all really," I went on, "did you manage to buy..."

"Oh yes, yes," she went on hurriedly, no doubt keen to get this awkward conversation over and done with as quickly as possible, " 'baby's fine, all fed and watered, she's at 'ome now, our Terry's lookin' after 'er."

"Good, I'm glad it's all sorted," I tried again, "now then about Michelle's school dinners, you do know that you're entitled to..."

"No need Mr. Critchley honest, no need at all – Michelle's dad's been out of work for a bit but he's got the offer of somethin' very soon so we'll be ok really – all done and dusted."

I did wonder for how many years and to how many folks she'd been offering this as an excuse for her insolvency – she must be truly dreading Christmas.

Michelle murmured something inaudible and turned her face to her mother who gazed down into the child's hood with a frown and listened.

"Oh yes Mr. Critchley, Michelle's just reminded me that I've lost that slip about party food, so can I have another one please?"

"Look Mrs. Constantine there's really no need to…"

"Oh no I'm not having any o' that," she went on indignantly, "we'll do our fair share like all t'others."

"Well to be honest I'm not sure I've got any…" I began, but she was in again like a flash.

"Well don't worry, I'll just send summat in on t'day instead wi' Michelle. Bye for now then and thanks for your time," this comment offered over her shoulder as she turned and made a hurried beeline for the door, her energetic departure fired no doubt by feelings of desperation, determination and family pride.

# CHAPTER FOUR – MORE JELLY ANYONE?

*The final week of term* – a phrase guaranteed to lend a spring to the step and bring joy to the heart of teachers everywhere, irrespective of age or location and that was indeed the point at which we were now arrived. I was sitting in a hall that was absolutely packed to the rafters – teachers were on chairs down each side whilst the floor was carpeted by two hundred cross-legged children once more. After issuing a stern warning that the audible breaking of wind again during the quiet bits of today's performance would simply not be tolerated I had gone on to threaten deployment of the ultimate deterrent – *staying in at playtime* - as retribution for any transgressors. Sean had actually been identified as chief suspect following a tip-off from one of his ex-mates and colleagues, and so I had him seated within an arm's reach, just in case. The Deputy Head meanwhile, wearing her second-best Jaeger burgundy two-piece and a fixed smile of welcome, sat in readiness at the piano, whilst at the back, countless parents risked permanent curvature of the spine, hunched uncomfortably as they were onto undersized infant chairs to watch the tale unfold.

Mr. Antrobus bumbled through some brief words of welcome to the assembled throng before sitting down too, as the Narrator strode on from the wings and the lights dimmed. Unwrapping a voice that belied her tiny stature and would certainly ensure no-one nodded off during the afternoon's proceedings, she picked a spot somewhere high up on the back wall and began bellowing at it:

"MANY YEARS AGO...IN THE FAR-AWAY LAND OF JUDEA...A HEAVENLY MESSENGER CAME DOWN TO EARTH...AND FORETOLD OF A SPECIAL BABY...A SAVIOUR... BORN IN A STABLE...WHO CAME TO TEACH US ALL!"

Pausing just long enough for a shy smile and a hesitant wave delivered from the hip to her proud mum on the front row and now easily recognisable by the streams of mascara cascading down both cheeks - the diminutive narrator marched smartly off stage which was the signal for the action to begin.

It's a well-known fact that the *awww factor* will always ensure that no matter what should transpire, you simply cannot fail to be onto a winner with an infant nativity performance. Be it angels with facial mucus-trails, shepherds wearing skewiff tea towels, or the mother of Jesus repeatedly exploring her knickers centre-stage, it's all part of the magic. Throw in a crowd-pleaser such as a pitch-perfect soloist to deliver a soaring rendition of *Away in a Manger* and you're home and dry, the audience will be weeping and baying for more – putty in your hands.

This was the third and final performance of the week, although at one point there had been talk of the possible need for another evening show to accommodate a group of disgruntled parents. Ticket sales had been absolutely manic with some folks sending in *ringers* to queue up each morning and bypass the maximum *two tickets per family* rule we'd had to impose. I'll bet most West End theatres wish they could fill seats with such ease. At the conclusion, the Head thanked one and all in his inimitable style, even remembering to give the scenery painter some recognition and I was gratified to receive a ripple of applause for my artistic efforts.

And that was that, - Festive hurdle number one was all over for another year. The knitted woolly sheep could all be boxed away along with the lampshade headdresses of the three wise men, Bill & Ada could start mopping up the odd puddle left behind in the area where the infant choir had been seated and we could all think about settling back to normal once again.

Bring on hurdle number two.

- - o O o - -

I approached the day of my first school Christmas Party with all the nonchalance of a lamb being led to the slaughter. Having been pre-warned by David about the potential for incident at such events, I had been fully expecting *lively*, possibly even *spirited* or maybe perhaps an outside chance of *boisterous*, but never for one moment, had I even considered the possibility for *frenzied*!

The morning had passed off pleasantly enough in the company of three helping mums come to set up the classroom for the forthcoming bunfight. Being veterans of similar events previously, these folks had far greater experience of such things than yours truly and I was therefore more than happy to assume the role of enthusiastic labourer, working diligently under their direction. I shifted tables, made cups of tea, emptied the stockroom of crepe paper and unrolled several yards of selloptape as we shared tales of Christmas shopping whilst transforming Class 2C into a veritable Winter Wonderland.

My helpers were back again too for the afternoon session, all fired up and ready to help deal with the logistics of mass catering. Dolled up to the nines and giggling broadly they certainly seemed happy to be taking part and unless it was my imagination, they were also rather more pink of cheek than earlier in the day. I felt it would require more than a liberal sprinkling of Coty L'aimant, to overcome the breathy undernote of alcohol about the three of them and as Mrs. Webster opened her bag to take out her apron, my suspicions were confirmed with the sighting of three bottles of Cherry B.

After depositing enough carrier bags of food to solve the famine situation in several developing countries, the children began to drift into the hall where I awaited their arrival. St. Paul's Cathedral Choir warbled carols from the gramophone as I greeted them all and congratulated them on just how smart they looked, and indeed they did, even the children from those families I knew were really struggling for cash were immaculately turned out.

This afternoon my class would be sharing the hall for the big event – three classes come together, meaning the hall soon became quite busy as the children dashed about the parquet in their bow ties, sticky-out frocks and shiny new shoes. All this activity, along with the tremendous heat pumping out from the old radiators and the scent of Sean's dad's after-shave being doled out furtively in the boy's toilets soon made the atmosphere quite oppressive. It was into this cauldron that my lower junior colleagues finally deigned to put in an appearance – better late than never I thought to myself.

Dorothy and Eleanor sashayed across the floor in dresses normally reserved for their Golf Club and Inner Wheel Gala dinners - dripping in glitz from head to toe they were greeted by an appreciative chorus of piercing wolf whistles. Studiously avoiding my gaze, they arrived at two cushioned chairs in the corner of the hall where they were to remain, steadfast and immovable for the entire afternoon. The realisation immediately began to dawn that the next couple of hours were going to be "awfully good experience" for me, as things suddenly began to liven up.

The Cathedral Choir was halted without warning part-way through the second verse of Good King Wenceslas and Slade's *Merry Xmas Everybody* replaced them instead on the turntable, this time at maximum volume. I had Mrs. Webster to thank for this as she had seemingly elected herself DJ for the occasion. Mrs. W, ("Oh call me Sheila please!") obviously had a real soft spot for Slade as I counted several airings of the song over the course of the afternoon. (*Even to this day, whenever I hear this being played, or Elton John's 'Step into Christmas' or indeed 'Wombling Merry Christmas' I still break out in a cold sweat.*)

The very instant the children heard Noddy Holder belt out the opening line, they went BERSERK!

It was their brutally competitive nature, which came as such a shock I suppose, a *win at all costs* attitude being displayed from the outset. Despite having used yards of sellotape and countless newspaper pages to wrap up a Fry's Selection Box earlier, a game of pass the parcel lasted barely three minutes. When the music stopped, timid, little Joanne Barton fell upon the tissue paper package like a demented terrier shaking a rat. Paper and tape shot in every direction along with little flecks of spittle showering from her mouth in raw, savage fury. I signalled frantically to Sheila to start the music again but as the rest were now screaming encouragement at the top of their voices, nobody even heard Little Jimmy Osmond continue singing *Long haired Lover from Liverpool*. Triumphant and more than a little sweaty, Joanne turned to hold the battered prize aloft to yet more cheering.

Musical chairs nearly resulted in a visit to Casualty as two boys made a frantic dash for the last remaining seat in the line. Even an almighty clash of heads though didn't put paid to an unseemly tussle as each retained a vice-like grip on two of the chair legs and refused to let go.

And if I hadn't abandoned the game of Musical Statues after twenty minutes, we might well still be there yet. Any child caught moving after the music stopped was deemed *out* and therefore required to retire to the sidelines. Of course the moment my back was turned, they recycled themselves by sneaking back onto the floor to continue playing, so desperate were they to be in with a shout of securing the winner's tube of Smarties.

At one point I sidled over to my two colleagues with a mind to requesting their more active involvement in all the fun, but as they were deep in festive conversation - I clearly heard Dorothy giving Eleanor directions to somewhere she was guaranteed to get a really good goose over the Christmas period – I decided to leave them to it.

One of my giddy band of three helpers announced a dancing competition requiring girl and boy partners to take to the floor together – this was of course the signal for an enormous collective shriek as everyone sat down in protest around the sides of the hall and refused to budge. Only the dangling of a truly special prize for the winners – two of the new-fangled and highly desirable Rubik's Cubes – managed to persuade a handful of reluctant couples to venture forth. There was precious little bodily contact during this however, those boys who really couldn't avoid holding their partners' hand, doing so only after rolling down shirt or sweater sleeve to protect their fingers from contamination by the opposite sex.

It was hot as Hades in there and I suddenly became aware of a steady procession of boys heading off into the corridor, only to return moments later in a considerably dishevelled state. Further investigation led me to the toilets in which a group of perspiring non-dancers were busy running their heads under the free-flowing cold taps. Their upper bodies and party shirts were now completely sodden, meaning that water pooled nicely onto the tiled floor and I couldn't help thinking that Ada was not going to be best pleased when three-thirty arrived.

And then it was time to eat.

Places had been set in the classroom on an alternating boy / girl / boy / girl basis in a valiant attempt at integration of those two seemingly alien species, an arrangement that was not received with much good grace. In this setting the helping mums were simply brilliant, filling paper plates with curling sandwiches and doling out crisps rather in the manner of croupiers at a noisy casino. Mrs. Cain strode around the room clutching a pair of five-pint jugs filled with diluted orange cordial, looking for all the world like a fraulein waitress at the Berlin Oktoberfest, repeatedly answering the calls for a refill.

"Where's my marmite butties?"

This comment indicated that, as with most dining experiences I guess, there will always be a less than satisfied customer, and today's moaner - surprise, surprise - was Maureen Pickavance. I was at pains to point out that as all the sandwiches had been pooled together before being divided up, there was no possible guarantee of what might arrive on the plates set before each individual diner.

"But I don't like meat paste," the irate little protester continued.

To be honest, I was with her on that one, but couldn't really admit as much. "Well do a swap with someone else then," I suggested in exasperation before my attention was taken elsewhere "...and Stuart, please eat your sandwiches before your jelly - there's a good lad."

Jelly eh? – there was masses of the stuff. It was present in every conceivable hue and in every possible stage of congealment. Some parents had sent it in still in its shop-bought, cellophane-wrapped, cubic state, whilst others obviously hadn't read the instructions properly and it was a runny, sticky, raspberry goo that trickled out of the carrier bag when picked up from the pile. Rest assured however, there can never quite be enough of this stuff on such occasions and so not a single plastic spoonful was left over at home time.

The mums bless them, got on with the task of restoring the classroom after the feast whilst I led the class back into the hall where the other guests were already assembled, seated on the floor. I offered a distant wave of greeting to Dorothy and Eleanor as they sat at the rear once again, sipping refreshment from the staffroom's best china tea set – well if you can't use it at Christmas when can you eh?

It had been announced to the children that they were to sit patiently and await the arrival of a very special visitor coming to visit at any moment now and I remember thinking to myself that if that door opens and a purple tracksuit jogs in, then I'm straight off to the pub. I needn't have worried though – as distant, jingly sleigh bells could be heard from afar and a well-rounded "ho-ho-ho" drew ever nearer.

It was a true delight to see the unadulterated excitement painted across so many small faces, even the hard-case-know-it-all-seen-it-and-done-it-all-before types had saucer-like eyes all aglow in surprise, when the doors swung open and a red-suited figure strode onto the stage. The crowd suddenly lunged forward and for a moment I thought he might be torn limb from limb, but no, they remained awestruck, calm and trembling on the floor at his feet. Unanswered questions immediately flashed into my mind: Could this really be the same rabid mob who had come close to ransacking the hall just a short time earlier? Am I the only one to recognise Bill's well-worn wellies sticking out from beneath his tunic? Will those two buggers at the back ever get off their backsides?

He asked them all what they would like for Christmas and the crowd then spent five minutes calling out their lists simultaneously at the top of their voices as Bill nodded and pretended to take notes on his pad before in a trice and with a cheery wave, he was gone once more and the happy band smiled at one another in contentment. Santa had left the building and they were all confident that December 25th would be sure to bring everything their hearts' desired – and I recall fervently hoping that indeed that would be the case.

- - o O o - -

Only an hour or so to go now. It was the afternoon of the last day and we were relaxing in class with the Christmas story, in surroundings that had been totally stripped bare of every festive branch and scrap of tinsel. In the old stock room, I'd recently discovered a mammoth piece of late-Victorian engineering hiding in the corner beneath a threadbare blanket. With its grey stove-enamelled frame and brass lens carrier, this nifty piece of kit was apparently an *epidiascope*, which could be used to project pages from books and illustrations up onto a screen. To the immense delight of my class I was now using this to hurl giant images from the nativity section of The Children's Illustrated Bible onto a sheet pinned to the classroom wall.

As they watched the Angel Gabriel deliver startling baby news to Mary and the shepherds scampered towards Bethlehem bearing their simple gifts, this was a wonderful oasis of calm after the madness of recent days, which left me feeling increasingly relaxed and in a positive frame of mind about completing my first term in school. Indeed as I looked around the room, there was but one fly in the ointment, one small obstacle to my achieving true innermost peace and tranquility, that being – just what in God's name am I going to do with Mary, Joseph and little Jesus still loitering over there in the library corner?

It was during afternoon playtime that I had a brainwave with regard to this and ran the idea past the class as they came back in to their desks.

"Now then Class 2, we really need to decide what to do with the Nativity figures before we go home don't we?"

Cue serious nods of agreement all round.

"I was just wondering, if there was anyone here who might like to take them home to keep?"

In an instant, twenty-nine backbones snapped into fully erect mode, two dozen index fingers were pressed firmly against their owners' lips to signify silent compliance whilst every spare hand was waved high in the air.

"OK then class," I went on, brandishing the book of cloakroom tickets I'd found in the cupboard, "we're going to have a draw to find a lucky winner today and the best bit of all is, it won't cost you a penny to take part!"

Pure brilliance on my part surely, to simply raffle off the Holy Family?

You could have heard a pin drop as I shook the bag containing all the tickets and then dipped my hand in to shuffle them again before drawing out a single blue ticket.

"And the winner is..."

- - o O o - -

Mrs. Horan stood in the classroom at the end of the day, her expression of amazed disbelief contrasting sharply with the beaming pride written across the face of her daughter.

"When our Sandra said she'd won a raffle Mr. Critchley, I was really pleased for her, but to be honest... well I never expected... I mean look at the state..." words apparently failing her at this point as she indicated the Holy Family group with an outstretched hand.

Part of me did feel for the poor woman, she'd no doubt got the house into absolute pristine order for Christmas and suddenly without warning, three lodgers arrive unannounced - would the turkey stretch that far?

"I mean, I've got all this shopping with me today an 'all and..." here she paused to try and pick up Mary from the floor, "I mean there's a fair bit o' weight to 'em isn't there?"

Oh yes I mused, I can certainly vouch for that, Mod-roc certainly isn't the most lightweight of artistic mediums.

"I'm not sure I can get them home, me an' Sandra won't be able 'manage 'em I know that much."

Bill had been sweeping the corridor but now popped his head in through the classroom door.

"Hello Eileen, maybe I can help?" He went on to explain, "Eileen, sorry, I mean *Mrs. Horan* is a good neighbour of mine you see Mr. Critchley, we only live two doors apart from each other."

"Hello Bill," piped up little Sandra cheerfully.

"Now Sandra," her mum scolded, "I've told you before that when you're in school you have to say *Mr. King* when being polite."

"Sorry mum, I forgot, sorry Mr. King," the child said glumly.

"Yes not to worry," Bill went on, " anyway my two lads are both off work today so I'll get them to come down to give me a hand later and we'll drop the figures off at your house Eileen before teatime, would that be ok?"

"I suppose so," replied Mrs. Horan without an enormous amount of enthusiasm, "thanks very much… er… Mr. King."

It was only later that evening as I sat at home cradling a chilled can of Younger's Tartan and watching Amy Turtle shuffle across the set of *Crossroads* on TV that a quite amazing thought struck me, prompting a whoop of delight which had mum running in from the kitchen.

"Why David," she asked in great concern, "what ever is the noise about – are you ok?"

"I'm fine mum, sorry about that, but I've just realised, if you were to walk along Morton Street just about now…"

"Yes, go on," mum prompted.

"You'd bump into *three Kings* delivering gifts!"

Priceless.

# CHAPTER FIVE – Nature, Red in Tooth & Claw.

Before I knew it I was back at school once more on a very chilly January morning but this time I was arriving in style. Mum had a new car, meaning that I was now the proud owner of her old one - a ten-year-old Hillman Imp in Tartan Red with just 120,000 miles on the clock, a vehicle that had served the family well (mostly) over countless holidays and expeditions across the years. Bill looked impressed anyway, providing me with me a mock royal curtsy as I drove in through the gates and gave him a New Year's handshake through the car's open window.

I'd been determined to do precious little over the Christmas break and there were reasons for this. Firstly I was totally knackered after my opening term (all that effort for just £93 per month after tax) and also, with wedding plans in the offing for next year, we'd aimed for an 'austerity Christmas' this time around. Christmas Day then had been spent round at ours, slumped in front of the box. With so many TV riches on offer however, staying in hadn't been too much of a trial to be honest and so, stuffed with turkey, and poleaxed by two bottles of Corrida red wine, we sprawled on the settee clutching glasses of Wanink's Advocaat to overdose on BBC1. Billy Smart's Christmas Circus followed the Queen's 3pm message and then later in the evening we had the twin delights of Bruce Forsyth's Generation Game and Mike Yarwood to look forward to. There was also a point around teatime when we switched over briefly to ITV in order to catch half an hour of Peters and Lee.

In fact New Year's Eve had been pretty much our one and only foray into the outside world, queuing as we did from around six pm on the 31st to be sure of a seat at the Local British Legion Club. Such a popular destination was this, that we had no shortage of company even at that early stage of the evening, our fellow queuers clutching flasks and sandwiches to see them through the remaining hours before the compere would bounce onto the stage to launch proceedings. The women in the queue held on tight to their headscarves as a stiffening breeze threatened to reveal the hair rollers hiding beneath. When the doors opened there was a mad scramble for tables, with the party-goers reserving places at these for their late-coming friends with a glass of something from the bar placed on a beermat in front of an empty chair. Meanwhile an enormous line of revellers snaked away from the ladies' toilet across the dancefloor and the air was heavy with the scent of hair lacquer.

Consequently, due to my extremely 'sensible' Festive period, I was now feeling refreshed, champing at the bit and ready to take the spring term by storm. The children seemed similarly full of beans and in a bid to get the Christmas memories over and done with once and for all, we spent the first half hour talking about what Santa had brought. Judging by the endless lists of gifts being reeled off by most of them, there would be several families now struggling to juggle the budget for a month or two for sure. Michelle wasn't joining in these conversations with much enthusiasm however and so I found a quiet moment to ask if she'd received anything nice for Christmas.

"Yeah we gorra new telly," she replied flatly, before adding with a proud beam, "a colour one!"

The boss led a 'welcome assembly' later in the morning and as staff settled into their chairs at the sides of the hall, DT leaned forward to whisper "Janus" in my ear. As this didn't mean a great deal I gave him a look of puzzlement but his reply was just a knowing smile as he tapped the side of his nose with a wink before Dorothy gave the piano keys a brutal January wake up call and we were off and running into 'Colours of Day.' It was a rather indifferent delivery of this song to be honest and as the voices dribbled away miserably with the final bars, Dorothy gave the assembled school a look over the top of her glasses which suggested that Wednesday morning's hymn practice might very well be retribution time. The boss stepped forward to the middle of the hall and spoke.

"Good morning school and welcome back to you all. You know, whenever I think of the New Year, I always think of a character from ancient times named *Janus...*"

I turned round to be greeted by DT's smug grin before he went on to mouth silently: "every single year  - without fail - he never misses."

Suddenly, all my initial New Year enthusiasm, and indeed that of the children began to evaporate rapidly and continued to do so over the next twenty minutes as the monotonous tone of our esteemed leader burbled on.

"Janus, the two-faced Roman God of beginnings & transitions...blah blah...guardian of gates & doorways...blah blah...representing the growth of young people... blah blah... born in Thessaly...blah...blah...blah!"

All this and more besides, wafting pretty much unnoticed above the steadily glazing expressions of teachers and children alike.

"and so everyone," a slight change in tone here indicating that the end may be soon approaching to bring release from the torture, causing most to sit up and take notice, "I'd like you all to turn to the person beside you and shake their hand to wish them a very happy New Year."

Pandemonium – I mean has the man learned nothing from 30 years spent in the company of children?

Getting together in the staffroom provided opportunity for yet more New Year handshakes as we all settled down with our cups of tea. Everyone tried very hard not to look bored witless yet again during Dorothy and Eleanor's blow-by-blow account of the little soiree for twenty guests they'd hosted over the break. Truly fascinating stuff indeed, and in stark contrast I have to say to the black pudding and chip butty refreshments with which we ourselves had welcomed 1975. I made a note to self that if ever I was in the need of exciting new recipes for canapés or needed advice on how to poach a whole salmon using the dishwasher, then these two characters would be my first port of call for sure. I'd never been so glad to hear a bell ring and as we trooped off down the stairs, DT reminded me about a lunchtime meeting we'd arranged with the top class to discuss the planned summer term outing to deepest Wales.

- - o O o - -

Well they were wildly enthusiastic about the whole project that was for sure. We had been aiming for about 15 participants in total, ie a minibus and a car's-worth, but the initial response suggested we may need instead to book one of the local coach firm's luxury 57 seaters to accomodate the crowds. After outlining the itinerary, cost, schedule etc. and doling out letters to take home explaining it all in greater detail, we asked did anyone have any questions. I was expecting these to possibly be concerned with the Welsh landscape and precise location or maybe about the activities available and so on, but no, Class 6 had rather different priorities.

"Can we tek money?"

"Why would you need money?" My friend David asked.

"To buy stuff."

"Last time I checked Stuart, Dolwydellan didn't have a Woolworth's or a Rumbelow's so why bother?"

Stuart was nothing if not persistent however, " yiss but can we though?"

"Can you *what* Stuart?"

"Tek money?"

"Sandra Maloney," David pointed to the rear of the group, "what's your question?"

"Will there be a telly there?"

"No there won't as a matter of fact," DT went on, "you see Sandra we'll be staying in a Youth Hostel way out in the countryside, not *The Dunroamin' Guesthouse B&B Prestatyn*."

This was met with some stunned and crestfallen looks as several members of the group immediately began to question the intensity of their desire to commune with nature first-hand. The notion of a weekend with no telly was a difficult one for many to come to terms with.

"OK that's enough for now, lunchtime's nearly over so get going eh? It's first come, first served for getting those £1:50 deposits in to school so think on, if you're going to leave those letters festering in the depths of your sweaty PE bag for a fortnight as many of you always do, then you'll probably be too late so forget it."

Cue sniggering and banter as the group made its way excitedly into the corridor and back to class, and we two headed off to continue teaching.

- - o O o - -

Ah the Spring term – a bit of a misnomer really as weeks at a time pass by without even the faintest whiff of anything remotely springlike. We were involved in a class topic about Africa, which would hopefully take our minds off the biting winds sweeping across the playground beyond the classroom window. At least there had been no snow worth mentioning. True there was just the briefest of flurries one morning, tiny flakes pirouetting down and playing havoc with my session on the properties of triangles as the news spread round the room like wildfire:

"It's snowin', pass it on."

" ' snowin, pass irron!"

"Gaz, hey Gaz... Gazzer...deaf lugs, it's snowin'!"

The news was immediately followed by the most important question of all, as Gaz looked up from his number square to ask pointedly:

"Yiss, but is it *stickin'* though?"

It wasn't sticking sadly, but that didn't stop the intrepid playtime explorers from trying to make the most of things anyway. Woolly-gloved and balaclava'd like Alaskan fur trappers, they dashed out at break-time to find disappointment rather than blizzards awaiting. The playground was completely clear apart from a tide mark of grubby flakes around one edge, where the wind had blown drifts against the school wall which, in some places, must have been getting on for almost two-thirds of an inch deep. Gloves were peeled off in haste and the backs of fingers skinned against the tarmac as a dozen hands frantically clawed together sufficient supplies to almost make a snowball.

It was cold though, that was for sure, but Bill saw it as his solemn duty to ensure the school retained a sub-tropical ambience throughout the winter months. On a daily basis he would shovel coke into that boiler with all the vigour of a stoker on The Titanic trying to outrun a crazed iceberg, surfacing regularly from the cellar throughout winter mornings to mop his perspiring brow and quaff heartily from a bottle of Sterilised milk. Outside it was Reykjavik, indoors we had The Congo basin. For God's sake nobody touch those radiators.

This was really quite appropriate however – the humid surroundings lending a real air of authenticity to the range of African artefacts gradually accumulating around us. There was a *frieze* along the back wall of the room – impossible to do justice to a topic I always felt without a good frieze. This one depicted an African village, mud huts roofed with artstraws sitting in a jungle clearing whilst cut-out cardboard monkeys capered about, some of them escaping from the jungle altogether to climb the walls towards the light fittings. I had attached these to the beige painted walls using a wondrous new material called *Blu-tack*. It was truly remarkable stuff and I had taken to keeping a ball of it in my pants pocket, warm, primed and ready at the drop of a hat to affix posters to any wall, anywhere, anytime – I felt truly sorry for those who had invested capital in drawing pin companies as surely these were now destined for history and the scrapheap. Oh yes indeed, I had glimpsed the future and it was Blu-tack. Above the frieze was a row of Zulu shields in assorted colours and a couple of dozen bamboo garden canes disguised as native spears. It was impressive I mused, and let's be honest, there's nothing quite like dealing in outdated, inappropriate National stereotypes when launching a topic.

School had a TV in order that we might from time to time, avail ourselves of the range of educational programmes on offer. Every class was allowed access to a maximum of two series per year, and teachers had to select these in advance from a BBC catalogue, thus enabling Dorothy to order the accompanying class pamphlets during that incredibly busy period of her professional life when she had to wrestle with 'whole-school requisition.' As Deputy Head this was definitely her biggest responsibility of the year and the burden on her meagre shoulders meant that she was both irritable and totally unapproachable during that entire fortnight. Removed from teaching duties, she would sit in the staffroom instead, surrounded by glossy catalogues from which to order industrial quantities of sugar paper, graph paper, tracing paper, gummed paper, wax crayons, plastic dispensers of *Gloy* paste, plastic scissors with rounded ends (absolutely useless and definitely not fit for purpose), plastic coins (for some reason there would always be considerably less of this remaining on completion of a maths topic on *money*), blackboard chalks (coloured and also the white variety, but always the *Cosmic Anti-Dust* brand) and so on and so on.

Co-ordinating the wish lists of every member of staff required a very high level of concentration, as any mistake could prove costly. DT told me that she'd been distracted whilst filling in a requisition slip a couple of years previously and inserted an extra zero into the quantities box by mistake. Whether that were true or not I couldn't really say for sure, but I do know there were enough eight-ounce packets of wallpaper paste in the stockroom to redecorate the entire street three times over. Everyone tiptoed around Dorothy for those two weeks, careful not to bump against the barbed wire fence she would erect around herself in the corner – oh yes indeed, an acute bout of PMT had *nothing* on requisition time that's for sure.

Anyway, one of the TV programmes I'd opted for this year was: 'Zig-Zag!', a kind of general interest series which coincidentally had 'Africa' as its principal focus this term. Today's broadcast was to be about African wildlife and flicking through the Teacher's handbook before the start, there was no indication of anything untoward or any potentially gruesome content that I should be made aware of. This was an important consideration of course as it would be another year or two before the VHS / Betamax home recording battle began, and so every programme, from whichever of the 3 available TV channels we were blessed with, had to be either watched live or not watched at all.

The class really looked forward to our weekly treat, and would hurry down the corridor to the newly-refurbished TV room after playtime, eager not to miss the start – my, how they loved to hum and sing along to the theme tune before the opening credits rolled. Today the music faded away and the screen opened to a shot of baobab trees, a lazily slinking family of lions and a background of chirping crickets, before announcing:

### Programme 2: Life on the African Plains.

Every pair of eyes was glued firmly to the TV and sitting at the back of the room, I was forced to wonder for the umpteenth time why it was that I was never able to command the class's attention in quite the same way.

All went well for the first few minutes – shots of mewling, cuddly lion cubs and newly born antelopes wobbling upright on stick-thin spindles of legs to suckle their mother's milk were all well-received. Sitting cross-legged on the newly installed carpet the children turned to smile at one another and a chorus of happy "awww's" could be heard, but all that was suddenly about to change.

The room was dark, warm and secure, almost womb-like I suppose, nothing there to worry about, no long division to knock the stuffing out of you, no tricky verb tenses to fret over, just fluffy nonsense on the screen to slip into and out of as the mood took you, with the added bonus of carpet pile too to fiddle with during the slower bits. On the screen, the young antelope's mother paused to scent the air, scanning this way and that to check for danger before tiptoeing on delicate hoofs down to the river's edge. There was a final cursory glance for approaching predators before the beautiful creature bent its elegant neck to the water and began to drink.

BANG!

From beneath the water's surface, the upper torso of an adult crocodile exploded upwards to clamp a pair of massive jaws around the head and face of the unsuspecting antelope – the poor thing didn't stand a chance. The front row of children suddenly jumped backwards as if dabbed by a cattle prod and glanced nervously at me over their shoulders for reassurance. I had none to offer. No one wanted to watch the action now unfolding on the screen, of that I was certain, but nonetheless, most eyes were drawn there involuntarily, with the exception that is, of Kelly Marie Tunstall, who had clamped her hands over tightly fastened eyelids in an attempt to shut out the horrors.

There was yet worse to come. The antelope's lifeless form was dragged from the riverbank to beneath the river's surface from where, unfortunately, the cameras continued to roll. Up until that point I'd never really given a great deal of thought as to how exactly it was that crocodiles managed to dismember and consume their prey. I had always wrongly assumed that they just used their formidable teeth to simply bite chunks off, as and when they saw fit – rather in the manner of the junior children eating sausages from their forks at midday in the canteen, a lunchtime display which always prompted a grumpy comment from Dorothy:

"Oh look everyone, the children are *lollipop-eating* again, it really isn't good enough. Eleanor, I think we ought to consider offering our after school 'table manners' classes once more, don't you think?"

Well I'll bet there's a queue for that one – what a choice eh, leg it home to catch Follyfoot and The Wombles on TV or spend another half-hour in school being taught how to hold a knife and fork. Anyway I digress.

We all watched aghast as the murderous amphibian fastened its jaws onto the upper thigh of the antelope, before beginning to spin its body violently in the water. Sadly, as the TV soundtrack had suddenly become silent, Kelly Marie had mistakenly interpreted this as the signal for the *all-clear* and risked one eye towards the screen at the precise moment Bambi's mother was having her leg forcibly removed. On the plus side however, the child's sudden and unexpected bout of vomiting successfully distracted attention from the river, which had now turned cloudy with blood.

- - o O o - -

Bill was very good about the whole thing however thank heavens.

I had returned to the TV room after school to apologise for the mess and watch him at work.

"A crocodile you say David?" was his curious comment as he sprinkled a shovelful of medicated sawdust onto a damp spot close to where Kelly Marie had been sitting.

"Aye Bill," was my reply, "absolutely no warning, the damn thing just shot out of the water and ate the antelope. I'm really sorry for all the …"

"Don't worry David, don't you worry now, it's really not your fault, blame the bloody BBC if you ask me. Anyway we'll soon have it right again."

"What will the boss say?" I asked fearfully.

The TV room with its 21-inch Rediffusion set, wall-to-wall carpet and cord-operated blackout blinds had been Ray Antrobus's pride and joy since the start of the year and was always the first port of call when showing visitors around the school. He was so proud of the whole thing, that he would regularly make disparaging comments about the paltry efforts made by other local schools to enter the age of technology.

At the start of a staff meeting for example, he might often open with a remark such as:

"Do you know, I was in St. So-and-So's last week and they have a 16 inch black-and-white set, *black-and-white* mind you, that they have to watch in a corridor – a corridor! That's not going to be a memorable experience for the kiddies now is it?"

"Don't you fret yourself David," Bill went on, " as my old mam used to say - *what the eye doesn't see, the heart cannot grieve over* – this'll sort it."

And with a conspiratorial wink he produced a can of Haze air freshener from his pocket, applying his finger to the button with a prolonged flourish. Thirty seconds later an asphyxiating cloud of *Roses from Picardy* descended to fill the little room and almost succeeded in masking the sour smell of bile.

## CHAPTER SIX – Infernal Combustion.

"Will you do that funny thing with your car again after school today Mr. Critchley?"

I requested further clarification - "And just exactly what funny thing would that be Alan?" Even though I knew exactly what he was talking about.

'You know," he went on, "when you pretend your car won't go an' that – it's dead funny, we all love it."

"Well we'll just have to wait and see won't we?" I added tantalisingly. "Now then settle down and eat your toast."

It was break time, but Alan Foster had to stay indoors – there was a reason for this.

The day hadn't got off to the best of starts, I'd opened the classroom door first thing this morning to discover an extended family of cardboard monkeys lying prone across the floor and desktops – bloody Blu-Tack – doesn't respond well to the cold apparently. I'd sought to overcome this deficiency in my new-found wonder adhesive by placing a ball of the stuff on top of the radiator, which, even at this early hour, was already belting out temperatures like midday in Nairobi. I reckoned too that applying extra pressure to the putty-like substance when re-affixing it to the wall would also be beneficial. To this end then, I was wobbling on some step-ladders placed precariously on top of two tables and using Bill's best claw hammer to hammer the things back in place when there'd been a knock at the door.

It was Mrs. Foster, holding Alan's hand, at least I think it was Alan, but the morning sun glinting off his shiny head made it difficult to be absolutely certain from this range. Mrs. Foster was definitely what you'd call 'old-school.' Approaching fifty I'd guess, Alan was obviously a late arrival into the extended family hierarchy, confirmed by the way in which she would never actually refer to him by name, choosing instead to always use the affectionate epithet: " 'little 'un." This morning she'd obviously risen earlier than was usual in order to beat the crowds – her hair was in some disarray beneath a headscarf, she was without her bottom teeth and a large nappy pin held a well-worn overcoat fastened tight against the cold.

I had a good idea what this would be about, remembering that Alan had gone home yesterday somewhat distressed to say the least, his discomfort prompted by an afternoon visit from the hygiene nurses. I'd been made aware of their arrival after lunch by Sean's comment of:

"Ay up everybody, it's Nitty Nora t'bug explorer, stand by your beds."

The children were lined up as per usual and the two smiling, uniformed ladies riffled expertly through their assorted scalps. There would be a pause in their progress if a problem were identified, with the child in question taken gently to one side and asked:

"And what's your name lovie? Take this envelope home tonight and give it to your mam, there's a good boy / girl."

It didn't take a genius to work out what this coded message signified and yesterday an acutely embarrassed Alan had been the recipient of such bad news, much to Sean's delight, and his subsequent stage-whisper of:

"Hey Gaz – Fozzer's got biddies,"

ensured that everyone else got the message too.

A wave of nicotine-heavy breath wafted over her gums as Alan's mother began to speak.

" 'Little 'un was upset yisterday Mr. Critchley."

"Yes I know, Mrs. Foster, I've had a word with some of the boys concerned."

"Yay," she went on, "anyroad it's not 'is fault, 'poor little bugger catches 'em from that tribe next door when they're playing out, and you can't keep kids apart now can yur?

"Indeed."

"Filthy 'er 'ouse is. We get cockroaches comin' in through our skirting boards from them, *they* know which 'ouse is 'cleanest. I've 'ad 'im to t'barbers anyroad and took it all off, so let's see t'nits stick to that now. It's cold out today though so will it be all right for 'im t'stay in at playtimes?"

"Of course Mrs. Foster, I'll find him some jobs to do."

"Arright cocker, be good for yur teacher," was her parting shot before planting a loving kiss on his glossy scalp and handing over several rounds of toast parcelled up in a waxed loaf wrapper for breaktime.

Alan busied himself sharpening pencils as he consumed his playtime snack and then the bell rang out on the yard and the children filed back into class once more. I had dispatched Alan to the office with the registers first thing this morning in order to provide me with an opportunity to threaten dire consequences for any class member foolish enough to pass an adverse comment about the lad's new hairstyle and the message had obviously got through as, thus far at least, peace & harmony reigned. In fact some class members were being extremely supportive of him, evidenced by the likes of Tommy Atherton's comment just before break started:

"Arright Alan, you c'n borrer my cap if yer want this playtime, it's fleein' cold out there y'know."

Possibly a shade tactless maybe? Oh undoubtedly, but it's the thought that counts surely.

Desk lids were opened and books taken out in preparation for the silent reading session, which always followed morning playtime. The whole school was involved in this simultaneously, which ensured an eerie silence throughout the school for twenty minutes or so. The Boss was keen on this initiative and would make random drop-in visits to check on how the children were progressing through the various reading schemes. I've already expressed my opinion about Ladybird Readers' Peter & Jane series, but my lack of patience wasn't limited solely to these books it must be said. It's the whole crazy notion of a *Reading Scheme* in general that makes me uneasy – the inevitable numbering and grading of sets of books that brings an air of hierarchy to the whole process of reading, when surely that should simply be a pleasure in itself. However, maybe that's the philosophy behind any scheme who knows – guarantee progress by exploiting the competitive nature of children.

All teachers were required to listen to every individual read aloud at least twice a week and log these occasions with a comment in a Reading Diary for inspection when required. I was just about to begin this process, when the door opened after a perfunctory knock and the Head Teacher arrived.

"Morning Mr. Critchley, 'morning class. I thought I might listen to one or two of your readers today, would anyone like to volunteer to start us off I wonder?"

Sean Bickerstaffe was always at the front of the line when volunteers were required and as per usual, his hand was first into the air.

"Very well Sean, come on then, let's see how you're doing with your book shall we?"

If Sean were a dog, he would be a terrier with that irrepressible desire to be involved in everything. Wearing an unruly shock of wiry hair he scampered out to take his place beside The Boss at a nearby empty desk, and I swear I could actually see an invisible tail wagging furiously with pleasure.

"So Sean," Mr. Antrobus began, "I see you're involved in our *Through the Rainbow* scheme, and what do you think of these books then?"

"Oh I love these stories sir, they're dead good."

*Fib* I thought to myself, you've had that one for the past five weeks.

'And do you read a lot at home?" the interrogation continued.

"Oh yes sir, I'm always reading and I go to The Library all the time."

*Fib* and *fib* again – Sean, how on Earth do you keep your face straight I wondered? The truth being that you really would struggle to find anyone who fits the title *reluctant reader* more perfectly than Sean Bickerstaffe does.

"Well that's so good to hear, because you know some children in our school hardly ever read at all."

Sean's response to this was a pious shake of the head as he tut-tutted at such a wasteful notion and raised his eyebrows in an expression of acute dismay.

"Now then," continued the Head in a let's-get-down-to-business sort of manner, "what do we have here then eh? Ahh, I see you're up to *Gold Book 5 – Thistledown & Cobweb*. Do you know what they actually are I wonder - Thistledown & Cobweb?"

Sean responded with his very best studious gaze.

"I know what cobwebs are Sir, they're a spider's house. I know that because mum has to sweep them out of the corners of the room at home with her duster."

"Very good Sean, well done indeed. And what about *thistledown* then?"

Sean responded well to this praise, and put his fingers to his chin in a pose to indicate the depth of his thought processes.

"I think I might know," he began somewhat uncertainly, "I think I might have heard my dad talking about thistledown when he's getting ready to go off fishing."

"Really," commented the Head, "so what do you imagine it to be then?"

"Is it...is it..?"

"Yes Sean, go on, don't be afraid."

"Is it when it's raining very, very 'ard outside?"

- - o O o - -

Anyway when hometime arrived, at least Alan and his bunch of chums were happy with the realisation that I may indeed be about to "do that funny thing with my car again."

Having loaded it up with three sets of books for marking, I sat in the driver's seat and found that, and not for the first time this week, my little runabout steadfastly refused to start. The car it has to be said, had proved *difficult* from its very arrival as part of our family in 1964. Dad had purchased it from the local Hillman garage, a location to where it would be regularly returned suffering from one fault or another as the months passed by. Dad's frustration finally reached the point at which he decided to go straight to the top, contacting The Rootes Motor Group for recompense. The fitting of a whole new engine was finally sanctioned and dad was initially triumphant at this result but his joy turned to absolute mortification as he opened the newspaper shortly after the car was returned to us, only to read that Lord Rootes had died suddenly. He was entirely convinced that it was his persistent complaints, which had in fact contributed to the poor man's premature demise.

Anyway here we are again I mused, ten years on and the thing's still playing silly buggers. With each unsuccessful turn of the key, I could sense the groaning battery gradually losing the will to live and also an escalating sense of expectation amongst the growing crowd of impatient little onlookers gathered around my vehicle. School had finished some time ago, but Alan had hung around the gates to recruit chums and passers-by, many of whom were dressed in a completely different school uniform, to witness the miracle I was about to perform.

A flattened battery is always a damned nuisance of course, but thankfully my father had always been a belt-and-braces sort of guy with regard to all things mechanical, meaning that I had a trick or two up my sleeve yet, and indeed it was just this that the spectators had come to witness. Reaching under the seat I found the starting handle that was always kept close to hand, and stepping out from the car, raised this aloft, rather in the manner of Chamberlain proclaiming 'peace in our time' in 1938 to cheering and tumultuous applause from an appreciative audience. None of the children had ever seen a starting handle before my arrival and so I guess it was true to say that I was something of an historical artefact. Neither had they seen a car with its engine at the rear and so there were gasps of amazement as I opened the boot/bonnet and squirted a puff of WD-40 into the air intake before inserting the magic device.

"What's 'e doin' Al," asked one confused crowd member, "is 'e windin' irrup or summat?"

"Shurrup an' keep watchin,'" was Alan's stern riposte.

Remembering to keep my thumb tucked out of the way as instructed by dad, I grasped the starting handle and turned the engine over for the first time to no avail.

A cry of **"ONE!"** immediately went up from my gleeful supporters.

I tried again, once more without success.

**"TWO!"** – my, how they were loving this.

The next attempt was successful however, and as the engine barked into life, a joyous shout of:

**"THREE!!"**

was accompanied by yet more cheers and clapping. Leaping back into the driver's seat, I flung the starting handle into the footwell, stuck the car into gear and headed off briskly towards the school gates like some demented, mechanised version of The Pied Piper, a trail of happy children galloping along behind, cheering and spluttering in the cloud of blue smoke being left in my wake.

# CHAPTER SEVEN – Vitamin C Season.

The winter of 1975 didn't cause anyone too many problems. School never had to close because of snow, (an achievement of which Ray Antrobus as Head Teacher was particularly proud) pipes didn't even come near to freezing up and I somehow managed to avoid the toxic clouds which would explode daily in my direction from two dozen hideously active pairs of nostrils throughout the chilliest months of the year. For some reason, the notion of covering the mouth when sneezing or during the continual nasal chorus seemed a completely alien concept to my class and I lost count of the number of times I would be required to call out:

"Tissue please!"

during the course of an average week.

Listening to prolonged inhaling through mucus-heavy noses from all corners of the room was not a pleasant experience, meaning that what amounted to a *symphony of snot* became the less than magical daily soundtrack which accompanied January and February in my first year of teaching, (and pretty much every year since too it has to be said).

Apparently though, the immune system of many class members was not so robust as mine, which would account for the rafts of empty places dotted throughout the room at this time. At playtime there seemed to be as many children dashing around outside in the chilly yard as there were indoors, wheezing and hawking as they kept warm with a comic book or sitting 'colouring in' beside the radiator.

I could paper the walls with excuse notes from home during these weeks, some of them actually proving fairly memorable. Sandra McCooey stood at my desk one Monday morning looking somewhat *peaky* to say the least.

"Oh dear Sandra, you don't look well at all," was my sympathetic opening gambit.

"Am ok Mr. Critchley," was her stoic, if somewhat adenoidal reply, "Sharon Stott won't be in today though."

This was surprising news indeed, as Sharon was a real class stalwart, a strapping member of our little band that on occasion I had even heard referred to as *hefty*. She certainly had a good appetite of that there was no doubting and my mind returned to the Christmas party when her contribution to the festive buffet had been a Gregg's steak & kidney pie teamed with a sausage roll side order that no other party member had a hope of getting their hands on.

"Oh poor Sharon, I do hope it's nothing serious?"

Sandra went on to fill in some detail. "Well we wus all at a Morris Dancing competition in Jubilee Park on Sat'day…"

I tried, without success it must be said, to picture Sharon Stott in a morris dancer's outfit, before continuing in sympathetic mode:

"Oh Sandra, not in all that rain surely?"

"Yay," she went on without pause, "it piss…, it *poured* it down all day din't it? Anyroad we got soakin' wet an' then that wind come an' all, so we wus all froze and had 'get back on t'coach in our wet things – Sharon wus shiverin' like mad her mam's sent a note in."

Holding up a crumpled piece of lined notepaper, she sneezed heavily all over it twice in rapid succession, wiped her nose with the back of her hand and then passed it over to me. It read as follows:

'Dear Mr. Critchley, our Sharon won't be in school today as she hasn't slept for 2 nights due to having chaps between her legs. Yours, Mrs. Stott.'

During morning break I stood once more looking out through the classroom window as the growing group of invalids behind me continued with the final rehearsals of their bronchial chorus. Eleanor & Dorothy were on 'playground duty' - elegantly swathed against the biting cold and deep in conversation, they strolled the length of the yard to the far wall before turning expertly on two pairs of kitten heels to return and process once more in the opposite direction. Not once during the five minutes I watched did they make any attempt to engage with the children careering about them or indeed even acknowledge their presence and I swear that they wouldn't even have broken stride had the Child Catcher himself pulled up to the kerb and used his giant net to scoop up the whole of Standard One into his cart.

At one point Dorothy did pause to adjust her headgear before turning again to face her like-minded chum for confirmation of the suitability of her appearance. This new addition to her wardrobe had caused a quite a stir in the staffroom first thing this morning.

"Oh Dorothy I'm SO envious of your new hat – miaow, miaow and miaow again!" cooed an enthusiastic Eleanor, pausing at the end of her row of knitting.

"Why thank you," was the immediate proud reply, "I have to admit to being rather taken with it myself."

"Is it a leopard print by any chance?" Eleanor went on, setting down her needles and ball of wool in order to stand and get a closer look.

"Well actually no, it's *ocelot* I'm led to believe. I *spotted it* on Saturday, if you'll pardon the pun," she tittered, "in the millinery department of Broadbents. Tres chic n'est ce pas?"

"Oh mais oui Dorothy, mais oui indeed - simply divine."

Outside the bell rang loudly and the playground came to a sudden, confused standstill, the children standing around in shivering knots to offer one another shrugs and looks of puzzlement at the early finish. The reason for this became immediately obvious as three of the girls from top class picked their way between the now stationary figures, towards the teachers waiting in the middle of the yard. The faces of two of the girls were an absolute study in concentration as they approached with the ladies' milky coffees, keen not to spill any of their morning beverage into the china saucers, whilst the third 'break monitor' tagged along behind with sugar bowl and spoon. When their drinks were sweetened appropriately, the girls were dismissed, the bell was rung once more, and normal service was resumed. I shook my head in disbelief at the antics as a voice spoke from the doorway.

"I know, they're a pair of corkers aren't they?" DT commented. "I need to get to the bank at lunchtime today, are you free?"

"No problem," I replied, "see you then."

Last lesson before lunch was handwriting practice and I was experimenting with newly arrived advanced technology in the form of an *overhead projector* or *OHP* to those of us in the know. To improve the quality of children's handwriting it is of course essential that they observe you forming the letters before copying these themselves into their books, rather than merely copying down a passage from the board. Using the old chalk and blackboard method means that your back is turned as you write on the board and, short of having a pair of wing mirrors fitted to your shoulders, you can never really be sure that the children are actually watching as you painstakingly form the letters. Chances are of course that the moment you turn away, silent though they may well remain, several class members will immediately begin dismantling one another.

With the OHP however, you are able to model quality writing with a pen onto an acetate sheet whilst still facing the class to continue first-hand supervision of individual behaviour. This in turn would lead to some memorable classroom exchanges such as:

"And now children as you can see I am practising a whole line of letter C's – starting beside the margin and then **up** and over and back and **up** and over and back and **up** and over and back and **each** and every one identical to the one before and **Sean** if I see you do that with your ruler again I'll get very, very cross…and **up** and over and back."

Mr. Antrobus suddenly appeared from nowhere to beckon me into the corridor and I instructed the class to complete two lines' worth of letter C's while I went across to the door.

"Thought I'd better let you know David, just had Mr. Lawrence on the 'phone. Apparently his PE course for new teachers is coming up shortly so he will pop in at some point soon to drop off an application form."

"Oh good, I'll look forward to that immensely," was my sardonic response, before turning back to the class and discovering Sean and Stuart standing at the front and using the OHP to perform an adult-rated shadow puppet show for everyone's amusement.

- - o O o - -

DT and I were out of the door and into the car almost before the lunchtime bell had stopped ringing. I was driving and first stop was the nearby baker's to pick up a spot of lunch. Unusually today, there was no queue of hungry workers spilling out onto the pavement and so in no time at all we were able to continue towards town, all conversation ended for the time being as we juggled scalding hot mouthfuls of meat & potato pie. Waiting on double yellow lines outside the bank I foolishly decided to start on my second course – a two inch deep vanilla slice. Experience had long since taught the folly of engaging with such a local delicacy ill-prepared but I simply couldn't resist the temptation a moment longer, meaning that DT's return to the car found me ankle-deep in flaky crumbs and with a hefty schlock of vanilla custard having slipped the length of my tie before coming to rest on the crotch of my trousers.

"That's not a good look DC if you don't mind my saying, maybe you need a drink to sort yourself out," was my friend's amused comment.

As our trip had been accomplished in absolute record time we decided this would definitely be a possibility and so I pulled up by the kerb outside one of the many local hostelries available on the return trip, in order to avail ourselves of a small glass of midday refreshment. Fifteen minutes later we were back out of the door again after my half-pint of shandy (or 'gill' as the elderly barman insisted on referring to it) and climbing into the car for the return to school in plenty of time for the afternoon session.

Just why the ensuing incident came as a total surprise to me I'll never really know as there had been plenty of recent warning signs of that there was no doubting. Plus of course, being a committed and fully-paid-up member of the North West Primary Teachers' Pessimist Society – aka 'The Glass Half-empty Club' I really should have been expecting only the very worst, but no – the car's stubborn refusal to respond to the turning of the key left me both dumbfounded and dismayed in equal measures.

We had just eleven minutes before the dinner ladies would vigorously signal the end of lunchtime. Two of these minutes were wasted in futile efforts with the starting handle and then after remembering I'd left the car unlocked, I wasted yet more time by turning back with the keys shortly after we'd commenced the long dash back towards school. Some unassailable logic from DT convinced me of the absurdity of such action:

"No-one can take it DC," he pointed out, breathless as he already was, "the bloody thing won't start, and there's nothing inside worth stealing apart from pastry crumbs so let's get going!"

It became a long and extremely brisk walking / semi-sprinting / painful limping sort of journey back to school, even before the rain began in earnest and as we turned the final corner we could see an empty playground waiting beyond the railings.

"Oh bugger," I exclaimed, before then going on to state the blindingly obvious, "they've all gone in already."

Indeed they had, some five minutes previously as it turned out. In a considerably dishevelled state - the heel from one of my platform boots having given up the ghost some five minutes into our trip - the two of us burst in through the front door and hurried, surreptitiously we hoped, past the tank of tropical fish standing in the corridor beside the Head's office. His thinking here had been that any parents coming in 'on the bounce' to complain about something, would have their anger and agitation completely erased by the calming influence of watching fish glide by from the comfort of nearby waiting armchairs. It didn't work for the two of us today though, but we were very relieved nonetheless to pass by the open door to his empty room.

On down the corridor we went at a considerable pace and passing Eleanor's classroom we glanced over to see her wave and attempt to attract our attention but we had no time for social exchange and carried on instead to hit the doors leading into the hall. Clattering across the wooden floor we were treated to a withering glare from Dorothy as she pummelled the piano keys and, although some time off yet, led her class through a premature Easter rehearsal:

"Look this way children and keep together now please –

There is a green hill far away,
Outside a city wall,
Where our dear Lord was crucified,
Who died to save us all."

We offered fleeting, feeble smiles by way of apology before exiting through the bottom door and into our home corridor at long last. My room came first, and as DT went on to continue his accelerated journey next door, I turned in to find a roomful of silent readers being supervised by a po-faced Head Teacher, which made me somewhat uncomfortable to say the least. There was worse to come however and as The Boss stepped to one side I was treated to an unmistakable flash of colour – African Violet Purple.

Mr. Lawrence looked me up and down, his eyes taking in my fragmented footwear, the dried vanilla stain now crusted and congealed on the flies of my trousers and the lank, rain-plastered hair before offering a caustic greeting of sorts:

"Good of you to join us Mr. Critchley."

Once more I am totally unaware of just exactly where my reply came from, maybe it was down to oxygen-starvation or possibly acute dehydration but in retrospect I really wish I hadn't said it:

"Just been out for a run Mr. Lawrence - to top up the stamina levels you know."

My tormentor stepped very close and pointedly sniffed the air by my mouth before adding:

"Really, and what was that then, three times around the taproom was it or did you really push yourself hard and go for several laps of the lounge bar?"

He pushed past me with a disgusted look and thrust some paperwork into my hand before lifting one impossibly spotless training shoe to step over the cardboard baboon which had just fluttered noisily to earth once more, and swept out, followed through the door by a disappointed looking Mr. Antrobus.

Their open reading books before them, every pair of eyes in the eerily quiet room was turned my way before Sean spoke up to break the silence:

"I can smell beer!"

## CHAPTER EIGHT – "We're Off in a Motor Car...."

We weren't the only school in the vicinity, our nearest neighbours being the RC establishment directly across the road from us – St. Cyril of Jerusalem's. For the most part relations between the two sets of pupils and staff were reasonably amicable – we'd take it in turns for example every December to visit one another's Nativity production and if either school ever ran out of something essential in their stockroom, the other would usually help out if they were able to. True there was the annual inter-school football match which would usually engender some fairly strong feelings – fuelled it must be said by groups of over-enthusiastic parents howling encouragement from the sidelines after a couple of mid-afternoon beers. Apart from that however, most was sweetness and light between the two establishments, with just the one traditionally bitter bone of contention.

My class was never entirely happy with the way the opposition appeared to benefit from more days off than they received themselves and you could guarantee the sight of their out-of-school chums strolling free on Holydays of Obligation and the assorted feast days which seemed to come around with envious regularity, would prompt some irate comment or other. On one such occasion as I recall, there had been considerable grumblings all morning about the empty classrooms readily visible across the way as my class steeled themselves instead for a tedious hour wrestling with the SRA box. In an attempt at appeasement I had promised some afternoon plasticine-time if they worked really hard up to lunch but it can't have been easy for them, particularly as the sun was shining and sounds of impromptu football games drifted up from the local green area which was known for some reason as the *Licker Field*.

Suddenly things got rather lively as an indignant Stuart jumped up from his desk and pointed an accusing finger in my direction. Within seconds he was joined by other class members on their feet, purple with rage and also seemingly directing their anger towards me. Stuart remained so incandescent that he struggled to get his words out until, an accusatory index finger indicating something truly dreadful taking place over my left shoulder, he finally let fly:

"Mr. Critchley," he spluttered, "there's...there's *Cath'licks* at t'winnder!"

And indeed there were. I spun round to look behind and was just in time to spot three grinning faces peering in at us before jumping down from their vantage point on an outside drain pipe, stooping to snatch up their abandoned bikes and laughing uncontrollably as they pedalled these at great speed back across our playground and out through the open gates.

Turning back towards the class I just managed to intercept a disgruntled Sean as he headed towards the classroom door leading a posse of willing vigilantes. The miscreants at the window had been identified as Bozzer and his chums, so Sean's gang was now seemingly hellbent on immediate search and retribution but were soon calmed by my explanation that our peeping Toms had heard such wonderful things about our great school and its children, that they just wanted to see the truth for themselves.

The days continued to warm up and we offered regular, fervent prayers that the good weather would hold for the forthcoming planned expedition to wildest Wales. All participants were now fully paid up, the money having come in gradually over the months, each of the children's growing totals entered onto individual savings cards every Friday morning breaktime by myself as duly elected accountant, (awfully good experience you know). After trailing in with bits & bobs of cash every week, the top junior children would always heave a mighty sigh of relief when I was able to write in the bottom of the final column: 'PAID IN FULL - £9:50.' It was as if this simple act signified that the trip couldn't now be snatched away from them and really would actually take place after all.

We'd issued lists of suggestions re appropriate clothing for the trip and stressed repeatedly to all the parents who'd bothered to attend our evening meetings that they should be thinking about packing only old clothes, as days spent outdoors would surely be the ruin of any newly-purchased outfits. There was also a heartfelt plea for all luggage to be kept to an absolute minimum as space would definitely be at a premium in the minibuses, but I had serious doubts that any of our advice was actually being taken seriously.

Whilst on playground duty for example, DT and myself would listen in disbelief to snatches of conversations drifting out from the knots of top junior children dotted around the edges of the yard.

"Michelle have you gorr' any new clothes for t' Wales trip?"

"Yay - I've gorra new green leotard wi' sequins all over, an' me mam's off ter Liverpool this affy for a frock 'ave seen in Blacklers."

"Ooh gorgeous Michelle, I've gorra new denim maxi-skirt, flurred you know, but I aft 'ave it shortened cos it trails on't floor and I keep trippin' up – even with 'igh 'eels on."

Mind you, the boys were every bit as bad judging from what we overheard.

"Worra you gunna wurr Stu?"

"Our Joanne's gunna stitch some tartan round 'turnups of my jeans - parallels yer know -18 inch bottoms – an' dad sez I can borrow 'is white braces if I look after 'em. Mam sez I can let me 'air grow a bit an' all - yer know – like Les McKeown."

"Nice!"

DT turned a pale exasperated face towards me:

"Oh dear God, you do realise that we'll be travelling into North Wales with The Bay City Rollers!"

We didn't let the non-starting car episode put us off regular lunchtime excursions, especially not on Fridays, which was always designated *banking day*. Lately though we had always driven in DT's vehicle just to be on the safe side, an early 1960's Morris Minor which we would take in turns to drive around the block whilst the other hurried in to the very impressive National Westminster building to cash a cheque. Usually mine would be made out to *self* for the totally extravagant sum of £5:00 – more than sufficient to see me through to the following week, including my spends for a couple of midweek nights in the pub and enough to take Anne out when she came home from College at the weekend.

True, DT's Morris Minor was a tad more reliable vehicle than my intermittently vindictive vehicle, but was still not without some little foibles all of its own. If you peeled back the carpet in the front footwell for example, you would see the gleaming white stove enamel of an old Creda cooker side panel used to effect a makeshift repair to a considerable gap in the car's floorpan and I had already ruined a perfectly good pair of Farah trousers by sitting too close to the spare battery DT insisted on carrying, also in the footwell. He held only slim hopes of success in this year's MOT, scheduled as it was in three months time, especially as we had already had the dubious pleasure of having the car's failings clearly pointed out to us in detail by the policeman who signalled us to pull over to the kerb during the return to school one Friday.

He spent some minutes walking around the car, poking and prodding, kicking the tyres, tugging at bits that looked as if they might become detached at any moment, his facial expressions ranging from disbelief through to downright amusement as he jotted in a notebook whilst shaking his head and *tutting* repeatedly.

"Switch your **wiper** on," he barked at one point, and his heavy emphasis on the use of the singular wasn't lost on either of us.

He grimaced as the lonely wiper blade dragged itself slowly and serenely across the screen before signalling that he'd seen enough and bending in through the driver's window.

"Take this piece of crap home and throw it in the bin," was his fairly direct instruction, "because if I see it on the road again I'll be a very angry boy!"

Well at least we weren't late for school.

- - o O o - -

Taking charge of two considerably more reliable vehicles a couple of weeks later then was quite a treat for the pair of us. We were in Liverpool – Upper Parliament Street to be precise – to collect the hired transport we would be using for our trip. Striding towards a brace of gleaming Toyota Hiace minibuses, 'M' registered with matching turquoise coachwork and relatively few miles on the clock, we climbed aboard to drive proudly off the forecourt back towards St. Helens thinking we were absolutely *the bee's knees*.

True, I did have something of a struggle attempting to manage the simultaneous twin terrors of manouvering an unfamiliar, oversized vehicle whilst coping at the same time with city-centre navigation, resulting in DT and myself parting company somewhere around the Old Swan area, hopefully this wouldn't prove to be an ill omen for the rest of our trip. My late arrival back into the school car park was greeted by whoops of delight and bouts of cheering as a distinctly 'party atmosphere' spilled over onto the edges of the field. It was mayhem, with troupes of over-excited primary children, (actually, many of those capering about in delighted high-spirits weren't even coming with us but had clearly become infected by holiday mania) and hordes of parents and grandparents who had come along to wave to their offspring at the start of their big adventure. It was certainly fun and who could deny any of them their excitement, particularly as I myself was experiencing a certain frisson of emotion but that may actually have been the result of unease and anxiety.

Reversing the bus carefully between the crowds and the school building, I switched off the engine in the shadow of an enormous mound, which I thought at first may have been a scale-model of Snowdon, constructed by grateful parents to wish us well on our trip. In fact this actually turned out to be the pile of waiting luggage in front of which DT and myself were about to stand whilst scratching our heads in disbelief. Right on cue yet more of the stuff arrived, carried along with enormous difficulty by a diminutive top-class junior boy named Stanley Brereton. Wearing a baggy pair of 'It Ain't Half Hot Mum', shorts, his skinny little legs could quite plainly be seen buckling under the strain of managing what could only be described as the world's biggest backpack. I struggled to keep a straight face and instead allowed DT to greet the heavily perspiring little lad:

"Well well Stanley, if you're going to get a rucksack get a good 'un that's what I always say!"

"It's a *Bergen*," corrected Stan, red-faced and breathless, "It used 'belong to Uncle Jack, 'e wus in't Paras."

The thing must have been at least 90 litres capacity and it was full to the brim with heaven knows what. Stanley looked mightily relieved as he added his bag to the pile before returning to stand between proud parents Mr. & Mrs. Brereton, the lad's t-shirt plastered to his back with perspiration even though he'd only carried the thing from the end of the street.

DT turned to me with a smile of resignation, "Well DC we'd better get started I suppose, as standing about like this won't help us squeeze a circus into a shoebox."

And that was exactly how it felt. The briefest of logistical planning sessions convinced us that the simplest way forward would be to get the children loaded into the vans and then arrange the luggage around them once seated – surely the easiest of tasks? Not so as it turned out, as rounding the children up was a bit like herding budgerigars, only noisier. The parents wanted goodbye hugs, then a photo taken with mum, dad, gran, little brother etc before getting on board, then some of the girls had to get back off again for a final hug or a wee, or both, then Esme Cotton couldn't find *Maisy* her cuddly monkey. I could tell DT was getting close to exasperation with his comment of:

"Look we're off to The Conwy Valley, it's not a one-way troop train to the Western Front, we'll all be back on Monday for God's sake."

Finally we got them nailed into their places and simply stuffed the luggage around them all as best we could – under seats, down the aisle, anywhere we could find - Stan's Bergen for example had pride of place lounging in the front footwell. There wasn't a scrap of spare space to be had anywhere and as we headed out of the school gates and along Morton Street, I was busy mentally composing a letter of complaint to the Chairman of Toyota concerning the complete inadequacy of accommodation within their minibus range. Meanwhile, Stu and the rest of *The Rollers* were waving rhythmically out of the back window and singing along to the chorus from Bye Bye Baby as several of the parents sniffled into their hankies.

Not for a single instant did the enormity of responsibility associated with this seemingly innocent excursion occur to me at the time, I suppose I was far too preoccupied hoping and praying that the traffic over the Runcorn Bridge wouldn't be too horrendous as we made our way towards the first planned comfort break at Chester. It was only much later in my life that I came to reflect on what it was I had taken on that day. There I was, just twenty-one years old, still struggling each morning to find sufficient facial growth to warrant the use of a Gillette, having never previously driven anything more capacious than a Hillman Imp, and completely unaware of how to reach our destination without hanging onto the rear bumper of my friend in front. Meanwhile the vehicle of which I was in sole charge was stuffed to the gunwales with that most precious of cargoes – the beloved offspring of a dozen families. Looking back now to that momentous occasion almost forty years ago, I am actually quite humbled by the abject faith placed in my capabilities by those trusting parents and so, overdue though it may be, I'd like to offer them a sincere and heartfelt thank you.

"We're off, we're off
We're off in a motor car,
There's fifty bobbies are after us,
And we don't know where we are..."

This, the traditional anthem of school outings for countless decades was being sung with increasing volume as I eased into the parking bay by the bandstand beside the River Dee at Chester. DT was parked alongside and the occupants of both buses pulled hideous faces at one another before slithering towards the rear doors across the suitcase assault course.

Within twenty minutes of arrival, to a man, each of our eager passengers had spent up every last cent of the money that they weren't even supposed to have with them in the first place. We had banned pocket money entirely for the trip as there were no shops where we were heading and primary children are notoriously poor at keeping hold of cash for any length of time anyway. At the point of departure however, mums, dads, grans, uncles etc had simply been unable to resist passing over quantities of cash, ("just in case – you know"), and this had lain smouldering in two dozen hot little palms until its release at Chester. It was a warm afternoon and surely the river had never looked lovelier. Shards of sunlight glinted off the water, couples strolled across the suspension bridge as rowers sculled by beneath and on the far bank, a scruffy heron made a great fuss about taking off with a beakful of perch. Our band of gallant troops however had far more important matters to attend to than scenic appreciation, as they raised their noses aloft to sniff the air for that most important of quarry – spending opportunities.

Clambering back on board later, each individual had a carrier bag, which certainly did nothing to ease the luggage situation and as we set off again, these were opened as they began eagerly comparing their trophies. Boxes of fudge for example, with lids depicting scenes of pleasure boats on the river seemed universally popular:

"This is for me gran," came one explanation, "she loves fudge me gran."

"Mine's for ar Sammy, it's 'er birthday when we get back," explained another.

Worthy sentiments to be sure, but as I recall, the contents of neither box actually made it beyond Queensferry.

There were sticks of rock also, and a snowstorm bubble dome containing a model of The Eastgate Clock that was to come to an untimely demise on the floor of the boys' dormitory next day. Stu had bought his mam a tea caddy spoon bearing the Chester coat of arms whilst his mate Frank had a small plaster owl that would apparently change colour according to the weather.

"Is it magic Mr. Critchley?" he asked.

I was about to reply - *No Frank it's cobalt chloride paint* - but checked myself in time so as not to ruin the mood –

"That's right Frank – magic!"

Their Bay City Rollers' repertoire thankfully exhausted, the bus grew quiet as we arrived in Wales and rural scenes began to appear thick and fast on either side. It was reassuring to listen to the children's comments and learn that a good many of them were very much taken with images of the countryside as indeed, that had been the principal objective of this whole exercise.

"Oooh look Joanne - sheep."

"Wurr?"

"Over thurr in that field."

"Oh yay, look, thurr's a black 'un an' all."

"D'you think they fetch 'em indoors at night or will they sleep outside?"

Speaking to the group over recent weeks, we'd discovered that for the majority this was to be their first ever time spent away from their parents whilst for others, it would be the very first taste of anything that could even remotely be deemed *a holiday*. Our overall intention had simply been to introduce the children to alternatives, to allow a glimpse of a world away from busy streets and shop fronts, where the wildlife was more varied than the curly-tailed estate dogs that roamed the pavements outside school. Early impressions seemed to suggest that this exercise in eye-opening was indeed being well-received, which was a great relief ay least to David & myself.

## CHAPTER NINE – Cymru am Byth.

Whilst our arrival at Lledr House Youth Hostel had been pretty unremarkable, the surroundings themselves were little short of majestic – DT had obviously done his homework well. Directly across the road from this imposing timber-clad house, an open field ran down to the banks of the River Lledr as it ambled past in gurgling eddies, and beyond that in the distance, could plainly be seen the wider landscape of Snowdonia. It was gratifying to notice that such beauty wasn't lost on our party either, as the group of appreciative children stood beside the minibuses and gaped.

"Eee I wish mam wus 'ere to see this," breathed Sandra Featherstone, "can we go an' paddle?"

"Not just yet, but later on, of course we can," assured DT, "first we have to unpack our bags and settle into the dormitory."

"What's adormitry?" asked a puzzled voice.

"You'll see."

Their excitement knew no bounds - beautiful surroundings along with the option of sleeping all together in a huge room using beds on stilts almost proved too much for some. Leaving them to the task of establishing group dynamics and ironing out the politics of their sleeping arrangements, we headed off next door to our own meagre accommodation – and I got the top bunk. We were separated from the adjoining rooms by the flimsiest of stud walls meaning that there would be no conversational privacy over the next few days, and there would of course be a good many conversations – including some taking place in the wee small hours.

We imagined that we'd run them all ragged on the field by the river that first evening in a bid to ensure they all slept.

(Suddenly from nowhere a rugby ball had mysteriously appeared and I was curious:

"Where did that come from?"

"Stan had it in his rucksack," came the reply

"Bergen!" Chorused Stan, DT and myself, in unison.)

Our efforts at organised exhaustion had all been in vain however, as they were all far too excited to be bothered wasting time with nonsensical fripperies such as sleep. I had to resort to using my 'big voice' around midnight in order to get them to pipe down and allow us a bit of rest but they were bright-eyed and bushy-tailed again well in advance of cock-crow next morning. I was awoken by a strange noise around 5 a.m. and it took a few minutes before my sleep-fuddled brain identified this as the sound of a suitcase being dragged out from beneath a bunk before being opened. This in turn was followed by a girl's voice:

"Hayley, Hayley, wake up. What 'yer gunna wear today Hayley?"

The person in question can't have helped but be startled to receive a reply not from her friend in the bunk above but from myself as I growled through the paper-thin plasterboard:

"If Hayley's got any sense at all she won't even be thinking about her wardrobe for another two hours at least now go back to sleep."

Peace reigned for a little while longer but as my watch showed 6:30 a.m. it was the turn of the boys' room to begin stirring. In the grounds of the hostel was a beautiful pony, a grey Welsh cob that had been a real-crowd pleaser yesterday afternoon judging by the reaction of the gang hanging over the fence trying to tempt it closer with handfuls of grass. Bernard Kelly had just noticed that the animal had now moved round to the rear of the property and wasted no time in pointing this fact out to his friend:

"Gary - you awake?"

"Yiss," the prompt reply.

"Have a look out o' winnder – 'donkey's gone inter ' back yard!"

Sadly however it wasn't only sound that filtered into our sleeping space as shortly after this exchange a distinctly malodorous air percolated through, prompting Bernard to comment once more:

"Phwoarrr! Who's let Polly out of prison?"

Cue great ribaldry and much laughter (bodily functions – remember?). Maybe it was time to get up after all.

- - o O o - -

The entire weekend was a tremendous success I have to say, particularly as we'd actually managed to choose days blessed with perfect weather for being outdoors. Sleeping at the appropriate time wasn't too much of a problem either after the first night, as we crammed so much into our brief stay and did our best to walk the children's legs to stumps each day. Next morning we yomped along the valley to Dolwydellan Castle, with Stan leading the way from beneath his enormous backpack. At one point he tripped over a tree root whilst attempting to guide us all by squinting with one eye through Uncle Jack's sighting compass and it took three of the group to right him and his oversized luggage once more before we could continue. On arrival, we attempted to bring history to life by explaining all about Motte & Bailey castles and sent the group charging up and down the hillside, a ploy which would surely pay dividends later at bedtime.

Whilst many of the group were much taken with grisly tales concerning the hardships of 13th century life, there were also a few who bemoaned the absence of a gift shop; whilst coming to terms with lavatorial arrangements in the great outdoors took some serious moral adjustments on the part of one or two children.

"Is there a toilet I can use?" This from Samantha Hardiman.

"I'm afraid not Samantha, you'll just have to find a quiet spot somewhere and use that."

This prompted truly incredulous looks from the majority of the group and indeed was such an outrageous notion that back at school, when they were asked if they'd had a good time, one of the first comments would be:

"Yay it was great – Samantha had a wee in a bush!"

Conwy Castle provided yet more opportunity for medieval re-enactments as they dashed along the battlements or up and down narrow spiral staircases. The whole toileting notion appeared once more on the agenda when DT asked if they knew what a *garderobe* was before going on to explain the function of the ancient chutes, which were used for transporting the inhabitants' excrement into the moat outside.

"So all t'water was full o' poo you mean?"

Our visit to Britain's smallest house on the quayside at Conway went down well too, but not quite as well as a stroll along Llandudno Pier where we treated them all to an ice cream each. We splashed about beside Swallow Falls, with Bernard Keenan splashing rather too far from shore and needing to be rescued by me. Driving the minibus for the rest of the day with soaking wet feet was not a pleasant experience to be honest.

We dipped for fish in the river outside Lledr House and Bernard had to be rescued again after falling off the algae-covered stepping-stones. Once again I was duly elected for this task as DT pointed out – with some considerable logic I have to admit - that as my lower body was already damp, he might just as well stay dry on the riverbank and act in an advisory capacity. Stan did offer me the use of an enormous loop of climbing rope fished from the depths of his Bergen, but I managed well enough without. Thankfully there were no real injuries or incidents to worry about, although on one occasion I did fear the worst. A breathless and obviously distressed Geraldine Cummings burst through the Youth Hostel entrance one afternoon and grabbed me by the arm.

"Come quick, come quick Mr. Critchley," she panted.

Accompanying her back out towards the river I attempted to find the cause of the panic.

"Whatever is it Geraldine – is someone hurt?"

"Yes, yes hurry up."

As we crossed the road my heart sank at the sight of one of the boys clutching a leg in agony as a curious group gathered around his prostrate form.

Geraldine went on to provide further information as we dashed in their direction:

"A duck's *bit* Geoffrey!"

Thankfully it wasn't a lethal peck and Geoff managed to pull through, much to everyone's relief. If he stretched the flesh on his shinbone extremely tight and you looked really hard, in bright sunlight, there was indeed a mark barely present which could I suppose to the generous observer, just about constitute a bruise of sorts. Despite the lack of severity of the injury however, Geoff became the toast of the group and for the rest of the term back at Morton Street he could often be spotted during playtimes, bravely re-enacting his valiant riverside tussle with a malicious mallard.

From my point of view, a real benefit of the weekend was getting to know the children better by observing them outside their usual habitat. It was edifying to recognise the real personalities of many, which didn't always come readily to the fore within the classroom setting. The brash, rufty-tufty, in-your-face, hey-look-at-me-aren't-I-a-hard-case types, often actually turned out to be rather more gentle souls who might need a comforting word to help ward off bouts of chronic homesickness. Meanwhile some of the never-say-boo-to-a-goose characters demonstrated genuine wit and a spirit of adventure that surprised us all. On several occasions we would notice individuals looking at some of their peers with new found respect, possibly actually seeing their chums in a whole new light for the very first time – it was as if a new order was being established, and just in time for the great exodus to secondary school. Turns out that a few days' trip to the Welsh countryside can be a great leveller.

The few days passed incredibly quickly, mostly in similarly simple pursuits to those described here, and in a shake of a lamb's tail the whole adventure was over and it was time to start packing again for our return home. Making sense of the boys' room was a bit of a nightmare as over the two and a bit days they'd simply elected to make a collective heap of all their clothes in the middle of the floor rather than try to maintain any sort of individuality relating to the assorted belongings. Eventually the pile was deciphered after a fashion, with DT and myself acting rather in the manner of auctioneers, holding each item aloft for claiming, together with a potted description:

"Red swimming trunks with a stripe down the sides?... Wigan rugby shirt with left sleeve completely torn off?...one brown shoe without a lace, looks as if it may have been a *brogue* in a previous life?… pair of green, nylon socks so stiff you can stand them up in the corner?…whiteish underpants of dubious quality…" and so on until the pile was all gone, apart that is from one well-loved teddy bear with a chewed ear that no Standard 4 boy would confess to owning even if his life depended on it.

These would be gratefully retrieved by their owners (or indeed those not actually the owners at all but instead, those reluctant to arrive home with a completely empty holdall) before being stuffed untidily into suitcases and bags, alongside unopened bars of Knight's Castile soap, virgin bottles of Vosene Medicated shampoo and pristine, bone-dry bath towels.

Not that there would be any likelihood of grey necks, grubby fingernails and missing underwear dampening the enthusiasm of the crowd waiting to greet us as we turned in again at the school gates on Monday lunchtime. The back doors of the buses burst open and a drift of sun-burnished arms, legs, hoarse voices (oh goodness me yes, there were voices all right) and assorted luggage, swirled out to fall into the waiting arms of various family members, some of whom had actually booked time off work in order to be at school in time for the homecoming. The air was heavy with the scent of fatted calves being prepared, whilst hugs-a-plenty, embarrassingly sloppy kisses from grannies and broad smiles were teamed with all manner of questions, one or two of which admittedly were in the manner of:

"Gary, why's your jumper on inside out… and who's are them pants?"

But more usually, the parents simply wanted to know:

"Ave you 'ad a nice time?"

The response to this was a unanimous *yes* as excited voices all around combined to give a reply in the form of a breathless outpouring stream of consciousness.

"There wus sheep all over t'place an' rivers wi' fish in an' I fed an 'orse with an apple. We 'ad an ice cream and never ad 'pay. Stuart fell off 'top bunk and banged 'is 'ead an' one night I stayed awake till after ten o clock. Castles 'ad no toilets an' we 'ad to wee on't grass. One day I 'ad a shower instead of a wash – can we 'ave a shower at 'ome dad cos they're great?"

It was an utter delight to witness such unbridled enthusiasm for what had been in essence, a simple weekend passed in a destination barely seventy miles distant. Parents and children alike came forward to offer their thanks for our efforts and I felt a real personal glow of good feeling about the whole event. I watched Stan's dad hoist the Bergen onto his own shoulder as they drifted off homeward along with all the other reunited families and DT and myself headed off towards the staffroom for a well-earned cup of tea. A breathless Joseph Patterson who came hurtling down the street at great speed halted us at the doors to school however, the anxious youngster glancing nervously around before blurting out:

" 'ave you still got that teddy bear?"

- - o O o - -

And then it was Tuesday morning.

My class were glad to see me back apparently as they hadn't much enjoyed being doled out around the rest of the school in small groups during my absence. Maureen Pickavance's hand was up in a flash as we got ready for the register, and she wasted precious little time in trying to bring me up to speed about some of their antics in my absence:

'Mr. Critchley, Sean Bickerstaffe got *done* when he wus in Mrs. Bates's class yesterday, he..."

"Actually Maureen," I interrupted, "I don't really want to hear what Sean has been up to, and if he was being silly somehow, I'm sure Mrs. Bates was more than capable of dealing with him."

Sean pulled a triumphant, sneering face across the class at his tormentor, but his smile was cut short as I went on:

"...but whatever it was that you did Sean, I have to say I am really disappointed in you yet again, so why don't we stay in together at playtime and discuss your behaviour eh? Now get out your reading books please everyone."

The fuzzy, warm feelings engendered by our successful weekend in Wales continued to grow as I listened to Angela read aloud at my desk, and marvelled at the progress she had made over the months. Maybe I'm not too bad at this teaching business after all, I mused, listening to her glide effortlessly through the content of Ladybird 5a *Where we Go*. Or maybe her undoubted literary progress wasn't entirely down to myself, but rather the other resources that had been at work, such as the one we would engage with later that morning.

After break we trundled down to the TV room once more, to enjoy the latest helping of this term's chosen series: 'Look and Read' and as with all televisual offerings, the class would sit spellbound in front of each programme. The format of this was fairly simple, an ongoing adventure story would be interspersed with cartoon characters whose catchy songs and antics were designed to aid the children's language development. After a teasing instalment about the alien child called Peep-Peep who'd been discovered near a meteorite in the countryside - the *Boy From Space* mentioned in the title - up onto the screen would leap Dog Detective, sniffing out new examples of punctuation, or Bill the Brickie, building his weekly word wall, whilst Wordie – a kind of oversized, alphabetic golfball, would hover around the studio to the delight of my viewers, repeatedly screeching out his rather irritating catchphrase of:

"Whoo – Hooo Wordwatchers!!"

Everyone's favourite however was surely Magic 'E' - a pointy-hatted wizard who would twirl his wand with a flourish before using it to transform a range of short vowel sounds and encourage the class to sing along each time:

"I'm magic, Magic 'E' – magic, Magic 'E' –
*Pal* becomes *Pale* with me,
*Cap* becomes *Cape* with me,
*Pan* becomes *Pane* with me –
Yes I'm magic, Magic 'E' – magic, Magic 'E'.

All harmless fun leaving many of the children chatting excitedly all the way back to class after the Boy From Space was left in some cliffhanging predicament along with his Earthling chums, meaning the gang of them would be dangling in danger until their inevitable rescue the following Tuesday. Other class members meanwhile carried on with the singing until suddenly, an all-too-easily recognisable voice began entertaining his colleagues with just a shade too much creativity:

**"I'm magic, Magic 'E' – magic, Magic 'E' –**

***Fit* becomes *Fite* with me,"**

(and here his fists were raised aloft, boxer-style)

**"Bit becomes Bite with me,"**

(now a menacing flash of teeth before continuing, but the crouching, squatting stance he adopted next in the middle of the corridor partly forewarned me about the quality of the approaching line, enabling me to cut him off mid-rhyme)

**"Shi…"**

"Sean Bickerstaffe I really am reaching the point at which I've had enough of what I am hearing, you will go too far one day. Please stay behind in class at lunchtime and I'll go through some of the things I'll be saying to your mum and dad at Parents' Evening."

- - o O o - -

There was no time to hang about after school, as I was due on the opposite side of town at 4pm to take part in the opening bout of Mr. Lawrence's PE course. I was absolutely determined not to further blot my copybook with any sort of vehicle-associated disaster or otherwise enforced lateness, which might thereby hinder any slender hopes of personal redemption. Clutching my trusty duffel bag of kit then, I was out of the door alongside the children, before sitting in the driver's seat of my car with fingers crossed and eyes pointing heaven-wards in prayer to turn the key in the ignition. No problems, the gods were indeed smiling, as it started first time enabling me to ease out into the street and return the cheerful waves of several passing class members as they hurried purposefully along the pavements towards the waiting TV delights of *Ivor the Engine* and *Jackanory*. Traffic was light too in those days meaning I was able to make unhindered progress across town towards the well-heeled, leafy suburban avenues surrounding the evening's school venue. Everything was going so incredibly well, and indeed it was only as I pulled into the well-scrubbed car park of the school venue that a disastrous realisation suddenly came along to spoil the party.

The associated paperwork had been quite clear in its instruction that all those taking part in the six-week course must attend wearing appropriate attire in order to enable full and active participation in the practical activities – tracksuit and training shoes then were absolute essentials. Presumably it was some form of miracle that I was searching for as I opened up my bag to peer inside, but the pungent, earthy, swamp stench that issued forth confirmed that unfortunately, this was not to be. My kit was of course, little more than a waterlogged, putrid slime, heavily contaminated with generous amounts of Welsh river mud and most certainly not fit for purpose, on this occasion at least. I was doomed surely.

The survival plan I cobbled together walking into the school was admittedly somewhat limited in its scope and revolved pretty much around hiding myself away amongst the other participants in order to avoid detection. Walking down the corridor I nodded to my peers and colleagues as they strode out of the junior classrooms, which had been designated 'changing area'. They were dressed to a man in faultless Umbro & Bukta sports gear, the afternoon sunlight glinting from the sheen of their glossy black training shoes and so I had to admit that my plan to remain inconspicuous wasn't looking terribly hopeful. Things got worse still as I arrived in the hall and took my place amongst them all on one of the plastic chairs that had been set out around the walls.

Without doubt the next two hours were amongst the longest of my life – every shred of self-dignity gone as I attempted to hold a range of weight-bearing positions on the PE mats, using body *points* & *patches* while dressed in a lime green Ben Sherman fitted shirt and a pair of flared Burgundy *Farah* slacks…with turnups. If ever Mr. Lawrence was in need of someone to demonstrate a particular move, it would be to me he would turn without hesitation and there can surely be few experiences in life more embarrassing than attempting to balance the length of an upturned PE bench wearing brown suede *desert boots* as a mirthful audience applauds your every step.

- - o O o - -

Next day I put the whole humiliating experience to one side as physical education was once again on the agenda, this time in the form of Sports Day Practice for my class. Dinnertime was spent in directing my trusty band of Munchkins as we hauled all manner of sporting paraphernalia out of the PE stockroom and onto the playing field. Bill was busy out there too, marking out a running track using an ancient roller-type device loaded with potentially debilitating amounts of creosote. Even though he was way over on the far side of the field, everyone knew he was happy in his work, evidenced by non-stop whistling of *The Hustle* by Van McCoy at maximum volume, his signature theme of choice over recent weeks.

Lunch over, Acme Thunderer around my neck, I began marshalling the troops who had by now, along with the rest of the school, been divided up into four groups using the familiar but spectacularly dull team names of *Red, Blue, Yellow* and *Green,* each child sitting impatiently on a PE mat with a band of tape in the appropriate colour looped over head and shoulder. They were all champing at the bit with excitement at the prospect of engaging in the potentially hazardous events that would always be present on occasions such as this during the mid-seventies. Whilst there is no doubt that the arrival of the Health & Safety executive did absolute wonders in terms of eradicating harmful practices across society; I have to say with some disappointment that its officers have also been responsible for depriving us of some truly memorable opportunities for slapstick humour whilst enjoying a typical Primary School Sports Day.

Take the now-outlawed wheelbarrow race for example, in which the children set off at a terrific pace but usually tend to run out of steam after about ten yards. Some judicious pairings at the start line can actually be extremely effective as a means of settling old scores from across the year. Anyone who has been a damned nuisance over the months should be designated *wheelbarrowee,* whilst *wheelbarrower*

119

– ie the one standing behind to provide the motive power – should ideally be chosen from the more robust class members and blessed with plenty of grunt. This model will ensure that it isn't too long before the one whose little arms are a-blur in striving to keep pace with the push they're receiving from the rear, gets a mouthful of daisies as their partner ploughs a deep furrow across the field using their nose. Immensely satisfying on so many levels.

Similarly with the three-legged race, in which the opposing limbs of two equally strong-minded children would be securely lashed together with a skipping rope. Blow a starting blast on the whistle and then stand back to admire the titanic tussle as the pair use their own individual mind-maps to gallop away in search of the finish line. Brilliant fun indeed, which actually only rarely ever results in a broken ankle or severed tendons.

For me though the gold medal event for laughter has to be the skipping race, especially if the participants in this are only ever selected from the group of boys in the *hopelessly-coordinated* category. Following the 'Ready, Steady, Go' they will each dash forward for a maximum of three paces before coming to an abrupt halt and dragging the skipping rope from behind their back and over the head then stepping over it as it lies like a lifeless snake on the grass. With this hurdle over, they then gallop on for a further three paces before repeating the process and the race can last several minutes as the gang of hapless individuals stutter towards the finish-line like a group of mime artists attempting to lasso a rainbow. Whilst those parents directly associated with the competitors will look on aghast at the display of total incompetence being publicly demonstrated by their offspring, the rest of the spectators are rendered positively incontinent with howling mirth.

Even though it took an absolute age to drag all the equipment outside, the practice session didn't last very long as my ribs were aching so badly from holding in laughter –

no, I really can't wait until late July and the actual event itself.

# CHAPTER TEN – What is it with Zebras?

It was early morning and I sat at my desk to savour the sense of achievement that only comes about after completing an enormous pile of marking. In this instance I'd been checking the results of yesterday's exercise from *First Aid in English (Revised)* which had been all about the use of the apostrophe to show possession. The past few minutes had clearly demonstrated that several members of the class had indeed been quite correct in persistently stating:

"I don't gerrit Mr. Critchley."

Whilst there were others whose misplaced confidence arose from playing safe by adopting a strategy of simply attaching an apostrophe to every word which concluded with a letter 's.' The same group had also overcome the thorny problem of whether this should come before or after the *s* by placing it in a hovering position directly above the final letter. *Ingenious* I thought, with results only marginally more successful than when I tried to get across the concept of *direct & indirect speech*.

I also reflected that furthering their proficiency in the use of tricky punctuation procedures would be a task which would now fall to others rather than myself, as the close of term was now but a couple of weeks distant. The room was looking good though, particularly the rear frieze, which now depicted scenes from *Willy Wonka's Chocolate Factory*, a spin-off from the class enjoyment of having a fifteen-minute dollop of the book read aloud each day. I had some time ago discovered the absolute joy of having children sit spellbound to listen to story, a situation in which I finally felt able to compete with the power of TV in capturing their attention.

Around the hastily-painted Chocolate River and dotted around some prancing oompa-loompas, I had mounted some of the children's creative writing and blu tacked these to the wall to complete a most pleasing display. They'd been asked to create other characters that might feature in the book and had entered into the task with much enthusiasm, particularly Angela, whose illustration of *Gabby Big Gob* (modelled apparently on her second-cousin from Cleckheaton) yawned down at me now from amongst a gang of similarly unsavoury delinquent friends.

"Cuppa David?"

Bill announced his arrival in a most acceptable manner as he approached carrying two steaming mugs before setting these down on the edge of my table and returning to the classroom door to bring in some essential supplies.

"Righto David," he went on, "there's a bottle o' water, a bucket, half a dozen sick bags – I used to use carrier bags but then found out the hard way that some o' these have holes in the bottom, not a good idea – a pack of paper towels, a bag o' sawdust and an air freshener, with a bit of luck you won't need any of 'em."

It was the day of the class trip and we were off to Chester Zoo later which explained why I was sitting there in my civvies – no tie, polo shirt, brushed denims, all teamed with the kind of jacket my dad would insist on referring to as a *windcheater* - all very casual, a state of affairs which didn't escape the notice of the class immediately I went out onto the yard to greet them. Angela was the first to comment:

"Oooh Mr. Critchley you look nice, dun't he look nice Samantha?"

"Oh yay, I wun't o' recognised you, you look really …*unusual*."

Accepting this somewhat neutral comment as a compliment, I returned one in similar vein.

"So do you girls I must say, and at least we won't lose sight of you in those bright orange sun hats, good thinking on your part."

The relaxed atmosphere and possibly also the proximity to the close of the year prompted a brave statement indeed from Sean Bickerstaffe as he grinned impishly at his close associate and accomplice Gareth Hughes before venturing:

"We know your real name don't we Gaz?"

Access to this monumental piece of information was indeed confirmed by his friend:

'Yay."

"But my name's Mr. Critchley, you all know that already," I pointed out teasingly.

"No, your *real* name I mean," the boys went on.

"My real name *is* Mr. Critchley lads, it says so on the classroom door remember."

"Yay but it's ... *David* in't it?"

"Well if you say so boys."

It was good that the class felt sufficiently relaxed to broach such subjects at all, but Sean had one last question which pushed things just a bit too far:

"Can we call you ... *Dave...* just for today I mean?" he asked shyly.

"No."

Strange how children have this ongoing fascination with the trivial everyday personal details of their teacher. For example it wouldn't be unusual for a hand to go up in class on a Monday morning to herald an awe-inspiring announcement:

"I saw you in town on Sat'day afternoon Mr. Critchley."

"Oh really, and what was I doing?"

By this time the whole class would be agog with excitement and quivering with anticipation for what was sure to be a rare glimpse into the intimate existence of their teacher. These were the days before the arrival of gossip magazines or *twitter* remember, and so such conversations at the start of the week were, I suppose, the mid-seventies version of *trending*:

"You wus crossin' t'road near Marks 'n Spencer."

Far from expressing disappointment at this rather banal item of news, the children would turn to each other wide-eyed with amazement to discover I actually had a presence in society as an individual.

It's a similar situation should I ever bump into one of my pupils while shopping in the supermarket. On such occasions even the most actively conversational, confident, outgoing child will be rendered tongue-tied, bashful and flushed with acute embarrassment as they fall immediately silent before attempting to become invisible behind their parent's coat tails. Indeed at such times it's normally mum who will feel strong enough to pass comment, usually something to the order of:

"Well Mr. Critchley, I could do with you being around all the time as that's the first time she's shut up gabbing since she got out of bed!"

It's as if they are just so confused to see you outside your normal setting, or possibly that they actually expect you to be hung up in the cupboard each evening by the caretaker, only to be taken down again like a well-worn overcoat before 9 o' clock next morning.

Goodness me though, they were just so excited at the prospect of today's excursion and of course it wasn't merely the prospect of getting up close and personal with a host of wild animals that was causing this:

"So children, which animal are you looking forward most to seeing?"

"The tapirs, or indeed any of the odd-toed ungulates."

Really Brian you ought to get out more I mused – there is a life beyond *Animal Magic* you know. Come to think of it, the lad did actually bear an uncanny resemblance to a juvenile Johnny Morris.

No, animals aside, they would also be savouring the thrill of a coach trip, shopping – of which more later – and a picnic:

"Wharr' ave you gorr'on your butties Ann-Marie?"

"Boiled egg 'n pickle."

A most disturbing announcement which prompted me to make a mental note to be well out of the way later when this particular lunch item was being unwrapped.

There would also be sweets, fresh air, the constant company of friends and best of all of course, no lessons for the day – could life get any better?

Another two-fingered gesture to Health & Safety was made as the class was loaded onto the coach, three children being assigned to each bench seat with reckless abandon and no seatbelts available either don't forget. Most sat with carrier bags on their knees, using these like nosebags as they carried out a continuous stocktake of their edible rations throughout the journey. Bill's anti-sickness aids were stacked ready to hand in the aisle, group lists were handed out to the helping mums who would now spend the next five or six hours relentlessly counting heads, dire warnings were issued to one and all about anyone caught eating sweets during the journey and we were off. Our driver turned out to be a kindly old soul thankfully, who made absolutely not a murmur of complaint as we drove around the block before returning prematurely to the gates once again in order that I might dash back indoors and collect the school cheque book.

Sitting near to the front of the bus, I passed the time in conversation with the helping mums until, feeling a pull at my sleeve as we approached the outskirts of Frodsham, I turned to find the imposing figure of Sharon Stott standing beside me.

"Stephen Gibbons sez 'e feels sick Mr. Critchley."

"Oh dear," I replied, "well I'm sure he'll feel better soon, tell him to look out of the window as we're nearly there."

Sharon was nothing if not persistent however:

"E's very 'ot and 'is face 'as gone all white."

I felt the colour drain from my own face too with this news; I was absolutely hopeless with vomit.

"Leave it to me Mr. Critchley, I'll go and sort the lad out."

This was the voice of my saviour from across the aisle and I watched with a grateful heart as the helping mum took a damp face cloth from her handbag and set off in search of the nauseous child. Oh thank you, thank you Mrs. Turner, I could kiss you I thought…were it not for your quite startlingly luxuriant facial hair.

There were no further incidents to report and in no time at all the class, including Stephen with his undeniably grey complexion, stepped down from the coach onto the car park outside the zoo, our number swelling the crowd of several hundred other primary aged children already present. Some of these were in faultless uniform, others seemed dressed for a day at the beach, several were in tears, one had been sick on his shoes - an act which had attracted quite a crowd of appreciative and curious onlookers drawn from schools across the North West - whilst others clutched clipboards to which were attached rafts of duplicated sheets containing zoo-based tasks for completion. I had avoided going down this route myself as previous experience in the local museum had shown me that in such situations the children merely charge around without actually looking at anything properly in an attempt to tick all the right boxes and answer totally pointless questions such as: How tall is an adult Rockhopper Penguin? Or: What is the dietary preference of the Madagascan Bamboo Lemur? Most pencils would of course be lost within five minutes of starting the whole exercise, whilst those individuals who did manage to hold onto their writing implement would be sure to jam this into an eye, (their own or worse still, that of some other passing unfortunate) at the earliest opportunity. No I was devoutly anti-clipboard myself, preferring instead to simply allow the children the opportunity to savour the whole experience unhindered.

With so much to see it was always going to be difficult knowing where exactly to head off to first, but I decided that a wise starting point might very well be the toilets. Setting off in search of the nearest ones I overheard Mrs. Turner asking her group where they would like to begin, with Brian wasting no time in making his recommendation:

"Might I suggest the pachyderm enclosure Miss?"

The boys emerged from the toilets refreshed, but also with tales of yet more misdemeanours from one particular group member:

"Sean Bickerstaffe was looking under all 'toilet doors Mr. Critchley an' a man inside one o't cubicles told 'im to *bugger off*."

It was time to take the lad to one side and really lay it on the line about how he was in danger of ruining the whole day for everyone, including myself and not to mention the poor zoo client presumably attempting to enjoy an undisturbed morning constitutional in relative peace and quiet. The message did seem to get through however and to his credit, Sean appeared suitably chastened and even a tiny bit moist-eyed.

Leading my little band through the wildlife of distant continents was a pleasant enough way to pass a morning, their relentless stream of questions keeping me on my toes throughout. The focus of these was really quite diverse, including for example, the usual fascination with superlatives in the animal kingdom:

"What's the biggest lion in the world Mr. Critchley?.. Which parrot has the most feathers?.. What's the fastest fish?"

Along with the totally bizarre:

"Could a boa constrictor swallow an ostrich?.. Do butterflies poo?.. Who'd win in a fight – a crocodile or a soldier?"

Important timetabling queries were also of course on everyone's lips:

"When can we eat our sweets?..Is it nearly time for dinner?..Will we be able to go in t' shop after?"

And not forgetting of course those questions lodged firmly in the awkward and embarrassing category:

"Why's that zebra got five legs?"

It really wasn't an opportune moment to launch into a discourse on animal physiology in my opinion and anyway, neither did I want to spoil the surprises that would lie ahead during the sex education lessons scheduled for the summer term of Top Juniors and so, on this occasion, I opted for a quite cowardly response:

"Hmmm, I think it's just one of those really, really special zebras...WOW will you look at the time - if we get a move on, I think we might catch the sea lions being fed, c'mon everybody let's go!"

Throughout the day there was the remorseless, repeated *click* of Kodak Instamatics being pointed at anything that moved, and indeed those subjects that remained tiresomely motionless, including a badly moulting camel, which must have been sixty yards away on the opposite side of its paddock. I felt certain that this would not provide the most rewarding of images when the photos came back from the chemist, but decided to pass no comment.

And then it was lunchtime – so far so good.

The other groups were already collapsed onto the grass by the giftshop and well on with demolishing the contents of their lunchtime carrier bags as I arrived with my gang. The two helping mums were sitting together, surrounded by munching children and I overheard Mrs. Turner speaking to her friend as I approached:

"Yay Pauline, who'd o' thought? - it turns out *pachyderms* are really elephants and rhinos and that – you live and learn don't you?"

130

Her friend paused mid-sandwich to reply:

"But don't you think elephants are the most majestic creatures though?"

Mrs. T mulled this one over carefully before replying:

"They're all right I suppose Pauline… but dear god they stink. Oh hello Mr. Critchley, everything ok? The children have been ever so good you know."

"Glad to hear it Mrs. Turner, thank you both for all your help. How's Stephen Gibbons holding up by the way, all ok on the upset tummy front?"

Both mums leaned to one side and I was treated to an unobstructed view of the boy in question through the gap they created:

"He looks ok to me Mr. Critchley."

An image of the anaconda we'd seen in the reptile house earlier sprang readily to mind as I watched Stephen cram the tail end of a family-sized pork pie into his mouth before glugging heavily from an old lemonade bottle now filled instead with full cream milk. Wiping a white, dairy semi-circle from his top lip with the back of his hand, he let out an enormous belch before reaching back into his carrier bag for yet more comestibles.

"Well if you ask me I think he'll live, what do you say ladies?"

Their response was a shared chuckle as they stood to begin clearing up their groups' lunchtime debris.

The appeal of photographing more lethargic animals lounging behind bars began to lose its magic part-way through the afternoon, to be replaced instead by the approaching attraction of what would, for many, be the undoubted highlight of the day…shopping. Throughout the lunch break, most eyes had been drawn to the nearby gift emporium as they'd looked on with great envy as other school groups piled in to part with their cash; and now at last it was about to be our turn.

This was the moment at which I first learned the importance of establishing definite ground rules surrounding available time limits and purchasing opportunities before setting a gang of primary children free in any commercial setting – it was manic from the instant their feet crossed the threshold. When faced with the chance to spend money, there is a set procedure that each child will always follow which goes something like this:

Step 1. Run round the shop scanning all the shelves to find something appealing.

Step 2. Pounce on an item and hold it high for inspection, possibly turning to a friend or colleague for a second opinion regarding its suitability:

"Aw look at this cuddly polar bear, in't it gorgeous?"

"Yay gorgeous, but look at this though – a plastic camouflaged jungle knife with binoculars and a water bottle."

"Ooh let me see… I'm 'aving one o' them instead."

Step 3. Pause to throw cuddly polar bear back in the general direction of where it was found originally.

Step 4. Stand impatiently in line waiting to pay whilst offering up a fervent prayer that you do actually have sufficient cash jingling in your hot little hand to buy said item.

Step 5. Place the item on the counter and pile up all your available cash beside it for the assistant to count.

Step 6. Gratefully accept the purchase and marvel at the bonus of also having some change handed back by the lady behind the counter, thus enabling a further spending opportunity.

Step 7. Go and find another prospective purchase and tag on to the end of the line once again.

Step 8. Repeat the above as many times as possible until all cash is exhausted.

They were all at it, with the exception of Michelle I noticed, who watched subdued from the corner of the shop.

"Everything OK ?" I quizzed.

"Yay Mr. Critchley am fine thanks, am saving mi money as I've not seen owt I fancy."

"Well that's very sensible Michelle, you wait until you see something really special eh?"

She responded to this with a glum nod, the reality being of course that as there was never any slack in the cash reserves of the Constantine household, pocket money was always going to be an early casualty. Turning a couple of silver coins over in my pocket, for a brief moment I toyed with the idea of passing these over to her, along with some fiction about having found them on the path with no sign of any owner. Very tempting, but then the poor kid would be torn between whether to accept my charity or not, and when she returned home carrying some new trinket or other she would be made to confess and next thing you know, her mum would be round to class in order to settle up her account. No, sad though it most definitely was, I had to leave well enough alone. Time to rally the troops.

"Right everyone, time's up I'm afraid, wherever you are now, stop what you're doing and let's see an orderly line by the door – well done on being first there Sean Bickerstaffe, but please step to one side as no-one is able to get in or out."

Several groans of disappointment greeted this announcement, but the majority did as they were asked, leaving me free to tour the premises and shoo the remaining hard-core consumers towards the door. Maureen Pickavance glanced fearfully over her shoulder at me as I approached the queue – she was now only three shoppers away from being served and obviously desperate to make a further purchase to add to the several she was already juggling.

"Didn't you hear me Maureen?"

"Oh yay Mr. Critchley, but I just want this one last thing, it's for mi Nan and…"

"Go and join the line by the door now, we're leaving, we've been in here forty-five minutes and it's time to go."

"Oh but please…"

"Open your hand please, and show me how much money you have," was my heartless reply.

The child's fingers unfolded to reveal just a few odd coppers.

"You've nowhere near enough money to pay for this set of tropical fish drinks coasters so go and put them back on the shelf this instant and join the others…NOW!"

She did as she was told, but I still had to keep an eye on her:

"Maureen, put down that Chester Zoo pencil case and do as you have been told please!"

- - o O o - -

There would still be several years yet to wait until the Falklands Conflict when Brian Hanrahan would famously comment from the deck of an aircraft carrier:

"I counted them all out and I counted them all back,"

but it was a similar feeling of relief that enveloped the adults as we sank into the well-worn upholstery of our *European Luxury Cruiser* after successfully loading an appropriate number of children back on board at the end of our day. The ladies, God bless them, having survived the trials of what they initially may have looked upon as a free day out, looked totally knackered. Mrs. Turner turned to her friend and managed a contented but weary smile:

"I'll tell you what Pauline  - am ready for a 'cig!"

# CHAPTER ELEVEN – Nymphs & Shepherds.

I suppose I should have known better to be honest, as Alan Foster wasn't the most reliable of boys, but I had thought the responsibility might have been good for his self-esteem. Yesterday afternoon after selecting him from the score of willing volunteers frantically waving their hands at me, I'd handed over the board duster along with an old wooden ruler and sent him out onto the playground to bang the living daylights out of the thing in order to render it dust-free and fit for purpose once more. He'd waved and grinned back at me from the corner of the yard through a cloud of chalk dust and after ten minutes or so I'd called him back into class. Moments later he returned to the classroom door clutching the ruler but no board duster, lord knows how you could lose something like that in a twenty yard journey, but Alan had somehow managed to do exactly that. Anyway, that was the reason I was now in the stockroom before school, rummaging around for a replacement.

Mr. Antrobus spotted me in there as he came up the stairs and called me into his room "for a chat". Stepping gingerly onto the elderly Axminster I was ushered towards a comfy chair beside the window, which looked out over the street and through which I could see a bunch of my boys kicking a tennis ball along the pavement.

"So David, the year draws to a close," was his opening gambit.

"Yes indeed," my non-committal reply. I was deeply curious as to where this conversation might be leading.

"Have you enjoyed your twelve months with us?"

"I certainly have Mr. Antrobus, very much so and I had hoped that would have been obvious to everyone, why, is there a problem of some sort?"

"Oh no, no, far from it, in fact David, I'm hopefully about to be *the bearer of glad tidings*, to coin a festive phrase, and please, call me *Ray*."

Curiouser and curiouser I thought.

"After discussion with the Deputy Head, we'd like to confirm that you've successfully completed your probationary year – so very well done to you," and here he leaned across to shake me warmly by the hand.

Finding myself at a bit of a loss for words, I just burbled on inanely for a few moments before managing to find my tongue again.

"Well thank you very much, that's really good news as I had been a bit worried to tell the truth…"

"Surely not?" he interrupted in reassuring tones, "you didn't imagine for one second that there would be any doubt about this? That's obviously my fault to be honest, in not reminding you at regular intervals what a truly splendid job you've been doing throughout the year."

"Not at all," now it was my turn to be reassuring, "it's just with the Mr. Lawrence thing you know, I thought he might have stuck his oar in so to speak."

"Oh that silly old sod," and here I must admit to being seriously taken aback to hear the Boss using such derogatory tones about one of the advisers, but there was even better yet to come.

"Always been full of his own wind & water that fella, loves the sound of his own voice and carries his brains round in a jockstrap – if he was made of chocolate he'd lick himself to death."

Brilliant! I suddenly felt as if I'd gained admission to an exclusive club of some sort, a kind of *behind closed doors society* as the Boss revealed his true colours to me - I felt really quite honoured to be privy to this exchange.

I had tried particularly hard to impress Lawrence during recent weeks, ensuring for example that there was no further incidence of the serious wardrobe malfunction, which had so clouded our opening evening together. Every session since that memorable encounter had seen my participation dressed in immaculate tracksuit bottoms, a Fred Perry polo shirt laundered to absolute perfection, (thank you mother) and a pair of Dunlop Green Flash plimsolls that positively gleamed beneath their abundant coating of Meltonian Wonder White. I felt in a way that an uneasy truce now existed between he and myself, but nevertheless, still looked ahead to his promised observation of one of my future PE lessons with more than a little trepidation.

The green numerals of the digital clock on the corner of the Head's desk announced 08:52 and so I made a move to get up from my chair.

"Oh, there was just one other thing," and he went on to make a totally unexpected announcement, a real out-of-the-blue moment. "We'd like you to take on responsibility for an aspect of the curriculum next year."

"Really? Me? On my own, kind of thing? This next year coming you mean? Well I…"

"Of course we wouldn't expect you to undertake something of that nature without appropriate reward and so we'd like to offer you a Scale II position starting from September."

Bloody Hell this was turning into some Wednesday morning. A Scale Two in my second year of teaching, at this rate I'd be Secretary of State for Education by the time I was thirty.

Trying to remain as calm as possible I pursued further detail:

"Any particular subject you had in mind?"

Knowing full well that it was highly unlikely for example to be offered for Physical Education.

"Well as you will know," he went on, "Science is very much the buzz word at the moment and so we'd like you to further the development of this subject over the coming months."

Science? Really? Me? I swallowed long and hard as in a flash my mind returned effortlessly to a catalogue of quite catastrophic school events at the hands of anything even faintly science-related, my total lack of aptitude in these disciplines summed up in a nutshell by an unwarranted caustic Summer report comment written by my fourth form chemistry teacher:

"David has elevated laziness to such a high degree that it has become for him an art form."

No, science certainly wasn't what I'd been expecting, nor would it have been top of my list in a free choice situation due to a chronically poor track record but hey – to be honest, if I'd been asked to abseil from the school chimney every week in order to paint the window frames before shampooing The Head's Vauxhall Viva and giving it a de-coke every other Friday lunchtime, I'd still have said 'yes.'

So I snatched his arm off.

With our 'little chat' seemingly now concluded, I was about to stand and take my leave when the door was suddenly flung back against the wall to herald a most amusing diversion as, with no prior warning, into the room charged a very red-faced Jimmy Patterson from Standard Three. He was obviously excited about something or other, but then that was very often the case with Jimmy, small in stature possibly, but large in personality certainly. Without waiting to be asked, he stood on the carpet between the pair of us and began accosting a really quite startled Head Teacher.

"Mis' Trantobus, Mis' Trantobus, I've…"

But he was cut off before even getting properly into his stride, as an extremely exasperated Head Teacher began firing questions at the lad:

"What on Earth is the meaning of this outburst James Patterson? Have you completely taken leave of your senses? I've never seen anything so rude in all my days, how dare you burst in here in this way? Get back outside that door at once, close it behind you, knock, and then wait to be invited in!"

Little Jimmy did exactly as he was told.

"Cheeky little tyke," Mr. Antrobus continued, "I'll teach him some manners if nobody else will. What he needs is…"
But then there was a further interruption as a frenzied knocking began on the other side of the office door. When, after a few moments he received no immediate response, Jimmy started rapping on the woodwork even harder still.

His eyes rolling towards heaven, the Head barked out an invitation of sorts.

"Come in… if you really must!"

Irrepressible as ever, Jimmy bounced back into the centre of the room and turned to face us both once again.

"Mis' Trantobus, Mis' Trantobus, please could you…"

"And you can stop that nonsense too," the Head cut in, "if you do wish to speak to me about something young man, then you will at least please do me the courtesy of using my real name."

"But Mis' Trantobus…"

"No James, there will be no further conversation until you are able to use my *proper* name if you please."

Crestfallen and impatient, Jimmy was momentarily nonplussed and stood there, racking his brains about what was actually wanted here, but then the light of realisation flashed across his features as he drew in a deep breath and tried for a third time:

"*Raymond*," he began innocently, "please could you give me mam a ring as I've forgot my baths kit?"

Now this really was my signal to leave and I chuckled off back down the stairs, leaving a totally perplexed Head Teacher seemingly at a loss for words.

- - o O o - -

Sports Day had been cancelled at the start of the week – such a disappointment for everyone concerned, as we were all in need of a good laugh - but the rain had poured down without pause from early morning leaving absolutely no alternative but to call it off. Now I had stupidly imagined that common sense would suggest to all and sundry that running and jumping on a wet field during an ongoing monsoon was a complete non-starter but no, and I was called upon to spend my lunchtime in the office responding to an endless stream of telephone queries. These are the responsibilities you have to shoulder I guess when you find yourself hurtling up the promotional ladder.

"Hello, am ringin' for 'check if t'sports will be on this afternoon or not?"

I wanted to say 'take a look out of the window will you, it's lashing down out there and blowing a chuffing gale, what do *you* think?' but managed instead to maintain a professional demeanour throughout:

"No I'm afraid due to the adverse weather conditions we have unfortunately taken the decision to cancel the afternoon's proceedings."

"So it's off then?"

"Yes."

There were some other callers however who adopted a rather more aggressive, indeed some might say truculent tone, obviously viewing the curtailment of the afternoon's entertainment as a purely arbitrary decision on my part:

"Off? What d'you mean it's off? I've booked half a day's holiday today and we've heard nothing else from our Ronald for a month now but egg 'n bloody spoon **and** he's ruined two of my best pillowslips practisin' for the bloody sack race up and down the landing. Can't you wait a bit an' see if it brightens up?"

A sudden spear of lightning momentarily lifted the gloom of the office whilst drapes of torrential rain continued to plaster the windows and angry clouds prowled the rooftops.

"Well to be honest Mrs. Atherton, if anything I think it's actually getting worse out there…"

"Bloody ridiculous!" And the phone was slammed down. Well you can't please everyone I always say.

- - o O o -

This afternoon however, there was a different al fresco treat to look forward to and the sun had returned in celebration.

142

Preparations for this were already in full swing as a few early bird mums drifted along to claim their place on the chairs that Bill and myself together with a crocodile of top junior porters had been busy arranging on the field throughout the lunch break. I continued with this task while Bill and the other David turned their attention instead to setting up the sound system by the car park. Strings of wires linked together by strips of insulating tape trailed from a pair of elderly speakers and passed through the open windows of the hall before disappearing into the back end of the school gramophone. I did have serious doubts about the potential success of this arrangement, but was proven wrong, as, following a sudden hiss and crackle, the whole thing burst into life and a deafening blast of accordion music startled the pigeons from their roosts beneath the eaves. Bill and DT gave one another a satisfied thumbs-up from either side of the glass and it seemed we were almost ready to go.

The blaring music was the signal for the stream of parents arriving through the school gates to turn into a flood and we were soon hard-pressed to keep up with an increased demand for seats. They were here to share in the afternoon's *Celebration of Traditional Country Dance* and, dressed in their summer finery with many carrying picnics, appeared determined to enjoy themselves.

The event was Dorothy & Eleanor's big project, but in fairness the pair had been pretty much conspicuous by their absence throughout the preparation stages, opting instead to relax in the staffroom, cooing enthusiastically over a knitting pattern for a matinee jacket planned for Eleanor's great-niece, while enjoying a Garibaldi biscuit and a nice cup of Earl Grey. Still, I'm in no doubt that staggering across a playing field courting a double hernia to carry an unpredictable pillar of post-war, wooden children's school chairs would be awfully good experience for me.

Thirty minutes later it was like a landscape from a Thomas Hardy novel that we gazed out upon, as spread across the field, every child in the school was poised to begin the afternoon's proceedings. The boys were splendidly attired in shorts and white tops whilst the girls in their lovely summer dresses, looked quite enchanting – indeed for some this was a sight that was proving rather too appealing:

"Mr. Critchley, Sean Bickerstaffe keeps lifting up my frock!"

The whole picture was an absolute delight and as the music struck up, each class moved as one into position for the opening dance – *The Circassian Circle,* with teachers close at hand to call out reminders about the steps:

"Into the middle two, three, four, & out again, two, three, four,
Circle left for eight – well done everyone,
Into the middle two, three, four, & out again, two, three, four,
Circle right for eight once more
GIRLS into the middle, two, three, four CLAP and return;
BOYS into the middle, two, three, four CLAP and return – well done everyone,
All Swing your partners and off we go again…"

It was simply wonderful, and with everyone seemingly happy to join in, I thought this a really lovely way to celebrate summer's arrival and the closing of the year.

Engaging though the scene undoubtedly was, it was true there were one or two notable differences between what was taking place before us and a similar pastoral scene from bygone days. Beyond the concrete panel fence surrounding the school field stood the sad rows of empty-eyed, derelict terraced houses patiently awaiting their fate. Actually, although I say 'empty', on this occasion as on successive recent afternoons, many of these were once again occupied, this time by a group of temporary residents. Substance abuse was a problem even back in 1975 and the local population of disaffected youth found the upper storeys of these properties a perfectly convenient venue for their antics. It wasn't amphetamines or cannabis that were the narcotics of choice in this instance however, but rather the frighteningly dangerous abuse of solvents that they opted for in order to provide the much sought-after high.

Consequently, from the broken windows hung a disturbing array of dishevelled youngsters, their red, streaming eyes and angry facial rashes providing a grim backdrop to our Celebration of English Country Dance. Clutching containers close to the face, they swayed disturbingly from side to side as they looked down onto the dancing below without actually taking any of it in, so completely *banged off their cake* were they with inhalants of every description.

Meanwhile the dancers were arrived at the refreshment stage of the proceedings and my class gathered round in the interval to collect their carton of pop. Michelle Constantine was very red of face and slurping heavily through a straw as I praised her efforts and made conversation:

So Michelle, and are you enjoying it all?"

"Oh yay Mr. Critchley, I love dancin' me."

"Good, you were all doing really well. Is anyone here today to watch you?"

"Mmmmm," (the straw was returned to her mouth at this point as the remaining drops of orange juice were vacuumed out,) "mi cousin Gerald's come."

"Oh lovely," I went on, "and did he manage to find a place on the chairs near to our class?"

"No, up there look," and here she pointed over towards the houses, "he's with that gang o' glueys, sat on't windowsill - second house in from t'left, the one 'oldin' a crisp packet up to 'is nose now, look he's wavin'.

And indeed in a way he was, a generous two-fingered salute being offered freely to one and all. As with Marley's ghost providing a vision of events yet to come, I shivered at the dreadful prospect of my class members providing replacements for these sad characters in future years and offered up a prayer for their safekeeping as they scampered away in the sunshine to prepare for *The Bridge of Athlone*.

- - o O o - -

Back home I allowed myself a celebratory glass of Double Diamond (works wonders you know) and reflected on a job well done in securing a totally unexpected promotion. I decided to give an old school chum who was also completing his probationary year a call, and we passed a pleasant enough half hour catching up on things. Without wishing to sound overly triumphant, I eventually broke the news about my advancement and to his credit, Barry sounded really happy for me:

"Oh well done you, that's great news and which curricular area will you be overseeing then?"

"Science."

Suddenly there was nothing from the other end of the telephone, apart that is from a faint rustling of tumbleweed blowing softly somewhere in the distance.

"Hello … hello … Barry ?.. Are you still there ?.. Hello …"

A slightly dazed voice picked up the conversation once again:

"Oh I'm still here David, don't worry" he went on, "I just wondered if you can hear that frantic whirring noise?"

"Well no actually I can't to be honest. What do you think it might be?"

"I'm pretty sure it's the sound of our old physics teacher spinning in his grave at the prospect of you taking responsibility for the science education of anyone," he chuckled.

*Unkind* maybe, possibly even to the point of being *cruel*, but a possibly legitimate comment nonetheless.

## CHAPTER TWELVE – "I do."

And there it was, all done and dusted; my first year of teaching was over. I hadn't mislaid anyone, nor had I left the school a smouldering ruin, so that's a result in anyone's book surely? The final hurdle of Parents' Evening had been successfully completed, although I had experienced considerable unease for a week or more leading up to that momentous event. This had started with the sudden realisation that the little people with whom I'd been engaging on a daily basis all year, actually had *significant others* attached in the form of mums & dads and these were about to subject me to searching questions concerning their little ones' progress – all very scary stuff.

I'd ensured the classroom was spotless for the big day, having successfully cajoled a group of house-proud girls for example to attack the less than pristine painting area. They'd been only too willing to roll their sleeves up and get stuck in, patiently soaking and massaging the solidly unyielding bristles of several dozen paintbrushes that had been standing to attention all year in grubby jam jars on the windowsill. After these had been rendered fit for purpose once more, next task was the scouring clean of the untidy tower of plastic palettes, most of which were heavily encrusted with countless seasons' worth of caked on powder paint.

The room was a good deal more pleasing to the eye as I laid out labelled piles of exercise books for inspection before attempting to smarten myself up a bit as well, with a change of shirt and a splash of Brut in the staff toilets, then returning to sit, jittery with nerves, at my desk. I needn't have worried however as the whole thing went really quite well and I was staggered to discover that for some reason, many of the parents were actually a good deal more nervous about the encounter than I was. Everyone seemed happy and there were some unexpected complimentary comments, which was nice and even some shared moments of humour to enjoy. Sandra's parents for example sat down at my table clutching one of her books and snorting with laughter:

"Eee Mr. Critchley, nothin's sacred though is it?" was the opening comment from her mum, "just wait 'til I get home tonight."

"Why's that Mrs. McCooey?"

"We've been reading our Sandra's *Christmas News*, here look, Monday January 3rd, listen to this bit – *and then my mam fell into the christmas tree and knocked all the baubles off after she'd had three glasses of Snowball.* Well I don't know where she's got that from d'you Charlie?"

"Naw, there's not a word of truth in it Mr. Critchley," her husband confirmed solemnly.

His appreciative wife nodded in agreement, before he continued:

"Everybody knows my missus only drinks rum 'n black!"

Cue more laughter.

I had been looking forward to finally meeting Sean's parents and as they entered the room, there was absolutely no doubt as to whom they had come to speak about. Mr. Bickerstaffe's red, wiry hair and generous flock of freckles showed their son to be a real chip off the old block, but there were apparently other shared family traits to be disclosed as well. As tactfully as I was able, I did try to express my concerns about Sean's seemingly constant preoccupation with all things bodily, going on to recount the underpants on the head incident, the inappropriate playtime offers made regularly to any girl within earshot, the uncannily lifelike over-excited zebra impression and so on. Mrs. Bickerstaffe didn't appear unduly concerned with these disclosures however, indeed if anything she seemed to stiffen with pride as she listened:

"Mmmm, he's always been a bit of a lad hasn't he Geoff … just like 'is dad, eh?"

And here they turned to exchange a disturbingly salacious leer before Mr. B reached across, squeezed his wife's thigh and whispered something in her ear, a gesture which, I must admit left me feeling quite nauseous and really quite keen to move on.

- - o O o - -

Traditionally, the final instalment of the summer term in school was designated *toy day* when the children were encouraged to bring in games from home to relax with, thus enabling staff to complete any last-minute tidying up and get on with preparations to welcome next year's tenants. It sounds like such a good idea, but in reality the whole thing's an absolute nightmare as the children soon get bored, or quarrelsome, or reduced to tears when some element of their favourite plaything gets lost or damaged – two instances of this occurring very early on that final Friday.

Sharon Stott had spent most of the morning completing a delightful landscape scene on her Etch-a-Sketch, but when Michelle bet her that she wouldn't be able to *etch* a monkey holding a bunch of flowers, she was immediately up for the challenge. Lifting the machine above her head, Sharon was shaking the thing vigorously back and forth to clear the slate in readiness for a fresh bout of creativity, when it slipped completely out of her grasp. Unfortunately, Alan Foster happened to be walking by at the time and the lad appeared really quite startled to receive an unexpected glancing blow to the head from a classic children's toy. Momentarily disorientated, Alan stumbled backwards, landing heavily with his left foot in the midfield area of a particularly competitive game of Subbuteo. Up until that point, it must be said that this World Cup final match between England and Brazil had been a tense and competitive affair, the score having remained at 2:2 for quite some time. With only seven minutes remaining now until the final whistle however, the sight of England stalwarts Trevor Brooking and Ray Wilkins lying prone on the pitch after being crushed flat by a wayward size 5 plimsoll, did in all honesty, appear to stack the odds heavily against a famous home victory.

Other games were in full flow also around the room. There was a four-handed game of Monopoly which would probably go on until home time, particularly as each participant could be quite clearly seen regularly helping themselves to a surreptitious banker's bonus from the box. These too were the days when it wasn't considered untoward to include sharp, pointy plastic rods in a children's toy and so *Kerplunk* tournaments continued in every corner.

Maureen Pickavance and a group of like-minded girls busied themselves at the sink, filling baby feeders from the tap in order to get maximum impact from their *dolls that could wee*, whilst a couple of other girls were really quite determined to deny active participation in their game to one particular class member:

"NO Sean I've told you before, you're NOT joinin' in our game of *Twister,* not after what 'appened at my birthday party. And any road, my mam says if you ever touch me there again I 'ave t'give you a good slappin'."

And then it was lunchtime.

"Yes Alan, you can stay indoors, I think that's a good idea, you just sit there quietly eh? That's it, remember to keep running the cotton wool under the cold tap and hold it against that lump, I'm sure your headache will soon go away."

After school I staggered out to the car lugging a box filled with all manner of gifts and presents from my class. More bars and boxes of chocolate than I'll manage to eat in a lifetime, a multitude of biros and propelling pencils in plastic presentation wallets and a bottle of *Whiskey Mac* were loaded onto the back seat for the drive home. So, six weeks holiday eh, however will I fill my time I wondered?

- - o O o - -

Not surprisingly perhaps, the small matter of a wedding along with moving into a new home did help the days pass reasonably quickly. All went according to plan on the big day, apart from the weather that is, which was distinctly *thistledown* for the duration. The rain, which soaked us as we left the church persisted also throughout our journey to Cornwall and for much of the week spent in a hotel in West Looe - indeed it was the lousy weather which I blamed for a minor motoring hiatus on our second day there. The fickle and unreliable Hillman Imp had been left behind for the marathon journey south and instead we travelled in style, using Anne's mother's new Datsun Sunny. Driving along a narrow country lane one rain-soaked afternoon I pulled over into a hedge to allow the passage of a giant tractor being driven at considerable speed by a ruddy-faced yokel psychopath, only to discover that Cornish *hedges* are actually in fact immovable limestone barriers covered with the thinnest veneer of grass and wild flowers. Still, as she'd only actually been my mother-in-law for seventy-two hours, I reckoned she'd be sure to overlook some minor front end re-modelling to her vehicle.

Back at home, I sat, pen in hand at the table and took a break from writing letters of thanks for our wedding gifts in order to survey my surroundings. The new house was a dormer bungalow purchased for the princely sum of £6000, sitting at the end of a quiet cul-de-sac. Only recently completed, the back garden resembled the battlefields of Ypres - only with considerably more mud, bricks and left over kerbstones - while the rest of the furnishings within were a motley assortment of cast-offs and donations from friends and family, with the occasional new purchase thrown in for good measure. Close by I could hear our gleaming Hotpoint twin-tub launch into spin mode as it began its weekly demented tango around the kitchen. Thankfully the machine was kept in check by a relatively short flex, preventing it from capering along the hallway to peep coyly at me around the door to the dining room. In the corner of the living room, stood a short wooden stool on which perched an elderly 19 inch black & white Pye TV set that always needed to be switched on ten minutes in advance of any programme in order to let it 'warm up.'

Elsewhere we were the proud owners of two-thirds of a black vinyl three-piece suite and I was sitting at an Edwardian dark oak dining table with its four almost matching chairs that once belonged to a great uncle. For background ambience there was of course my faithful Dansette record player, benefitting from a recently installed replacement stylus, supported by a Grundig reel-to-reel tape recorder – not much admittedly, but it was home. Returning to the task in hand I put the finishing touches to a card thanking the staff for the gift they'd presented after school on the last day of term. On that occasion, we had been gathered in the staffroom for sherry and Twiglets and as Eleanor raised her glass of Amontillado before passing the present over, I had found Dorothy's explanatory comment somewhat confusing:

"It's often a common error to overlook the inclusion of these in any decent canteen David, but I think you'll find that *fishers* are really terribly useful."

Some time later though it all made sense, as we unwrapped a set of matching fish knives and forks to add to our collection of Viner's *Love Story* cutlery.

And before I knew it, September had arrived once more.

# CHAPTER THIRTEEN- Déjà vu.

For every recently qualified teacher, there comes a point when the realisation will suddenly dawn that having survived / endured / enjoyed / managed / mastered the challenges of their career's opening twelve month period, they are then required to repeat the whole process over - and indeed, over – again. For myself this moment only really occurred when I walked back through the doors of the school at the start of September to find the place exactly the same as previously - only different, if you see what I mean.

It was a touch of déjà vu then that I experienced while standing in the hall, a wedge of charcoal in hand, gazing up at a huge blank backcloth pinned across the back wall behind the stage, as I tried without success to conjure up another masterpiece, this time with an appropriately *Harvesty* flavour. I was flanked by the imposing figures of Dorothy and Eleanor, both keen to act in an advisory capacity, however I had realised over time that when dealing with this pair, for *suggestion* one should actually read *instruction*.

"I'm seeing it develop in my mind's eye," Dorothy began ominously, "a giant *cornucopia* spreading diagonally downwards across the wall beginning somewhere top right, what say you Eleanor?"

And here she turned towards her co-conspirator, as did I, and my look of total non-comprehension, evidenced by an expression as blank as the wall in front of us, was immediately recognised.

"A cornucopia is a *horn of plenty* David," Eleanor explained patiently before going on, "Oh yes indeed Dorothy, a charming thought, with the gifts of nature's abundance spilling out from the open end – fruits of every kind, a host of vegetables, maybe a sheaf of barley, a plaited farmhouse loaf and so on."

These were the words issuing from their mouths but what my brain was actually receiving was more like: "blehbleh bleh bleddedy bleh." I had absolutely no clue what they were talking about but it was to get worse still as Dorothy was just getting into her stride:

"I'm really not seeing solid colours you understand David, no blocks of green or orange here, but rather the whole thing will surely work to greater effect if we ensure that we take *subtlety* as our watchword, don't you think?"

Just nod, I thought to myself as Eleanor picked up the baton:

"Oh indeed, indeed. I think we use *eau-de-nil* as the principal hue supplemented by accents of ivory, taupe and toning grey. We must be sure to limit our palette to neutral shades, possibly with occasional highlights of coral perhaps for dramatic effect."

I was much encouraged to hear this talk of "**we** must use" and "**our** palette" and was poised to enquire about a shared timetable for completion of this project, but I was too late, the moment had passed as they headed off towards the staffroom and I couldn't help but think that their involvement might actually now be at an end.

"Ah – a cornucopia David," repeated my friend DT at lunchtime, mimicking Dorothy's plummy accent to perfection. "Well we may as well make a start this evening I suppose after school, although the colour scheme all sounds a bit *pastel* for my tastes though, but…ours not to reason why - you start sketching it out and I'll mix up ten gallons of beige."

The Harvest Festival was of course the first major celebration of the season. It wasn't something I'd had much experience of previously to be honest, but here in school it was a big event. In order to develop a sense of community, the children were asked to bring in harvest gifts and then suggest worthy recipients from around the locality to whom a share of the foodstuffs would be distributed.

My new class knew the system well enough, and soon, slips of paper started to arrive as they began the process of nominating a pensioner of choice. Graham Morley's suggestion appeared rather unusual I thought, as the lady's postal address was actually in Widnes, a location several miles distant from school. I was curious:

"So how do you know this *Mrs. D. Roberts* then Graham?" I enquired after calling the register.

Before he could answer for himself, one of the girls jumped in first to supply the necessary information:

"It's his Auntie Doris Mr. Critchley, he always tries this on, last year it was his gran & grandad he put forward."

"Well I'm not sure that's really in the spirit of..." I began, but Graham was far too busy to listen, as he turned with venom onto the whistleblower, issuing dire threats, mostly along the lines of:

"I'll get you after," and d'you know in all likelihood he probably would.

I had discovered over the opening weeks of term that Graham was a bit of a handful and not exactly at the top of children's guest list for birthday parties and social gatherings due to a somewhat volatile nature and tendency towards creative violence. He was hard work in class too thanks to a span of concentration that was every bit as short as his temper and he and I had already had some memorable run-ins, and staying in at playtime had become pretty much the daily norm for the lad. These were the days before the invention of helpful labels such as *Attention Deficit Hyperactivity Disorder* and the like, so Graham was allocated residency in the *Downright Bloody Nuisance* category instead.

Truth was that I was missing last year's class terribly. I had been totally fazed by the fact that whilst I was in the same classroom and surroundings as previously and the children were of the same age and number with a similar gender distribution, it all seemed very different nonetheless. They seemed much *younger* somehow and more immature than last year's happy band, which of course they were I suppose, but still… I couldn't quite put my finger on it, but it just wasn't the same.

- - o O o - -

As Harvest Festival services go it was pretty much standard fare I guess, the hall being packed with parents as each class took it in turns to entertain. On a rota basis, classes were alternately *Bright & Beautiful* as we *Plough'd and Scattered* our way through the programme. Costumed children hopped, clucked and slithered in celebration of *All Creatures of our God & King* - the cockerel fitted with yellow Marigold rubber gloves on his feet being an absolute show-stopper - and we acted out the parable of *The Sower* through the medium of mime. It passed a pleasant enough hour I suppose, but I'm not entirely convinced all the agricultural connections will have had much resonance in an area which had only the threadbare Licker Field as its sole point of reference to green spaces.

David & myself had spent some considerable time sorting all the harvest gifts into cardboard boxes to which had been attached neatly printed address labels prior to distribution. The biggest headache with this task had been in attempting to ensure some parity of content across the board, a problem which led to some quite memorable exchanges between the two of us as we scrabbled about amongst assorted groceries piled up on the floor of the library:

Me: "That box has two eggs in it and this one hasn't got any."

DT: "That's because there aren't enough eggs to go around."

Me: "Well split the difference then and let's have one each."

DT: "You can't give someone a *single* egg, it just looks mean."

Me: "All I'm saying is it doesn't seem fair, we'll have to add something extra to this box to even things up."

DT: "Here then, take this tin of pilchards and an onion, how does that look?"

Me: "Hmmm… better I suppose, what d'you think?"

DT (distractedly, holding up a can of vegetables for closer inspection): "D'you know, I've never seen tinned asparagus before now – well, well."

Despite our best efforts though, there was still dissatisfaction apparent in certain quarters. At the end of the service some parcels were handed out to those nominated recipients who had actually managed to attend, the children presenting these reverentially to our special guests on the front row. After gratefully taking receipt of these, the next action was then for each of the OAPs to lean over and see what their immediate neighbour had been given. Peering into the adjacent box, they were certainly not averse to voicing grievance if they felt they had been subject to individual discrimination of some sort:

"Here, she's got a tin of Bird's Custard Powder, so where's mine eh? AND this turnip smells funny."

There were also several boxes left over and it fell to DT and myself to deliver these around the neighbourhood over lunchtime. These were duly loaded into both our cars, along with a couple of hand-picked children and we set off up and down the streets, pulling over to the kerb and sending the children off to hand over the goods. On one occasion I sat and watched as my two, carrying the loaded box of Nature's Bounty between them, stood and knocked at a door down the street. There was no reply.

"Knock again," I encouraged, desperate not to have to take any boxes back to school. Still no answer came.

"One more time," I called to them through the open car window, "harder!"

At this point the door to the adjacent house opened and an elderly lady stuck her head out to speak to the children:

"There's nobody in lovie," she announced, "Martha's on a Nile cruise – she'll be back a fortnight next Wednesday."

I made a mental note that possibly in future we might consider investing rather more time exploring the concept of 'needy' with the children in advance of Harvest Time. I mean it was extremely unlikely that anyone capable of funding international travel to this level would be an appreciative recipient of a cauliflower, a quarter of Co-op tea and several assorted tins of veg.

Next day I had to deal with Graham Morley again. It had been a wet playtime and I'd sat at my desk to catch up on some marking while the children just got on with things. Comics were being swapped, some children played clapping games and others were munching the toast they'd brought in from home when the peace was suddenly shattered by a blood-curdling squeal from Angela Maloney.

It turned out that Graham had suddenly experienced an urgent need to use the very same brown felt-tip pen, which Angela was using to finish colouring in a picture of her dog

*Benny*. Reluctance to hand this over rewarded her with a serious dose of arm-pinching from everyone's favourite monster-child, which immediately reduced her to tears. Remembering the oft-quoted adage that it was important always to label the action and never the child, I pointed out that it was a nasty, spiteful thing, which he'd just done and that I would be left with no option but to call his mother in for a chat after school. A pair of heavily shrugged shoulders suggested that this action held no real fears for the lad.

At three-thirty Graham skulked angrily in the corridor whilst Mrs. Morley sat across the table from me, wearing a distinctly resigned expression. Things really can't have been easy for her, a frail, spindly single parent, who was dwarfed by her oafish son and looked all of seventeen herself, she limped unhappily through life relying on handouts and benefits, unable as she was to enter the world of employment:

"I'd love go t'work Mr. Critchley, but what would I do wi' Graham? 'E can't be left in th'ouse on 'is own as e'd wreck t'place and I can't find anybody for't look after 'im; I mean… would you?"

I could see her point.

"I dursn't turn my back for a minute or he'll smash summat. On Sunday 'e knocked 'telly over and now it's broke so we 'aven't even got owt to watch."

My heart really went out to her.

"Last night I could 'ear 'im bangin' about upstairs, but then after a bit it all went quiet so I knew 'e'd be up to summat. Any road - when I went up e'd got my new lipstick and wrote 'is name all over t'bedroom wall."

Her eyes filled up at this point so I passed a tissue over from the box on my desk and did my best to sympathise:

160

"I'm so sorry Mrs. Morley, I really am, it must be so difficult."

"Aye well, these things are sent to try us," was her stoic reply, before suddenly brightening a little, "but d'you know I was that proud, as it all looked so neat, 'is 'andwriting's really come on a treat since e's been in your class!"

It seemed to be a week for parental visits as I found myself offering yet more after-school counselling just two days later.

Another class character that had come to my notice - in this instance for totally contrasting reasons to Graham - was Francis Reid. He was a gentle soul with an endearing lisp whose interests included reading and needlework. A great favourite with the girls, he was regularly to be found in their company either skipping around with them at playtimes or joining them to perform handstands and make daisy chains in the outfield during our games of rounders, and it was Francis' mum who sought my help now.

"I hope you don't mind me coming in Mr. Critchley but I wanted to have a word about our Frank."

"Not at all Mrs. Reid, what exactly was the problem? I mean he seems happy enough in class."

"Oh yes, he's happy enough and he's always talking about you, but I'm just a bit worried about him all the same."

"Really?"

"Mmm. Well me *and* his dad to be honest, no well actually it's my husband who really wanted me to come in to school. You must have noticed our Frank is a bit...well... a bit *different* to the other boys?"

"Well he does seem a rather sensitive soul wouldn't you say?"

"*Sensitive*," she repeated, taking a few moments to mull this one over, "yes I like that, he's definitely *sensitive* all right. Anyway his dad is really keen to make him perhaps a bit less sensitive and a bit more, how shall I put it...*manly* if you get my drift? It's been a real struggle to be honest. Steve – that's Francis's dad – took him fishing a while back but he squealed like a little girl when the tin of maggots was opened and then rugby turned into a complete non-starter after he slipped over and got his shorts muddy."

"I see, it must..." I began but was interrupted once more.

"It was when he broke his heart all weekend after not being allowed to join the Morris Dancing Troop that was pretty much the last straw for Steve."

"So what would you like from me then Mrs. Reid?"

"I'm not really all that sure Mr. Critchley to tell the truth. How about if you looked for any opportunity to give him jobs and responsibilities, get him involved in games and PE a bit more p'raps – get him mating with the lads a bit more maybe rather than girls all the while?"

"I'll do what I can Mrs. Reid, but you really shouldn't worry you know, all children are different and Francis is a lovely boy. Let's see how things go eh, why don't you pop in again before the end of term and we'll have another chat?"

Continuing with what I hoped were reassuring noises, I led her out to the cloakroom where we discovered a smiling Francis relaxing with the copy of last week's *Jackie* he'd borrowed from Elaine Butterworth.

- - o O o - -

Days for me in school had become even longer than usual as I began to shoulder the burden of my curricular responsibilities, starting with a valiant attempt to restore some sense of order to our much-neglected *Science Equipment Resource Centre*. In reality this was a large plywood cupboard covering most of the back wall in the staff room and the fact that I had been unable to open its locked doors was a possible indicator of the state of science education throughout the school. Bill came to the rescue however, aided by a large Peek Frean's biscuit tin containing keys of every description through which he patiently sorted until locating one that would fit.

Like Howard Carter and Lord Carnarvon standing before the Pharaoh's tomb, we held our breath as the handles turned and the doors creaked open allowing the light of day to fall once more upon contents that had lain undisturbed for oh so many a year. On this occasion however our gaze was not rewarded with the sight of "wonderful things," but rather fell on what appeared at first glance to be a pile of old tat as it was absolutely filthy in there. Thankfully, Bill had his shovel with him and skillfully scooped up the decomposing rodent lying pop-eyed and rigid on the second shelf:

"Well I think that's about enough for today David don't you?" he suggested.

"Absolutely Bill - couldn't agree more, same time tomorrow then?"

Nodding agreement, my friend picked up a pair of empty milk bottles from the draining board before bursting into a hearty rendition of Jonathan King's *Una Paloma Blanca,* thus clearly demonstrating the pleasure he was taking in this task.

And that was why I was in the staffroom again, at a quite unearthly hour next morning, pulling on a pair of rubber gloves. Bill wasn't far behind me though, dashing up the stairs armed with a pile of bin bags:

"I can only stay a few minutes David - there's a coke delivery due any time and... blimey what's that smell?"

"Oh sorry Bill, it's my plugs, I did mean to open the window."

The acrid stench was down to my efforts to prepare myself for the drive home later and address yet another motoring malfunction which had recently become apparent. Shortly after setting off on the drive to school each morning, the good old Imp would suddenly succumb to a violent coughing fit before launching into an uncannily lifelike impression of an asthmatic sewing machine, signifying that one of the spark plugs had oiled up yet again. Being the spiteful, malicious piece of scrapyard fodder it undoubtedly was, the front three cylinders would continue to fire away quite cheerfully leaving me instead to face the chore of changing the rearmost, virtually inaccessible plug in order to continue with my journey. Over the five mile trip from home to work, an uncomfortable and highly inconvenient replacement procedure would usually need to be carried out twice on average, as indeed it had been earlier this morning. Kneeling on an old piece of lino at the roadside, wearing collar and tie, in the rain, I had been required to shove my arm deep into the engine compartment, rather in the manner of a vet examining a cow's rectum, in order to put things right. I had learned the futility of hurling invective at the car as it was totally immune to any insult or expression of contempt, so I simply got on with the job. On the plus side though, at least this accursed vehicle was blessed with capacious door pockets enabling plenty of spare plugs to be carried around and kept readily to hand until required, and it was several of these that I had arranged on the gas ring in the staffroom kitchen to burn off their Castrol residue and fill the place with blue smoke.

"Oh dear God," exclaimed Bill, "there'll be some wrinkled noses if E & D come in to these fumes later for their morning coffee and scone."

Over the space of several weeks I dealt ruthlessly with the science cupboard detritus, filling the bin most days with all manner of antique bits & bobs that may, once upon a time, have fired the imaginations of budding young Einsteins. Into the rubbish would go battered microscopes with missing eyepieces along with hundreds of accompanying cracked and grubby slides showing *scales from a butterfly's wing* or *sting from a bumble bee*. There was an enormous amount of broken laboratory glass, including flasks, retorts, test tubes and stopperless bell jars. There were tripods with a leg missing (*twopods* maybe?) and dozens of torch batteries encrusted with chemical leakage around the terminals. There were countless metal bars, variously shaped and brightly painted in vivid red and blue, suggesting that at some point in their distant past, these may well have enjoyed a life as magnets – sadly though, their days of attraction were now long gone. Some items were able to be rescued for future use it was true, and these – sets of pulleys and the like - would form the nucleus of a new and updated equipment centre – *The David Critchley Resource Bank for Investigative Scientific Research* maybe - supplemented by a range of new purchases at requisition time.

Evenings then would see me sitting up in bed, riffling through the glossy pages of Educational Suppliers' catalogues, eager to spend every penny of the generous £75 grant I'd been allocated for the year – it was almost like Christmas.

And then - lo and behold - it was.

## CHAPTER FOURTEEN – Result!

Even though I had learned last year just what a madly busy time it could be, I was still really pleased to witness Advent's arrival in school. One of the undoubted benefits of the approaching festive season was that it would finally see the demise of the depressing, crumbling *Autumn Displays,* which Dorothy had insisted every class must present on the shelves outside their room back in October. These had all started off well enough I suppose but in an alarmingly short time they'd degenerated into a manky pile of curling sycamore leaves and dried out, wrinkled acorns. Horse chestnuts had been an early casualty too from these tableaux, stuffed furtively into pockets and pump bags when no one was looking, (Graham Morley was particularly adept at this) the irresistible appeal of conkers of course, being their considerable value as autumn playground currency. Ada too was glad to see the back of these exhibits, tired as she was of chasing wayward rose hips and hawthorn berries the length & breadth of the corridor each evening with a broom. DT had at one point received the offer of a grey squirrel for his display, hunted and shot dead in the local park by an air gun-toting older brother. Well at least this showed that the children were paying some attention to what went on around school I suppose.

I had attempted to enliven the shelves from time to time, for example by adding a witches' broom come Hallowe'en time, but it didn't really make a great deal of difference. There would also have been a couple of carved turnip lanterns as well, but after almost opening a vein with a carving knife whilst attempting to hollow out a particularly stubborn swede on the kitchen table at home, I decided to give any further embellishments a miss. No matter how I tried to improve things, the stench of decay would hang about the late November corridors, Autumn's fading fruits providing a macabre daily reminder about the fleeting nature of mortality.

So Bill's early morning request:

"Can you give us a lift putting the Christmas tree up David?"

was cause for celebration indeed, promising as it did a ray of brightness in the enveloping gloom and I began by helping carry a zinc dustbin full of bricks and sand into the hall.

"It's mucky work though David," he warned, " I've got some gloves here and you'll need to be careful with your white shirt too."

"Too late I'm afraid Bill," I replied ruefully, looking down at my dishevelled appearance, "today's journey in was a *three-spark-plug nightmare* and then I had to wrestle with the copier when I arrived."

Just by means of a change, it hadn't been the Banda spirit machine that had caught me out today, but instead the Gestetner ink duplicator in the secretary's office. In order to print things using this device of the devil, you began by typing out your text on a special *skin,* with the typewriter set to *stencil* mode. This was then attached to the machine's rolling drum and as usual whenever I came to use the infernal thing, I'd discovered this morning that it needed filling with ink. Despite my very best efforts at keeping clean, I usually ended up completely slathered in the stuff, and this morning was no exception. Using the handle, I'd carefully set the drum roller so that the filler hole was positioned upright at the top and, with the aid of a paper towel to insulate my fingers from the grubby screw cap, removed this with ease - so far so good. My luck is definitely in today, I thought as I discovered the last remaining squeezy bottle of printing ink in the stockroom and, after managing to peel off the foil cap without mishap by holding it at arm's length, inverted this over the filler hole and began to squeeze – ever so gently.

It was all going so well; I could feel the plastic bottle gradually collapsing beneath my fingers accompanied by the kind of oozy, moist, farting sound that would have had my class rolling in the aisles. These were clear indicators that the gelatinous, treacly contents were going just where they should. Job done, the empty bottle ended up in the bin and I congratulated myself on remaining absolutely pristine and spotless throughout the whole process, but then as they say, pride often comes before a fall. After refilling the thing, the knack then is to turn the drum rapidly a few dozen times without the paper tray being engaged in order to let centrifugal force distribute the ink around the inside. This I duly did, only actually noticing on its third or fourth revolution the plastic cap to the ink reservoir still sitting on the windowsill and I looked down at an inky Armageddon with viscous, black goo coating much of the secretary's desk and also large areas of my clothing.

Bill & myself chatted away as we manhandled the Douglas Fir into its dustbin in the corner of the hall.

'You'll miss the other David here in school won't you?" He remarked.

"I certainly will Bill, that's for certain."

My friend, mentor and confidant from the class next door was moving on. He had successfully secured a Scale III post at a school on the other side of the Borough and would be taking this up at the start of January; it was certainly the case that I was going to really miss him around the place.

The bell rang for the start of school, (it's no wonder I'm knackered each evening I mused, having done two hours work every day before the kids even walk through the door) and I went out to collect them from the playground. The classes stood in silent lines as all around, like a scene from Hitchcock, flocks of scruffy starlings and screeching gulls arrived to pick over the remnants of crisps and biscuits strewn across the yard. Graham Morley stood at the front of our line wearing a huge, beaming smile and carrying a bin liner that resembled a giant green hedgehog thanks to the branches poking out through the plastic all around. I'd been searching out opportunities to react positively to him for weeks now, patiently looking for those times when I was able to *catch him being good* and so this was a perfect occasion for celebration:

"Why Graham, whatever do you have there?" I cooed.

"It's a Christmas tree," was his proud reply, "mam sez we can 'ave it for class."

"I bet 'e's nicked it," was one less than charitable observation from further down the line.

It was pleasing to note however that Graham managed to find it within himself to rise above this possible slander, maintaining a fixed grin rather than reacting instead with his knuckles and / or feet as he would have done not so long ago. Once back in class I continued with the flattery:

"Look everyone, Graham has brought in a tree to brighten up our classroom at Christmas, wasn't that kind? Let's give him a big clap to say thank you."

This instruction was met with some sporadic, cynical applause, which seemed to suggest the lad might have some way to go yet in securing universal appeal and ready displays of affection. My attempts to include the rest of the class members in a project initiated by Graham continued thus:

"The tree's lovely, I'm sure we'd all agree wouldn't we children, but what we really need now are some decorations to bring it to life; is anyone able to help?"

Hands shot up from all sides promising a veritable *cornucopia* of festive delights; it seemed that my plan to foster an atmosphere of mutual respect and enthusiasm appeared to be working.

After dangling the carrot of a possible afternoon spent enjoying Christmas crafts - should we manage to get through sufficient amounts of work first of course - a studious engagement with the delights of *Modern Comprehensive Arithmetic* before playtime was guaranteed – with only the occasional clicking of wooden Cuisenaire rods disturbing the peace. After break I sat with a group trying to catch them out with a set of flashcards linked to the reading scheme, whilst the rest of the class sweated away in the silent purgatory of Haydn Richards' *Junior English*.

They had worked hard, admittedly and so lunchtime was spent preparing the room ready for the afternoon's creative onslaught by covering the tables with sheets of newspaper. My mind returned to the time last year when I'd foolishly asked Sean Bickerstaffe to carry out this simple task and he'd wasted no time at all in snuffling through the cardboard box containing multiple back copies of the tabloid press, like a pig in search of truffles. On that occasion we'd arrived to start the lesson after lunch to find a bevy of busty page 3 lovelies smiling provocatively from every horizontal surface.

It was like spending the afternoon in Santa's workshop today, with a host of seasonal activities taking place on all sides. There were squares of grey sugar paper for example, onto which we created monochrome winter landscape scenes with sticks of charcoal and white chalk before then spraying these liberally with hair lacquer to prevent the masterpieces from smudging. The windows were thrown open wide to lessen the potentially hallucinogenic effects of hairspray, and anyway, as Bill was once again in demented winter stoker mode down in the boiler room, feeling the cold was not likely to be a problem. Once these were dry, miniature calendar tabs would be stapled to the bottom edge to provide stocking-filler gifts for unfortunate relatives and friends. Glitter was being applied by the shovelful to home made table centrepieces for the Christmas party whilst the first-aid cupboard had been ransacked for the yards of cotton wool required to transform empty toilet roll tubes into a miniature regiment of identical snowman clones. Meanwhile saliva glands worked overtime on strips of coloured gummed paper to create the paper chains that would later hang from the light fittings. Actually the production of these wasn't as far ahead as it might have been, after something of a false start, which had resulted in twenty minutes' worth of hard work going straight into the bin. It was my fault I suppose for not supervising blue group's efforts more closely. From the start they'd worked at quite a rate of knots, cutting, licking and sticking the strips together, but unfortunately they'd overlooked the need to link these together first, resulting in the production of several dozen individual gummed paper rings.

- - o O o - -

Next morning the festive feel continued as the class arrived carrying bagfuls of items with which to decorate Graham's tree. These were piled up in the library corner and I hinted that I may very well be on the lookout for a couple of lucky volunteers to carry out this special task over lunchtime, adding that anyone chosen for this honour would of course only be selected from those who'd worked particularly hard all morning. Consequently our handwriting lesson produced some quite beautiful results as they all paid considerably greater attention to letter formation than was usual, laboriously copying out a passage from the board about The Annunciation.

Sensibly perhaps, I withheld the snippet of information that Santa's chosen lunchtime helpers would actually be working alongside – or possibly under the direction of, it being his tree after all – Graham Morley. So keen was I to move progress with regard to the boy's total rehabilitation, that I looked for any and every opportunity to integrate the lad with his classmates. As the bell rang for lunchtime the whole class perched on the very edge of their chairs, ramrod straight and with wide, staring eyes as they tried to mentally *will* me into awarding them what was without shadow of doubt, the festive season's absolute plum job:

"And so children," I began, as from all around the room came a strange, muffled chorus of desperation, being chanted loudly from behind tightly pursed lips:

"Mmmmm! Mmm! Mmmmmmmmmmmmm!"

"As I said earlier we really need some sensible people to attend to our tree decorating this lunchtime,"

"MMMMMMMMMMMMMMMMMMM!!!"

"And I thought it might be rather nice to have one boy and one girl…"

**"MMMMMMMMMMMMMMMMMMMMMM!!!"**

By this point, as the grunting chorus had lifted a few octaves and every face began to turn puce, there was the distinct possibility of several eyeballs actually popping out of their sockets before rolling about the desks below:

"So what better way to sort this than to allow Graham himself to pick two lucky children to help him with our special task."

A moment's confused silence, signified the class's rapidly waning enthusiasm and this was followed immediately by the collapsing sound of two dozen pairs of shoulders slumping in bitter disappointment. I left them to it and retired to the staffroom.

I felt certain that even Graham could manage to behave himself for the short time it would take me to eat my lunchtime sandwich, but nevertheless I opted not to linger over my coffee and so left part-way through Eleanor & Dorothy's graphic account of the Rotary Club's recent Charity Gala dinner. As this was the third time of telling, I knew every detail by heart already, from the arrival of the Lady Mayoress dressed in an outfit that Eleanor "wouldn't have worn to weed the garden," right through to the visiting Swing Band's glittering climactic rendition of *Boogie Woogie Bugle Boy* and so didn't feel too deprived. There was a certain amount of trepidation as I returned to the classroom once more, but appropriately enough in this season of goodwill, all appeared to be sweetness and light. Graham was standing to attention in the corridor as I approached, his two deputies positioned dutifully alongside. Drawing closer it was reassuring to note that where once there would almost certainly have been blood and tears, today there were only smiles from all three. Ellen Fitton was first to speak:

"We've finished Mr. Critchley an' it looks lovely."

Sentiments that were echoed by Georgie Appleton:

"Yay it does, we've used all t'stuff."

And indeed they had. Thankfully the tree stood on the floor in the library corner, as there probably wouldn't have been a table in the room capable of supporting all that weight. In a bold break with tradition, rather than being crowned with a lone fairy, the top of the tree had instead a pair of these sellotaped to its uppermost branches. This arrangement may have looked quite magical I suppose were it not for the fact that as they bobbed to and fro in the waves of heat pumping out from the radiators, the smaller of the two gave the impression of repeatedly head-butting her winged colleague in the face. Somehow my festive co-ordinators had also managed to cram three sets of fairy lights onto a tree which was actually only four feet tall, meaning the early December gloom was easily dispatched as these twinkled away in fierce competition with one another. Elsewhere, extravagant baubles of every shape, size and colour fought for breathing space, often needing to be arranged three or even four to a branch in order to ensure no item was left over, whilst skeins of glittering tin foil Lametta tinsel in red, green and silver had been draped, somewhat heavy-handedly it has to be said, from top to bottom. A further wintry touch was lent to the whole ensemble courtesy of the cotton wool carpet laid beneath the tree's branches in an attempt to recreate that *deep and crisp and even* look, so should anyone suffer a bumped head or split lip between now and early January, then we would unfortunately need to resort to the use of a wet paper towel I suppose.

This shimmering monument to kitsch left me at a complete loss for words and the children likewise were stunned into open-mouthed amazement as they drifted back in after lunch, shielding their eyes from the room's lustrous new addition, or *Graham's tree* as it would come to be known for the next fortnight. Audrey Lafferty probably came closest to summing up the mood of the moment with her perceptive observation:

"Bloody 'ell it's like bein' on Blackpool North Shore!"

Indeed what more was there to say?

- - o O o - -

Apart from the prospect of losing my friend and colleague this December, there was but one other blot on the otherwise luminous horizon of my second school Christmas – that being a visit from Mr. Lawrence to sit in judgment on one of my lessons. This time it was to be an indoor session, so unusually, given the time of year, Nativity and carol concert rehearsals had been cancelled for the afternoon. I was taking no chances this time around, with no stone left unturned during my painstaking preparations for the big day. My kit was laundered, polished, pressed and waiting on coat hangers in the Gent's, Bill had been called upon to double-check the hall had been swept free of any lurking foreign bodies surreptitiously deposited earlier by Reception Class during Assembly and, most importantly, the class had been primed, threatened and rehearsed into a well-drilled troupe

174

of peak performance athletes – what could possibly go wrong?

Amazingly - nothing, as it turned out. The children showed themselves to be enthusiastic and extremely capable *Educational Gymnasts* and the lesson went off without a hitch. Lawrence granted me the blandest of smiles from his chair beside the piano and it was pleasing to note that his biro was nowhere near as busy as it had been on our previous encounter. There were even some nods of approval from my erstwhile tormentor as the children perched on mats scattered around the hall to hold balance positions using body points & patches. Thankfully he was too far away to hear Peter Billington's stage whisper:

"Are we doing better than when we practised yesterday Mr. Critchley?"

and as the lesson drew to a close, Lawrence approached and shook my hand warmly on his way out of the door to the car park:

"A truly excellent lesson David, really effective, I don't think I could have done better myself."

Result!

It was certainly true that I'd learned a good deal during last year's PE course, and not just about the art of teaching it either. The six weekly sessions had provided the ideal opportunity to observe the great man himself at close quarters and begin to work out what really made him tick. Being unsure exactly what to include in today's lesson, I'd eventually decided to take the easy option and simply deliver verbatim one of the sessions I'd seen being delivered last term. Copying his lesson exactly had obviously been a smart move on my part, the monumental arrogance of the man being clearly demonstrated as he gratefully accepted my most welcome Christmas present to himself – a gift-wrapped copy of one of his own lessons.

- - o O o - -

Achieving success in the face of an adversary, toasting my friend's departure to pastures new and marking the imminent arrival of the festive period were surely events which warranted some form of celebration and so DT and myself had a pub lunch planned. Consequently we were out of the door and hurrying along the pavements once again almost before the dinnertime bell had stopped reverberating throughout the school. First stop was the fish & chip shop on the corner of the street, an establishment known locally to one and all simply as *Sarah's*, this being the name of the proprietress who, together with her long-suffering husband Frank, had been attending to the community's dietary preferences for decades past. It was always a delight to stand in the queue in front of that magnificent, tiled 1950's frying range and absorb a bit of local colour. As parents and grandparents will have done before them since time immemorial, legions of housewives stood in line, clutching dinner plates wrapped in a tea towel, to exchange gaudy banter whilst Sarah expertly sloshed chunks of cod in the tray of milky batter before tossing these into the sizzling oil. A desperate plea came from one customer obviously keen to secure lunch for her other half waiting hungrily at home.

"Oooh Sarah love, 'ave you got no sausage left today, on'y I've promised 'im one for 'is dinner?"

This would be Sarah's cue to launch straight into one of her dearly beloved stand-up routines from behind the counter, much to everyone's delight.

"Did y'ear that ladies? It's true what they say about them randy cows on the estate, they're allus at it – this one's off back 'ome now to give her husband some hot sausage time – and in't middle o' day an' all – you dirty mare. It's no

176

wonder your Charlie looks as if a puff o' wind 'ud knock 'im over, you've wore 'im out!"

Ribald, cackling laughter, loud enough to rival the sound of frying fish would greet this, but Sarah wasn't done yet. Turning from the range for a moment, she called behind through the open doorway to where her husband could be seen standing in their own kitchen, frying pan in hand, attending to his own lunchtime meal:

"FRANK!"

"Yiss, whatever d'yer want now y'aggravating woman?"

"Tek that sausage out o' your pan, I think we've got a buyer!"

More laughter.

Today thankfully there wasn't much in terms of a queue, meaning we could be served reasonably quickly. The large, matronly figure in front of me turned to offer a broad smile and I instantly recognised the well-polished gums and woodbine breath of Mrs. Foster, standing in her trademark tartan *beddies* to part with her money.

"Oh 'ello Sirs, fancy seein' you two, am just gerrin 'little un's dinner. Alan, say 'ello to yer teachers."

Alan's shy little face popped out from behind his mother's considerable bulk to give us a hesitant wave before continuing to empty the vinegar bottle from the counter into a newspaper containing a popular lunchtime delicacy.

*(More than ten years later whilst walking through the town centre, I bumped into Alan Foster beside the Council Offices. Obviously we'd both changed somewhat over the intervening period but he was quick to recognise me, and came across to shake hands:*

*"Oh, Mr. Critchley, I wus only thinking about you t'other day, blinkin' 'eck it's gud t'see you."*

*I recognised him too at close range and, as they say, you never forget your first class.*

*"Hello Alan, fancy meeting you after all this time. What are you up to these days?"*

*"Am still workin' for't council - parks an' gardens an' that you know. Eee them wus 'appy days in school though wun't they just? an' d'you know, to this very day there's one thing tha' allus sticks in my memory, it's summat I think about all't time."*

*How gratifying to have childhood influence recalled with such obvious affection I mused, now which occasion might he be referring to exactly – his part in a Christmas play perhaps? An end of term trip maybe? The day I taught him how to use a pair of compasses to construct a circle of specified radius without spattering his geometry book with blood? The afternoon he was rendered semi-conscious by a wayward Etch-a-Sketch in full flight across the classroom? Who can tell which momentous events might remain in the dormant sub-conscious of the adolescent? I was curious indeed.*

*"And what was that then Alan?"*

*He turned to face me and with a serious face confessed to his life-affirming experience from years long gone:*

*"No, I'll really never forget that dinnertime when I saw you in't chippy with me mam an' I 'ad a steak puddin'!")*

Our chips were eaten on the hoof and a few minutes later we were able to relax in the lounge of the pub, two pints of bitter shandy in front of us and the jukebox belting out *Hold Back the Night* by Trammps – they don't write them like that any more. Sated by our lunchtime feast, we were easily able to refuse the otherwise tempting offer of *"Cockles? Mussels? Prawns? Assorted brightly-coloured crab-effect snacks?"* being hawked around the tables from a huge basket carried on the arm of a ruddy-faced salesman wearing a white coat and matching trilby, whilst a warm, mellow feeling enveloped the pair of us and we reminisced fondly about the past year in school, savouring the moment…and the drinks.

"I'll tell you what DC, those chips must have been really, really salty, could you manage another pint?"

"Oh I think so David, don't you? It is Christmas after all."

The second drinks went down a little more slowly than the first had done and the clock moved on until we reached the point at which duty began to call once more.

"Come on then DC, time to sup up and head back to the ranch."

Draining the remnants from our glasses, we stood to leave as the barmaid tottered unexpectedly towards us carrying two more pints of shandy:

"A friend of yours has sent these through from the Bar Side."

Bill's cheery faced grinned at us through the hatch across the counter and he gave us a cheery thumbs-up before mouthing *Happy Christmas lads!*

Nothing for it then but to get stuck in, and as we lifted the glasses to our faces and *Bohemian Rhapsody* burst out from the jukebox, I reflected that by the time this record had finished playing in just six minutes' time, we needed to be back in class. It wasn't easy but we managed it, gulping down the dregs before waving to Bill and dashing out of the door, hurrying along the pavement with all the poise and elegance of a pair of water filled balloons, the sound of Queen still ringing in our ears. Indeed to this day, whenever I hear Freddie Mercury begin to sing, I still experience an immediate and irresistible urge to empty my bladder.

- - o O o - -

It was a somewhat mixed picture, which emerged concerning the progress of a certain two members of my class, this becoming apparent following discussion with their mums after school during the last week of term. Good news was apparent in Graham's case at least and it was a bright-eyed and totally transformed Mrs. Morley that sat beside my desk one afternoon.

"Oh Mr. Critchley I can't gerr' over 'im, e's that changed 'e really is."

The boy in question who was also sitting in on this conference blushed as his mum continued with her praise:

"He's such a sensible boy now, aren't you love?" she went on.

"Oh shurrup mam," being the embarrassed lad's response.

"Well I'm really pleased to hear that Graham's behaviour at home has got better as he really seems to have grown up in school, that's for sure."

It really had been an improving picture over the term, with just the occasional lapse from time to time coming along to blot his copybook. As I couldn't see much point in raking over recent indiscretions however, I chose not to mention last week's *locking all the boys' toilet cubicle doors from the inside* incident. After all, It hadn't taken Bill long to open them all again with a screwdriver and so no great harm was done, with possibly one exception, but even Kenneth Donnellan had now managed to forgive Graham and was mostly recovered from the afternoon's trauma. Besides, as

Graham quite rightly pointed out, how was he to know that Kenneth was suffering from an upset tummy?

"I'm thinking of looking out for that part-time job an' all," went on Mrs. Morley, "and givin' Graham the chance to show 'e can be trusted on 'is own."

This would still be a huge challenge for the boy I felt certain, but why not give it a go? Surely he just needed a bit of incentive:

"That would be good wouldn't it Graham?" I suggested, "that way your mum might have a bit more money to spend on some little treats to reward you for being so sensible."

Now it would seem, I was really speaking Graham's language and I could see him rolling this notion around in his head and considering the possibilities and benefits that might accrue from continued conformist behaviour. Bribery and corruption – that's the way to move progress with some individuals for sure.

It wasn't such a rosy picture in the case of Francis Reid however and I had to report to his mum that a decidedly gentle nature was still very much in evidence.

"So he's still hanging about with the girls all the time then Mr. Critchley is that what you're saying?"

"Well now...let's see...erm...most days he...to be honest I..." my blustering and prevaricating was soon cut short however by Mrs. Reid:

"It's ok really, we know the way it is with Frank. I'm guessing for example there weren't too many other boys looking forward to Elaine Butterworth's sleepover last weekend were there?"

"Oh I wouldn't know I'm sure but..."

"Don't worry," she went on, "we've come to accept our Francis's *sensitive* nature and the fact that he's a bit different to most other lads. It's his dad I feel sorry for to be honest – Steve was so chuffed when a lad came along after we had Catherine and Suzy. I can remember him going on about all the things he was going to teach him, fantasising about stuff like the day Frank would score the winning try at Wembley, instead of which..."

She paused at this point so I encouraged her to continue, which she did with an endearing chuckle.

"It was Saturday evening Mr. Critchley, and Francis had asked Steve if it would be ok to borrow his razor. Well, his dad was really pleased that Frank was starting to think *manly* so to speak, so he unscrewed it and took out the razor blade then he wouldn't cut himself and we left him to it in the bathroom. After a while though Steve couldn't cope and so we both crept upstairs and along the landing to peep through the crack of the door and see what he was up to," here she paused again.

"And?" I asked, obviously curious.

"Well," she went on, "there he was, standing beside the sink, a towel wrapped round his head in a turban, singing that Tammy Wynette song, you know... *Stand by Your Man*...with one foot up on the edge of the bath so he could shave his legs!"

So one moment I'm doing my damndest to exert a calming influence over a great lump of a lad like Graham Morley, and the next I have parents begging me to get their son to behave in a way which is totally alien to his personality – it's a strange old world, it really is. I was completely at a loss as to what the problem was with Francis, as he was such a lovely boy with a heart of gold and the kindest nature, which made him pretty much universally popular with his peers, of both genders. Throughout his days in the junior department he achieved a great deal both academically and socially, culminating in the award of Head Boy status when he was in Standard 4 and, let me see now, that would have been... ah yes – 1979, a memorable year indeed.

## CHAPTER FIFTEEN – Fast Forward.

Looking through the window onto the car park, I admired my new VW Beetle as it gleamed canary-like amongst the drab greyness of a mid-November morning. Ah the sheer, unadulterated luxury of being able to climb into a vehicle without first double-checking that a plug spanner was near to hand, then feel the door close with that reassuring Teutonic *clunk* before turning the key with the assured confidence of an impending stress-free journey to work. There was even a radio installed in the dashboard enabling the likes of Peter Powell and Kid Jensen to keep me company during my journeys – absolute bliss. True, the heater was reluctant to begin throwing out too much in the way of *kilojoules* until the car had completed a journey equivalent to its arrival in Aberdeen, but hey – a small price to pay for total reliability and absolute peace of mind surely?

The car was just one of several new items and circumstances with which I found myself now surrounded, including for example the classroom, school, staff and children, as this was 1979 - the year I flew the nest to sample fresh pastures.

- - o O o - -

Although I'd loved my time in my first post and learned so much over five short years, the lure of trying to apply this knowledge in a new situation was just too much to resist. To his credit, Mr. Antrobus had seemed genuinely sorry when I announced my intention to apply for another post across town:

"You'll be terribly missed here at Morton Street David as you've achieved so much during your time with us."

"Oh I'm not sure about that…" I began modestly.

"Nonsense," he interrupted, "for one thing, just look at how Science has flourished under your guidance."

It was true that I had worked very hard at enhancing this much-neglected area of the curriculum, shoring up the gaps in my own understanding by attending courses after school and spending periods of leisure time in the local library. The updated resource centre was a triumph of which I was particularly proud, along with the scheme of work that had been completed over a Summer break. This now sat on a staffroom shelf, alongside all the other *curricular statements* in their matching folders emblazoned with the school crest. These did look mightily impressive (if, disappointingly somewhat under-used) and it was to these that The Boss would draw visitors' attention rather than to the Television room, as he would have done in years past. I'd started a Science Club too after school, thus providing the children with an alternative to *staying behind* for football or netball and this continued to be very well attended, despite a minor potential Health & Safety incident.

'Electricity' had been an extended topic we'd studied after school, and for this I took as my bible a Ladybird book entitled *Magnets, Bulbs & Batteries* that I'd dusted off from childhood days. It was filled with engaging projects including how to turn a six inch nail into an electro-magnet and transforming a Saxo salt carton into a model lighthouse – all exciting stuff – well, Peter & Jane seemed to enjoy it judging from the illustrations. First off however we had attended to the basics of circuitry, using lengths of bell wire, assorted batteries and bulbs in their dinky little holders and it was truly wonderful to see the glow of delight cross the children's faces as they learned how to make a tiny 2.5 volt torch bulb come to life.

What with stringing sets of bulbs together, or joining several batteries in line to make a bulb glow more and more brightly before eventually going off *pop*, we were getting through Ever Ready batteries at a quite alarming rate of knots. It was then that I had the brainwave of using rechargeable batteries instead; buying several sets of these along with their charging units, using the dregs of the year's requisition allowance for their purchase, and it was this attempt at saving funds that had been my undoing.

It turns out that there is one considerable drawback when using batteries of this type to construct simple circuits, the problem being first brought to my attention one evening by a comment from a Standard Three boy:

"*JESUS TONIGHT* – that's 'ot!"

A chorus of similar expressions of dismay soon echoed round the room and as curiosity got the better of me I was forced to investigate further. It would appear, that when connected into a circuit by holding the bits of wire to each end of a rechargeable battery, the terminals begin to heat up extremely quickly resulting in several sets of badly singed fingers. Ah well, surely science is all about learning from your mistakes, and at least no-one actually burst into flames.

As my departure would coincide with the close of the year, a grand summer celebratory finale had been organised in the form of a Junior Department Talent Show to be performed in front of the whole school. A committee of children from the Standard Four classes had assumed responsibility for the management and coordination of this prestigious event, leaving staff free to concentrate on the traditional chores associated with the end of year winding-up. Posters and programmes advertising the scheduled attractions were displayed round school a week or so before the show was due to take place, these no doubt designed to whet the appetite of the audience. Apparently we could look forward to a range of delights including:

- Gymnastic display – Girls from Standard 2
- Joke telling – Peter Kenny Class 3H
- Disco Dancing – *The Boogie Girls* Standard 4

- Judo demonstration – Geoffrey Partington Class 1A
- Footie skills – Jimmy Corcoran Class 2C
- Song from Grease – Francis Reid & Friends Class 4T

Having sat through the relentless purgatory of comparable events over the years (awfully good experience though) I did have mixed feelings about having to endure the torture of similarly embarrassing individual performances – with one obvious exception of course – the programme's final act which already had me quivering with anticipation.

I was really quite moved by the gifts and good wishes lavished upon me during that final day from pupils past and present, and similarly by the sentiments expressed by the staff at lunchtime as they presented me with a new Dunlop squash racquet as a parting gift. How I'd love to confess that I still have this trusty old sporting relic, unfortunately however our association turned out to be somewhat short-lived as, following a particularly enthusiastic attempt at backhand, I smashed the frame against the back wall of a court at the Squash Club a fortnight later. It was Bill however that really had me moist-eyed as he passed over a gift-wrapped pair of cufflinks at the end of the afternoon:

"This is from me and Ada, just to say a big thanks David for all the support you've always given to us – it's been a real pleasure to work with you, you're a true gentleman," and here he cleared his throat before continuing. "Anyway, must get on, stuff to do and all of that,"

and then he was gone, striding away up the corridor whistling *Brown Girl in the Ring*.

The concert had been all I'd expected and more besides – a truly memorable experience with which to end my time at the school. The hall was packed to bursting yet again, with the Junior classes crammed like sardines onto the floor in front of the stage and the teachers seated on chairs down each side. The majority of the school appeared cheerful and in mightily good spirits, an exception to this perhaps being some of the Standard Four children. For several of these, the realisation was beginning to dawn that this was the point at which early childhood was being left behind along with their pump bag and reading book, so tears for some - and not just the girls it must be said - were very much the order of the day. They brightened up a bit however when the Head introduced two of their top class colleagues as our masters of ceremony for the afternoon, thereby signalling the start of the concert, and the fun.

It's never easy being first act onto a stage, but the Standard 2 girls did us proud. What they may have lacked in gymnastic expertise was more than compensated for by an undeniable enthusiasm for task, and if a measure of success is to finish the routine and exit with all limbs mostly intact and only minimal bruising, then theirs was indeed an accomplished performance. Every forward roll, somersault and backward walkover was met with rapturous applause from the assembled throng – mind you, I always say that if you can't please an audience that is looking down the barrel of six weeks off school then it's a pretty poor show.

Now as for stand-up comedy – that's a completely different kettle of fish. The odds were stacked against Peter Kenny from the outset I guess as he bravely attempted to simultaneously massage the collective funny bone of a crowd whose tastes ranged from the easily-amused, slapstick-happy, ready chucklers of Standard 1, right through to the sophisticated expectations of our elder statesmen seated at the very back of the hall. It was a complete disaster from the off as poor Peter demonstrated precious little in his repertoire of off-the-cuff, put-down remarks for dealing with hecklers:

"Knock, knock" he began cheerfully.

"Come in!" yelled a group of boisterous Standard 4 leavers sitting on a bench against the wall bars.

This fazed the lad completely. Standing centre-stage, his mouth opened and closed codfish-like as he gave me a bewildered stare. I tried to throw him a lifeline:

"Who's there?" I called aloud.

"Aardvark," he blurted our gratefully.

"Aardvark who?"

Nothing. A blank look was all he had to offer. The poor soul looked over towards me and mouthed "I can't remember" before turning to trudge away disconsolate. This surely wasn't the way it will have been during the endless hours of rehearsal in front of the wardrobe mirror at home when his timing no doubt, would have been faultless. Suddenly, as he reached the edge of the stage he paused, his face briefly illuminated once more as he retrieved the missing punch line from somewhere deep in his subconscious:

"Aardvark a million miles for one of your smiles!"

Well *I* thought it was funny anyway and offered him my very best grin of consolation, but it was too late for Peter, the moment had passed and things had moved on. Alas, 'tis true – a primary school audience can be that most cruel of beasts and it would appear the afternoon's proceedings might just be a case of *no turn left unstoned*.

Not so with the *Boogie Girls* however who were welcomed on stage with whoops of delight from their fans at the back, and this even before they'd shimmied a sequin-spangled leotard or dangled a spotless dancing pump in earnest. A momentary hiatus with the sound system at the start meant there was a need for urgent commands hissed offstage to Aileen Murphy who had been left in charge of the cassette player:

"Pssst, **NOW** Aileen."

"What's up wi' 'er? Tell 'er't push 'button."

"Aileen, turn the soddin' thing on will yer, we're all waitin' 'ere!"

Finally the music burst into life and the girls were off into their well-rehearsed routine. It was a polished enough performance I suppose, if a trifle repetitive and up until that point, I'd never realised just how long the Bee Gees' *Stayin' Alive* actually lasts. They finished eventually though and there was welcome applause, which the girls took as encouragement for an encore, but as they launched straight into *Native New Yorker*, a forest of hands suddenly appeared around the hall requesting a visit to the toilet.

Geoffrey Partington's demonstration of the martial arts was brief... but brutal. He walked onto the stage in his judo suit complete with its orange belt, carrying one edge of a PE mat. On the other end of this was his assistant / unsuspecting victim, Eddie McGinn, known to one and all simply as *Little Edward* dressed in his football kit. With the mat placed in the middle of the stage blocks, Geoffrey turned to bow to his audience before proudly announcing:

"I will now demonstrate *O Goshi*, also known as *the large hip throw*."

And with this he approached an innocently smiling, unwary Edward to place an arm around his shoulders and upper back in an apparent display of affection. Then, in a blur of motion that Eddie for one certainly didn't see coming, Geoffrey grabbed the lad's free arm and hurled him onto his back where he remained for several moments, wide-eyed, gasping for breath and savouring the welcome sanctuary of the PE mat against his spine. Indeed after regaining his composure, it may very well have been "*O Goshi*" or something quite similar that Edward muttered whilst hobbling back to take his place among the crowd.

Jimmy Corcoran's demonstration of footie skills mainly consisted of bouncing a school match ball up and down on various body parts, a skill that nowadays would be known as *keepie-up*. It wasn't a tremendously fluid display however, as the wayward ball had to be repeatedly fielded from the laps of spectators in the front couple of rows, and with a personal best tally of just four consecutive bounces onto head, knee or foot, I didn't think Jimmy was yet ready to grace the hallowed turf of Anfield or Old Trafford. He appeared happy enough however with some rather sporadic applause as he dribbled the ball off and we all settled down excitedly to welcome the final act.

*"A song from Grease"* I mused, now which of these exactly might Frank go for I wonder? Maybe it would be the iconic *Summer Nights*, performed as a duet with his best mate Elaine Butterworth taking on the Olivia Newton-John role?

No, no, surely he'd opt instead for that plaintive love song, *Sandy*, as the audience would be putty in his hands as he crooned about being stranded at the drive-in.

Of course, how stupid of me, whatever was I thinking about? Certainly the only song of choice simply had to be *We Go Together*, that sparkling, exuberant homage to long summer days and the close of Rydell High School, simply perfect for the occasion. As in the film, the bouncy *dinga da dinga dong* refrain and infectious hand jiving would soon spread through the hall like an anthem of freedom and class after class would stand to join in with the dancing. Maybe we'd all finish up outside, the entire school spilling out through the doors to perform excited cartwheels of pleasure across the cinder track and onto the field, with Bill and Ada leading the way twirling their mops like a pair of drum majorette's batons, closely followed by Dorothy, Eleanor and The Boss shaking their tush in a Watusi masterclass. Wouldn't that be a truly momentous climax to the school year and one that would certainly live in the collective memory for generations to come?

Maybe others were experiencing similar thoughts as an excited buzz could be felt around the room, before suddenly the waiting was over. The doors flew open and three girls from Standard 4 skipped onto the stage – No, wait, wait I tell a lie – two girls and Francis Reid from Standard 4 skipped onto the stage – it was an easy mistake to make though. Whilst the rows of Standard 1 & 2 children nearest the front of the hall stared up in open-mouthed confusion, the top classes were immediately on their feet, standing on the benches to clap out a frenzied beat whilst chanting:

"**FRANK! FRANK! FRANK!**" at the top of their voices.

Meanwhile, Dorothy & Eleanor's facial expressions were an absolute picture as they tried to make some sense of the vision that was Francis Reid. His costume mostly involved clothes borrowed from his sisters - a short frilled nightie and flesh-coloured tights that disappeared into a pair of pink fluffy mules. On his head an extravagant brunette wig was peppered with plastic rollers, the whole gorgeous ensemble being set off to perfection by appropriately lavish applications of lipstick, nail varnish and mascara. Already this was looking to be an absolute showstopper, but the boy wasn't even started yet.

The hall suddenly hushed into appreciative silence as, led by Francis, the three *girls* moved to the apron of the stage. Dorothy and Eleanor's eyes were by this point like dinner plates as the music began and Frank offered us all his warmest smile followed by a perfect rosebud pout, before dropping one hip and launching into *Look at Me, I'm Sandra Dee*.

This venerable school hall had stood since 1912 and will have played host to countless hundreds of assemblies, drama productions, Nativity plays and the like but I'm willing to bet that nothing to rival this will ever have been witnessed by the generations of pupils that will have perched cross-legged in expectation on the glowing parquet. There was absolutely no doubt that everyone was enjoying the performance, but no-one it would appear was having quite so much fun as Francis Reid himself who was literally in his element.

For one brief moment, as I listened to the lad deliver lyrics which included a desire to remain intact and virginal until after wedlock, before going on to warn Elvis that the proximity of his pelvis was indeed unwelcome, I did wonder what might be the outcome should one of Her Majesty's Inspectors of Schools decide to make an unscheduled visit just at this moment? He may for example raise an inspectorial eyebrow to discover a mini-transvestite belting out songs laced with wholly inappropriate sentiments in front of an appreciative crowd that included several teachers of previous good standing. Ah, what the heck, it was a glorious event, and surely it's the duty of educators everywhere to recognise and celebrate talent when they see it and oh boy did this young man have talent!

He finished with a twirling curtsy and clapped his hands to his face in appreciation of a cheering ovation that really did almost raise the roof. My hands too were sore from clapping and I offered up a fervent prayer that Frank's mum was fully aware of what a treasure she had in her family, a boy with intelligence, and wit, her son was such an accomplished performer, please stop trying to change that Mrs. Reid. Yes indeed, It was a truly wonderful moment on which to end my association with a great school and a fantastic bunch of children.

- - o O o - -

And so what of my new setting - well let's start with the positives should we? Top of that list must go the fact that I was once more reunited with my old chum and colleague DT as I'd followed him across the Borough. *Briar Field County Primary* itself was just five years old and equipped with several innovations and resources that made my last place appear fairly antiquated. There were no blackboards for example and obviously therefore, no chalk either meaning a considerably cleaner classroom environment and an end to my regular bouts of conjunctivitis brought on by the circling clouds of chalk dust. Instead, teachers wrote on shiny wipe-clean whiteboards using special pens. Unfortunately this wasn't pointed out to me on arrival until after I'd neatly printed the date at the top of the board in my room using a spirit-based permanent marker. Consequently it had been *Monday September 3rd* for several weeks until Lionel the caretaker finally managed to erase it with nail varnish remover and a Brillo pad.

The walls weren't the beige gloss painted plaster that I'd become accustomed to but instead the bare brick had been left as a *contemporary* finish, which I thought looked really quite attractive. Every class had its own stockroom too in which could be found, along with the reams of paper, books and pens etc, an overhead projector belonging to each individual teacher. Imagine the luxury - an OHP of one's very own, no more the need to arrive early in school each morning to kidnap the thing then wheel its trolley secretively down to your room where it would be camouflaged under a sheet until needed in order to hide its presence from anyone else wanting to use it.

There were other differences too, like the fact that all the *Ronalds* and *Sharons,* the *Maureens* and the *Edwards* had now been replaced with *Simons* or *Kimberleys*, maybe a *Jason* or a *Wendy*, which was only to be expected I suppose given the very different nature of the school's catchment area. The old terraced rows and corner shops didn't feature here, instead the school stood in the middle of a sprawling new housing development with avenues of dormer bungalows, all fronted by neatly trimmed gardens. There were open green spaces dotted around too and a large central car park around which stood rows of shops linked by a covered walkway, meaning that even on the rainiest of days, shoppers could dawdle from beauty salon to florist without ruining their expensive new hairdo.

I suppose you would best describe the local population as *middle-class aspirational* - there were pot plants at every windowsill and a Ford Granada on many driveways. Although separated by only a very few miles, my schools past and present were actually indeed continents apart on so many levels which made for a very different working experience. It had taken me several weeks to come to terms with the principal change here I suppose, eventually recognising that this was not actually down to classroom materials or geography or indeed the fact that I now worked for a female Head Teacher - Mrs. Richardson - but rather it was the children themselves, which provided the starkest contrast.

With their neat, grey school uniform and gleaming, well turned-out appearance, my class now seemed a completely different species from those of previously. Most of these children wanted for very little in their lives, apart that is, from maybe a sense of loyalty and kinship, as they seemed to be forever bickering, and constantly on the lookout for opportunities to snipe at their classmates and try to get them into trouble. The way they interacted with teachers too was very different. They weren't rude or aggressive exactly, but certainly lacked the warmth that I'd always been conscious of from my old classes. I felt they looked on me rather as they might any other school resource, treated in the same way they would a desk or a set of books - to be used when the need arose and then pretty much ignored for the rest of the time.

There were noticeable contrasts too, between my colleagues from both institutions, the new place seemingly populated by what I can best describe as *strong characters.* One of these was a woman called May Brennan who to be honest really never seemed to greatly enjoy being around children all that much. She'd first come to my attention on the very day I arrived as I witnessed a rather less than positive interaction between herself and a top junior boy standing in the corridor with his hand raised.

"Please Miss Brennan, can I go to the toilet?"

"I don't know Robert, you tell me, *can* you go to the toilet?"

"Please Miss, I don't understand."

"Well you see Robert," she continued, firmly locked into heavily pedantic mode, "what you've just asked doesn't really make sense, it's what we might describe as a rhetorical question."

Actually I didn't think she was entirely correct on that point but opted not to get involved as none of this was helping out poor, distressed Robert who hopped from foot to foot in obvious discomfort. Miss Brennan wasn't finished yet either:

"Strictly speaking Robert, the word *can* infers the physical or mental ability to carry out an act, whilst *may* on the other hand denotes permission or authorisation. You should use *may* then when asking such a question."

He looked confused. But then I was finding it hard to concentrate too and I wasn't the one bursting for a pee.

"Well go on then," she said to the boy, and he turned to dash off but was halted again in mid-stride.

"Hold it right there young man. What I actually meant just then was, 'go ahead and ask the question again; but properly please this time'."

"Please Miss Brennan, may I go to the toilet?"

The evil cow prolonged his agony yet further still by appearing to give this desperate plea some serious thought before graciously replying:

"Yes you may."

As the boy hurried away towards relief, she turned to me with a sardonic grin and I can remember thinking to myself, why don't you go and do something else with your life to which you might, (or should that be *may*?) be better suited? A career at Marks & Spencer perhaps, or possibly head slaughter man at the abbatoir?

It had taken a while to adjust to my new situation but I felt now that I was beginning to get a grasp of things and had moved on from the total despair I'd experienced on arrival, when sleepless nights convinced me I'd made a terrible mistake in deciding to move. It had been the timetabling and classroom organisation, which had provided the biggest headaches initially, indeed the first time I observed a typical morning set up in school I thought I may well have stumbled into a parallel universe. Classes were divided into groups – oh boy there were groups all right – and these drove the way in which learning took place. Most classes worked on a four-group system and a typical morning session for English might unfold as follows:

**Monday**.

**Group A - Audio comprehension**. For this, the children would sit around a cassette player and listen to a story through sets of headphones before then going on to answer questions about what they'd just heard. It was designed to benefit the skills of listening and concentration and the children were encouraged to jot down notes as they listened. Now one could be forgiven for imagining that this would be a peaceful, low-maintenance type of activity – but oh dear me no, not a bit of it. Isolated from the real world, the children would often ask one another questions at the tops of their voices, rather in the manner of old ladies in the hairdresser's shouting over the noise of the driers. Thus, the peace of the classroom might be disturbed by:

**"JONESY, WHAT DID THE WIZARD'S ASSISTANT SAY JUST THEN?"**

**"I DON'T KNOW, I MISSED IT TOO, I'LL REWIND IT A BIT."**

This would of course cause outrage among other group members who wanted to get to the end of the story.

**"WHARR' AVE YOU DONE THAT FOR, I'VE HEARD THIS BIT BEFORE?"**

**"OH SHURRUP GIBBY YOU'RE ALLUS MOANING."**

**"AAAAGGGHHHH!! – YOU TIGHT SOD!"**

The scream would be the result of one group member tweaking up the volume control to the point at which his neighbour's ears had begun to bleed. This then could be a very noisy activity and would also mean considerable extra work for the poor teacher as four sets of questions, differentiated according to difficulty would need to be produced each week to support the different stories.

**Group B – Library Skills.** Sets of reference books linked to the particular topic being studied would be delivered to each class from the School's Library Service in town for a half term's loan and the teacher would design question cards for each of these non-fiction books. These were intended to develop referencing and researching skills such as indexing and the use of contents / glossary pages etc. Trouble is the group would never replace the question card in the correct book and indeed the books themselves were always going astray leading to a twice-termly inquisition from fiercely confrontational Library Services enforcement officers as they arrived to investigate the whereabouts of missing volumes.

**Group C – Junior English (Haydn Richards).** Progress through these tedious books was supposed to develop the *nuts and bolts* of grammatical understanding. Well at least it didn't require supplementary inclusions from beleaguered, battle-weary teachers.

**Group D – SRA.** Enough said.

There were also other organisational issues to add into this mix. Those children identified as needing extra support with their work would also be withdrawn from class on a regular basis by a Local Authority *Remedial Teacher*. On seemingly random days this person would appear unannounced in the doorway with a list of clients before whisking away these class members to an alternative location, presumably still somewhere on school premises. I never actually found out what these characters were doing when away from their peers and for all I knew, the woman might simply have taken them out shopping. A definite downside to this was that as the children were often away during my instructional input, I'd have to take time on their return to repeat my explanation of what I wanted them to do, which was extremely time-consuming and disruptive. The same would be true of those children called to the staff room for their weekly music lesson. On Mondays then, I'd have to run through a repeat set of instructions to the returning group of violinists, Wednesdays would be the clarinetists, Thursday morning would be the cellist (note the use of the singular here, Curtis Patterson being the only child big enough to singlehandedly lug such an instrument through the streets, but she was a nice enough girl despite her ample proportions) and on Friday morning it would be the saxophonists of which there were now upwards of a dozen – it would seem that Gerry Rafferty's recording of *Baker Street* had an awful lot to answer for.

As the week progressed the groups would rotate through the different daily activities, a similar range of mathematical-based group tasks being engaged with after morning breaktime each day. Although I had by now started to come to terms with this potential logistical nightmare, most days I still felt like a plate-spinner in a variety show.

- - o O o - -

Other notable differences were associated with the notion of daily morning assemblies. At the last place, these were always the sole responsibility of the Head Teacher, with Dorothy as his Deputy grudgingly assuming the role of stand-in if ever The Boss was unavoidably detained. In her eyes, valid reasons for his non-availability might include: singlehandedly fighting a massive blaze in the roof space of the Junior corridor or negotiating with a gun-toting psychopath during a Nursery Department hostage siege-type situation, anything less, and assemblies were always expected to be down to him. In this school however, all members of staff were expected to share the burden. I soon discovered a real fondness for my early mornings spent leading whole school assembly every couple of weeks and the children too seemed to enjoy what I laid before them at these times.

The key to success here of course is to choose your material with the greatest of care. Each story must obviously contain some kind of moral or lesson but of far greater importance I feel, is to select a tale, which contains elements likely to appeal to one and all right across the spectrum of ages seated before you, a task all too often easier said than done. There was one obvious common denominator however, which, if included, would usually guarantee the attention of the majority audience and unite one and all in unanimous appreciation of your story-telling skills, that being: stories involving animals. Be these either of the domesticated or of the wild and angry variety, they are always well-received. Should the creature in question be required to display incredible bravery or selflessness in the face of overwhelming odds then so much the better and your audience-engagement quotient will benefit accordingly. Introduce an element of acute peril or better still, potential injury to the innocent creature in question, and you will have the whole school eating out of your hands.

It was with supreme confidence then that I stood at the front of the hall on the morning of my very first foray into the world of whole school assemblies, impatiently awaiting the school's arrival and fully prepared to deliver an award-winning rendition of *Barry the Mountain Dog* – a stirring tale of canine fortitude and gallantry from The Bernese Oberland. *Winter* by Vivaldi tinkled away agreeably from the sound system and I'd closed the hall curtains to shut out a watery November sun – *atmosphere*, surely another key ingredient of the whole assembly experience. Standing beside me at the front of the hall was a painting easel onto which I'd trained a stage spotlight in order to pick out my glorious technicolour representation of a handsome St. Bernard dog, complete with obligatory keg of brandy fastened to his collar and distant snow-capped peaks glistening in the background. It had taken me most of the previous evening to complete this illustration but initial signs were that the effort had been well worth it as the children focused on this as they entered before folding themselves into a sitting position:

"Aw look at that lovely dog."

"Mmmm, it's a Golden Retriever, my Auntie Sandra's got one just like that."

"That's not a golden retriever you divvy, it's a Husky, I know because…"

"All right everyone, remember we're in assembly, we can talk about this in a little while."

The classes were in, the teachers had made a hasty exit back to class where they would, no doubt, be juggling resources linked to the morning's group activities for later, Vivaldi had put down his fiddle and we were off.

For those unfamiliar with the story, I won't spend time unravelling the intricacies of the plot in great detail here, but suffice to say it is a saga that will tug forcefully at the heartstrings of dog lovers everywhere. The principal action takes place one stormy night around the monastery of The Grand St. Bernard Pass in Switzerland, and as I began painting a lurid picture of hardship and adversity, you could have heard a pin drop around the hall. Expressions of intense disquiet were apparent on many a child's face as they listened aghast to the unfolding story:

"… the brave animal, undisputed leader of the pack of dedicated St. Bernard rescue dogs, bravely turned once more back into the teeth of the fierce blizzard, determined as he was to seek out the missing soldier, lost somewhere out there in the inky blackness of the bleak mountainside…"

A concerned exclamation from a front row listener was heard at this point: "Oh no – please take care Barry."

Encouraged by the attention being shown, I really got into my stride and the mood took an even more sombre tone with narrative which included:

"As a feeble scratching was heard at the mighty oak door of the monastery one of the monks hurriedly flung the door wide to the howling night air, only to be greeted by a truly dreadful sight. There before them stood brave Barry, his thick coat streaked and matted with blood from what looked to be truly terrible injuries…"

"Christ Almighty" came as a whispered comment from the same child on the front row.

There was worse to come however as we approached the chilling climax of the tale:

"The abbot himself sat on the cold stone floor of the entrance hall, cradling Barry's mighty head in his lap. Through half-opened eyes, the faithful dog managed a feeble whimper before reaching out his pink tongue to lick the back of the old man's hand in gratitude. The Abbot continued tenderly stroking Barry's blood-stained muzzle, as the rest of the monks gathered close, so great was their concern for the well-being of their trusted old friend. After only a few moments more however, the brave dog's breathing grew ever more shallow and the group watched with tremendous sadness as Barry the Mountain Dog, closed his eyes for the last time and slipped peacefully away, finally at rest."

The children, who had up until that point been holding their breath in a determined, collective effort to somehow *will* the arrival of a happy ending, breathed a disappointed sigh which, alongside the occasional sniffle of mourning, was the only sound to be heard. Usually at this point in the proceedings there would be a discussion about the lessons to be learned from what we'd been listening to, (in this case it was all about mistaken intention and jumping to the wrong conclusion) but today they were all far too subdued to join in, trudging away disconsolate after a short prayer as Vivaldi picked up the rhythm once more. Packing away the easel and switching off the lights, I was more than pleased with the way I had engaged two hundred-odd primary children in today's story, a real success surely in terms of whole school involvement? Well *I* thought so at least, but my colleagues it would appear, didn't share similar levels of enthusiasm for my story-telling prowess, making their feelings quite plain in the staffroom at break time.

"Well well, Mr. Critchley, it seems you surpassed yourself in your first assembly, I've heard nothing but *Barry the sodding Mountain Dog* ever since," being the opening gambit.

DT grinned across the room at me as the good-natured scolding continued.

"Fiona Pearson's been sobbing a leg off all morning - says she's going to ask Father Christmas for a St. Bernard puppy and will never, ever let it out of her sight."

"There's almost been a massed revolt in my class," announced the Standard Four teacher, "they've all asked if they can stay indoors this playtime to continue working on their petition to the RSPCA of Switzerland – and I don't even know if such an organisation actually exists."

"I sincerely hope you didn't let them know that the remains of Barry the Mountain Dog can still be seen, stuffed and mounted in Berne Museum David, because the next thing you know they'll be organising raffles and fund-raisers to pay for a visit!"

## CHAPTER SIXTEEN – "Sausages!"

Primary schools are incredibly busy places and so it is imperative that effective channels of communication be securely in place in order to keep everyone abreast of just what's going on day-to-day. Mrs. Richardson, my new Head Teacher was especially keen on this element of school management, seemingly to the point of obsession. Every teacher for example, had been issued with an academic year diary, and these would be dutifully brought along to the weekly Monday morning pre-school briefing meeting to be filled in. A messages book would also be sent around the classes from time to time during the week with any alterations / additions to the master plan, this needing to be signed by every class teacher to indicate that they'd actually seen what was written there, and there was a whiteboard in the staffroom on which would be written daily schedules:

"If it's not on the message board, then it doesn't happen," being the grave warning issued by our esteemed leader on numerous occasions.

It was very early morning and I found the Deputy Head busy in the staffroom, writing up the day's itinerary as I entered to make a brew. It seemed that The Head was going to be absent all day, but I didn't need to rely on the notice board for this information as there were other much clearer indicators that this was to be the case. The Deputy, Mrs. Picamole - aka *the crimpeline vision* - was a dumpy little woman of around four foot six, not overly-endowed with personality it was true, but she was a cheery little soul, always friendly enough and approachable except on certain days that is, when all that I've just written about her would change dramatically, and today was just such an occasion. It's the role of the Deputy of course, as their title might suggest, to stand in, or *deputise* for the Head Teacher in the case of his or her absence and whenever this situation arose, Mrs. P would emphatically announce her temporary change in status to one and all in a quite remarkable way.

For example, Mrs. Picamole never normally bothered too much with make up in school, but as she turned from the board to face me this morning it was the vivid, crimson slash of inexpertly applied lipstick that first alerted me to her newly-assumed high office. Her expression too was somewhat chilly, not today the usual smile of greeting, as apparently, being a stand-in Head Teacher is a deadly serious business. Watching me reach for a teabag from the cupboard, she issued a deadpan reminder about the perils of abandoned crockery:

"If that cup is going out of the staffroom Mr. Critchley" (what had happened to the usual *David* I wondered?) "then please make sure it also returns at some point as I seem to spend far too much of my time collecting dirty mugs from around the place."

There would be other accoutrements of power on display too if you knew just what to look for. For example, when left in charge she would always clutch some sort of security blanket in one hand whilst striding about the place - a clipboard, a bulging diary, a copy of the latest NAHT bulletin, this week's Times Educational Supplement, and so on. Today she brandished a sheaf of papers and now handed one from this pile across to me together with an officious comment:

"These are the arrangements for the school photographer's visit today, please familiarise yourself with them; the hall will of course be out of action until three-thirty."

But it was as she swept past me towards the Head Teacher's office that I became aware of the final, unmistakable symbol of sovereignty. Only on days such as this would our eyes meet at a common level as her usual comfortable brown loafers had been exchanged for the pair of shiny black court shoes kept in her cupboard for those times when she was left in sole charge of the school's destiny. Whilst these stilettos would successfully elevate the wearer to virtual nosebleed altitude, they also ensured an unnatural and uncomfortable gait and as I watched her clatter unsteadily out onto the tiles of the corridor, rather in the manner of a character from a Dick Emery comedy sketch, I was really tempted to call out a comment concerning her ridiculous demeanour. In my imagination this would of course be extremely witty and cutting, probably something to the order of:

"You want to get over yourself you do love…you do realise don't you that in those shoes you look as if you're permanently running downhill?…AND by the way, you've got lipstick on your teeth."

- - o O o - -

Back in class as the morning session started, I realised that I'd lost the instructions concerning the photographer's visit but hey, how difficult could it be? Get all the kids in, take the photos, flog all these to friends and family in time for Christmas - job done. I'd seen several photographer mornings at my last school, I mean surely it couldn't be too different…could it?

Yes, as it turned out.

My mind returned to similar previous occasions and the fairly straightforward procedure which had ensued, ie:

- Kids line up in the hall, licking their hands to try and flatten down wayward locks of hair that had seen neither comb nor brush since this time last year.
- Photographer beckons first child forward to sit on a PE bench thus providing a three-quarters frontal view towards the lens.
- Photographer directs his subject to repeat a simple word or phrase – "*sausages*" being a time-honoured

favourite — which will guarantee an appropriately smiley mouth.
- Click.
- Child walks off back to class and the next in line is called forward.

This ensured the whole school could be snapped in a trice, all done and dusted in no time with any photographer worth his salt polishing off the whole school before lunch, so what's with all this "...*the hall will of course be out of action until three-thirty,*" business I wondered?

As already mentioned, I was daily coming to terms with the really quite marked differences between my current situation and those of a previous existence and I was about to discover that yet another startling contrast was evident in the way in which today's events would unfold. *Family Groups* is at first glance I suppose, a pretty innocuous statement, non-threatening and simple enough, but boy can it lead to a logistical nightmare when linked to school photographs.

I had the morning fully organised, all the group activities were sorted — the cassette player was loaded with a compelling tale about a runaway pony that escapes from its cruel owner to discover instead a life of peace and harmony with a loving new family in an appropriately rural setting. They'd be on the edge of their seats listening to that one. I'd even found time to alphabetise the coloured pencils in the SRA box before school started and now I was running through my expectation with the class before the lesson began, when I was interrupted by a knock at the door.

A group of Junior Four children stood in the doorway wearing clean shirts and expectant looks.

"Yes?"

"S'cuse me Mr. Critchley but we're starting off the family groups."

"Yes?"

"Well we need our brothers and sisters for the photos."

"Oh…right…well… of course you do…er…" I really should have kept hold of Mrs. Picamole's script.

My children seemed to know the ropes well enough though and several members of the class stood to join their older siblings before trotting off towards the hall, busily spitting on their hands as they went.

No sooner had I turned back to resume my input with the class than there was another knock at the door and this time it was a gang of Standard Three children come-a-calling. Now I was getting the hang of this situation, obviously a *top-down model* as children from progressively younger classes hunted the corridors for family members – dead easy, soon it will be the turn of my class to go in search of kid brothers & sisters. The downside to all these interruptions was of course that by playtime I'd repeated the same sets of instructions four or five times whilst the heartwarming tale of *Star, the Happiest Pony* had to be continually rewound for the benefit of returning group members.

Five minutes before the end of the lesson a group of my children sauntered back in through the classroom door.

"Good, so you've had your photos taken then?" I enquired as they returned to their places.

Ben Smart gave me a puzzled look: "No Mr. Critchley, we've not had ours done yet."

"Well where have you been then?"

"Clarinet lesson."

Oh bugger I thought to myself, of course, it's Wednesday, I should have realised.

"Do any of you have a brother or sister in school?"

To my extreme dismay, there were several replies in the affirmative.

"Well there's nothing for it, you'll have to go and collect them from class, then hurry along to the hall and explain the situation to Mrs. Picamole."

"Awww do we have to?" bleated Jasmine Beaumont, "she'll be in a really bad mood."

"And how on Earth can you possibly know that Jasmine?" I asked.

"Because I saw her on the playground this morning and it's a *high heels day*."

Ahh - what perceptive little souls children can be, I mused.

Things didn't get a whole lot better after playtime either; a hand waved in the air signalling the commencement of yet more confusion.

"Mr. Critchley?"

"Yes Jack, what is it?"

"I can't remember if I'm supposed to have my picture taken on my own or with our Chantelle."

"Well what did it say on the slip you brought in Jack?"

"I can't remember, do you still have them?"

God knows, haven't seen them in days I thought. Plan B was needed in a hurry obviously, along with a healthy dose of lateral thinking:

"Right Jack, go and find your...er..."

"Chantelle," he prompted.

"Exactly, go and get Chantelle and take her along to the hall for a family group photo and then when it's time for individuals, go to that as well and then when the pictures arrive, your mum can decide which she wants to buy. Oh and don't forget to tell Chantelle to do the same thing."

Surely this was nothing short of an absolute triumph of *thinking on my feet*, but the sight of seven other children wrestling with a similar dilemma soon wiped the look of smug self-satisfaction from my face. They all trooped out to follow Jack, leaving me to entertain the remnants of the class. I was just making a mental note reminding myself of the need to establish a foolproof system for filing reply slips in future when Emily Pearce raised a questioning hand.

"Yes Emily, what is it?" I sighed.

"I was just wondering Mr. Critchley, do *cousins* count as family too?"

- - o O o - -

As predicted, the hall was indeed out of action for the entire day. *Individual Photos* followed *Family Groups* and then it was the turn of *Teams* & *Clubs*, the Cricket Team clattering past in their whites, carrying bats and balls to add a bit of interest, signalled the start of this innings. Team captain, Nigel Fairhurst, wearing an enormous pair of batting pads to indicate his status, fell flat on his face outside my room. Surely this didn't bode well for success in matches for the coming season, I mean if the lad can't walk down a corridor without courting personal injury, what hope of galloping between the stumps without incident? Mrs. Picamole's *Needlework Society* was next up, offering a tastefully arranged group image. Mrs. P. positioned herself front centre wearing a sickly smile, whilst a shard of sunlight glinted from the pointy toes of those fearsome stilettos, and around her sat the rest of the group - "*my girls*" as they were always referred to - striking a forced and unnatural pose. Each child held in one hand a square of coloured sewing material or *binka* whilst the other hand merrily brandished a needle threaded with colourful embroidery silk. By the time the shutter snapped closed to capture the scene, the poor souls had aching faces and arms from remaining with a motionless smile in *mid-stitch* for so long.

*("Oh my God, it looks like a scene from The Prime of Miss Jean Brodie," being DT's comment when the photo was displayed in the staff room some weeks later, and indeed I'm sure that's just how the woman saw herself.)*

Educationally speaking, the day had been somewhat fragmented to say the least and as the close of play approached, the class relaxed whilst I read aloud the next instalment of *Stig of the Dump*. Suddenly I was aware of a lessening interest in the antics of Barney and his stone-age chum Stig and looked up from the book to try and determine the cause of this. At the window, peering in from the yard, was a face, or rather *two* faces and it was to these that the children's attention had shifted.

"Does anyone know that lady at the window?" I asked.

The children were cooing and giggling at the antics of the tiny baby held in the woman's arms, but someone did eventually manage to provide an answer:

"That's Calum's mum and his new baby sister."

"Oh I see. Does she need you for some reason Calum, as school doesn't actually finish for another twenty minutes?"

The poor lad looked mortified as the class gathered at the window to continue waving out at the recently arrived family member.

"Perhaps I'd better go and speak to her Mr. Critchley. I thought she was only joking this morning when she said she wanted a family photo taken with our Jessica."

- - o O o - -

The day's events were picked over during the rest of the week in the staffroom and I was pleased to discover that I wasn't alone in feeling exasperated by the manner in which the whole day had been disrupted. May Brennan was never slow in offering an opinion:

"I've said it before and am sure I'll say it again before I'm done, that bloody woman couldn't organise a p...p...party in a brewery..." before adding as an afterthought, "...with someone else's money!"

"Would that be *Lofty Picamole* you're referring to in such derogatory terms I wonder?"

This came from behind a magazine being read by the occupant of the armchair situated furthest away from the door. Over past months I'd come to recognise that any comment issuing from this particular location could normally be relied upon to be humorous...or caustic...or laced with sarcasm...or more usually just dripping with plain filthy innuendo. The chair in question was ancestral home to Mr. Molyneux, *Malcolm* to his friends, and no one ever dared to occupy the seat, even if Malcolm happened to be absent – it just wasn't the done thing.

213

Not a million miles away from retirement now, Malcolm was indeed quite a character, who had, in his very own words –

"been there, seen this, done that… twice."

It was presumably this *wealth of experience*, which required him for most of the time around school, to wear a permanently fatigued and wearisome expression of total disinterest. Give him any opportunity to *perform* however, and his apparent ennui would immediately be swept away in a wave of enthusiasm for task, as had been evidenced at the end of last week. All the teachers were required to take turns in leading the Friday afternoon Reward Assembly and as a preamble to what was essentially a quite tedious event involving the distribution of stickers and the presentation of a really quite mouldy attendance award, this term we were each expected to say a few words about our own out-of-school weekend interests and pastimes in an attempt to enliven proceedings. As well as the children, staff too had found this brief insight into their colleagues' outside life quite interesting and so turned up in their numbers to listen. DT for example had spoken about his love of sailing – *spinnakers and schooners*, I'd brought in my collection of cameras - *f-stops and shutter speeds* while Mrs. Picamole had bored everyone witless with an extended discourse on her countless years spent with macramé - *not knitting but knotting*. She attempted to inject some excitement into this with the aid of several decorative pot hangers hanging from the wall bars to display a varied collection of spider plants.

"Now children, we're going to move on from the basic *overhand* and *lark's head* knots as I attempt to demonstrate the more complicated *horizontal double half hitch.*"

My how their little hearts must have soared to hear that piece of news. Next in the series came Mr. Molyneux, but he had remained mysteriously tight-lipped about the content of his presentation, insisting that we must all just "wait and see."

It was therefore an expectant hush that descended across the hall as Malcolm signalled the children to be seated before beginning his much-awaited delivery.

"Now everyone, you're probably wondering just exactly what I'm going to speak to you about today?"

Cue anticipatory smiles and vigorous nods, these coming mainly it must be said, from the staff seated around the edges of the hall.

"Well now everyone, Mr. Molyneux is going to tell you all about one of his very, very favourite activities - something I started to do many years ago in fact, as a young teenager and have actually continued with to the present day, managing it now probably two or three times a week. There's no set rule about just when you can begin this activity, in fact looking around the room today, I would imagine that some of you are approaching the age when you will soon get into it, or possibly some of the older children may have already begun. But don't worry about that, you'll know yourselves when the time is right for you."

No real alarm bells at this point, but some teachers did sit up in their chairs, curiously attentive.

"And usually I have to say, it does tend to be the boys more than the girls who will first develop an interest in doing this, but can I make a plea at this point – come on now girls, why not give it a try yourselves eh? You might just find it enjoyable. It doesn't cost anything, or need any expensive special equipment, which is a good thing, and really you can do this whenever you feel the need – great for filling those spare times when you're sitting around alone with nothing to do, feeling just a wee bit bored."

Now there were some puzzled looks between staff, as they turned round in their seats to offer that: *can you see exactly just where this might be heading?* kind of expression. Malcolm was just getting into his stride:

"I say this can be done alone, which I certainly always did at first, but then I found that it's actually really good fun also to think about joining a group of like-minded people so you can all do it together. Over time too, it's true, some people may very well grow out of this pastime, particularly in their later years when other things come along to fill the time, but I find personally that the whole experience still really, really excites me, particularly as you know I live alone, just me and my Persian cat Salvatore, so it's good to have something enjoyable like this to look forward to in the evenings and at weekends."

By this time, the expressions on staff faces ranged from incredulity to profound amusement with more than one of my colleagues watching the whole scene unfold through the fingers, which covered their faces.

"When you do take this up children, as many of you surely will, it is important never to feel you are doing anything at all to be ashamed of, as there are too many people out there who will try to tell you this is not something you should be spending your time doing; that it is somehow terribly wrong. This is just nonsense, as it is a perfectly natural activity, all part of the whole process of growing up."

Heads were now being shaken in disbelief as troubled teachers perched on the edge of their seats, whilst Mrs. Picamole, obviously unable to take the pressure any longer, scampered out of the hall by the rear door. The strain of expectation around the room was almost palpable as Malcolm ambled towards the culmination of his introduction:

"That's right boys and girls, today I'd like to speak to you all about trainspotting!"

- - o O o - -

Today then Friday had come round again and as usual it was *The Radio Times* behind which Malcolm had been busy with his biro, planning out his viewing programme for the coming week. Nibbling on a lunchtime sandwich we would all chuckle away at the weekly commentary he provided whilst making his all-important selections:

"Oh my… *All Creatures Great and Small*, on BBC1 - now that's an absolute must, of course. My Sunday evenings just wouldn't be the same without a stroll through the pastures with Tristan Farnon. I'm fond of a good quiz too I have to say and there's nothing I wouldn't be prepared to do for a Blankety-Blank cheque book and pen. Do I ever watch Paul Daniels I hear you ask? Not a lot. *Grange Hill*? No I think not somehow darling, *far* too much of a busman's holiday sort of thing, but *Rumpole of the Bailey*, now we're talking – happy memories there of my own days spent in the corridors of Crown Court, oooh talk about a well hung jury!"

Suddenly the pages of the TV guide were closed and after glancing at the time Malcolm gave an enormous stretch and yawn before leaping to his feet in mock alarm.

"Well sitting here won't get the baby in the bathtub now will it?" he announced to one and all. "We're busy making glove puppets in Class 1 this afternoon, so I really need to pop into the stockroom and get felt…" and here he paused briefly to let the laughter die down, "…anyone fancy coming along?"

I really can't imagine how Dorothy and Eleanor would have coped with the unashamed raucous ribaldry that was regularly on offer behind the closed door of the staffroom, and therein lay another huge contrast with my previous experience. Malcolm was professionalism personified - miserable with it though it has to be said – as indeed were the rest of the staff beyond the confines of these four walls, but once that door was closed at break times, it was a case of *anything goes* and on occasions, the place could be a real bear pit.

--- o O o ---

My classroom during the afternoon was nothing less than a creative cacophony and I'm pleased to announce that Mod-Roc was back on the agenda. This time though it wasn't being used to fashion unerringly lifelike caricatures of the Christ Family but that same process of applying the material over a chicken-wire frame was instead being employed to create an enormous boar's head. When complete, this was to form the centerpiece of our medieval banquet and at this point perhaps I ought to offer a word of explanation.

Christmases here weren't the big deal they had always been previously. It was considered nothing short of wanton extravagance for example to *deck the halls* with all that foil and glitter at the start of the festive season only to have the whole lot consigned to the dustbin around a fortnight later. Whilst understanding of course the need for frugality with public funds, I did have mixed feelings about this whole situation, being also a firm believer in making Christmas that most special of occasions in school and indeed have always sought out any and every opportunity to focus on the non-commercial aspect of the whole event. But there we have it, with the exception of a token fir tree in the far corner of the school hall, there was to be but limited frolicsome festive fare to enliven those bare brick corridors.

Late November this year however also coincided with the planned extravaganza of our class assembly and so for some time now, afternoons had been given over to preparations for this. Throughout the year each class would take it in turns to put on a show related to the topic being studied, drawing together several curricular disciplines under the banner heading of *Colour* or *Countries of the World* or *Keeping Healthy* and suchlike. For the past term we had been exploring *The Middle Ages* and so our classes were preparing to lay the sum total of our medieval understanding before an assembled audience of school and parents.

I say *classes* as DT and myself, working as we did in parallel had been given special dispensation to combine our efforts on this occasion, a situation that hadn't gone unnoticed by colleagues.

"Well, well, it looks as if we have a right pair of blue-eyed boys in our midst," this being the lunchtime staffroom comment from May Brennan, "smacks of favouritism if you ask me – twice the bodies equals half the workload, what say you everyone?"

Replies to this came in the form of nodding heads and mutinous growls from some quarters, but Malcolm Molyneux at least appeared reasonably supportive of us, although naturally he couldn't resist lowering the tone somewhat:

"Oh I think it's an absolutely wonderful idea personally, I've always been partial to an early morning two-hander."

As I'd come to expect, many children were displaying only average levels of enthusiasm for the whole project and even an event such as this, which aimed to foster a spirit of working together in pursuit of a common goal, failed to engender too much in the way of harmony and co-operation. This attitude was in part evidenced by the exchange between two boys currently up to their elbows in wet plaster of Paris:

"D'you think this is ever really gonna look like a pig's 'ead?"

'Naw, but am not all that bothered anyway are you?

"Naw, I'm dead *boared* with it – d'you gerr' it?"

"You think you're funny don't you?"

The group using the pile of library service books to research interesting aspects of life from the period did appear to be rather more actively engaged on task, however on closer inspection their *Alphabetical Guide to Medieval Pastimes* clearly demonstrated a somewhat morbid fixation:

- **B** – Burning at the Stake / Death by Combustion
  Boiling Oil and its many uses

- **D** – Dismemberment & Mutilation
  Disembowelling: The process

- **G** – Gibbets of The British Isles
  Guillotines

- **H** – Hung, Drawn and Quartered: The Facts

- **M** – Mutilation & Dismemberment (see above sections)

- **T** – Thumbscrews & Other Instruments of Torture

- **W** - Trial by Water
  Witchcraft & Herbal Cures

Joshua Robertson, a pale and inoffensive little boy had taken it upon himself to painstakingly illustrate several of these procedures, including within this undeniably gruesome series a quite worryingly specific level of detail. I was just about to try and explain to the lad the possible inappropriateness of exposing an impressionable group of infant children to a grisly, technicolour representation of decapitation when I was distracted by a very curious question from another group member:

"Mr. Critchley, in those days was it considered shameful to be seen wearing anything on your feet?"

"Well... they weren't big on shoes it's true... but why do you ask?"

"Well it says here," and at this point he began to read aloud: "... *a favourite form of punishment was to convey those*

*convicted of any crime to a prominent site within the village*
*where they would be placed in socks.*"

"Actually Ethan, I think if you read that more carefully sunshine you'll find that it does in fact say: ...**stocks**."

Meanwhile Bryony and Charlotte were attempting to choreograph a fairly lacklustre *quadrille* being performed by other girls in their group:

"Oh c'mon Alice, Stephanie, liven the dance up a bit will you for God's sake?

"We're doing our best with this crappy music Bryony, but it's not exactly Donna Summer or Chaka Khan now is it?"

I'm sure it will all be fine on the day I thought to myself, and on the plus side, surely that cardboard and papier mache scale model of a Motte & Bailey Castle will be an absolute triumph.

As I have suggested here, enthusing this set of children on any subject was never an easy task but DT and myself had given it our all in terms of attempting to get them all fired up. For example we'd had them over to Chester by coach, this time to tramp the ancient walls and stand before the gates of the city, there to try and imagine the trauma of being locked outside in the wilds after curfew, risking unwanted interference and potentially invasive molestation by posses of Welsh bandits and unsupervised packs of wolves. We'd stood them all on *The Rows* to look down and sketch the half-timbered buildings and we'd sat beside the mighty River Dee listing a myriad possible uses of its waters in a medieval domestic setting.

On the way back, we'd stopped off at a working farm along a leafy Cheshire lane, there to be lectured on the subject of ancient agricultural techniques - the children being given the opportunity to practise the important life skills of hoeing, winnowing and broadcasting. When even this failed to lift some spirits, the ever-patient guide paraded a host of different cattle breeds for them to pet and stroke whilst simultaneously quizzing the children as to how they thought each one might have come by its name:

"And how do you think *The British White* came to be named?"

Sadly this was far too easy to even warrant a response of any sort beyond raised eyebrows and yawns of boredom.

"...and the *Shorthorn*?"

"Is it because it has *short horns*?" this the sarcastic reply from Felicity Nolan as she sat peeling a tangerine.

Next to be dragged across the field was an enormous black beast with a hugely broad, off-white cummerbund about its middle:

"And so children, why do you think this beast is called *The Belted Galloway*?"

Apart from sorely perplexed expressions, there was little else by means of a response for quite some time.

"Oh come on now," our resident famer cajoled, "can you not think how it came by its name: The *Belted* Galloway? - look more closely now, use your eyes and your imaginations."

Eventually a hand was offered from the middle row.

"Here we go at last, so what do you think sweetheart, eh, why is the Belted Galloway so called?"

Miriam Stewart continued to think about her answer before suggesting:

"Is it because it's just a naughty, aggravating little sod that will never do as it's told?"

Classic.

- - o O o - -

Once our big event was over with, I for one was looking forward to a nice quiet run-down to the end of year. Whether this would materialise or not would depend in part on the content of this evening's staff meeting. There was certainly a cheery atmosphere apparent, helped along by The Head Teacher who brought in a tray of home-made mince pies for general consumption. The final agenda item concerned *End of term arrangements* and Mrs. Richardson was first to speak about this:

"Traditionally we've never really gone overboard on this one, no full blown Nativity etc, but I really think we need to mark the message of the season in some appropriate manner don't you everyone?"

There were nods of agreement, and Mrs. Picamole gave her input at this point too:

"Something…*tasteful* I think wouldn't you agree?"

There were nods all round again, and of course The Head was all in favour of this suggestion:

"Oh definitely…goes without saying…*tasteful* must be our watchword at all times."

Mr. Molyneux it would appear however wasn't exactly totally tuned in to this particular wavelength:

"I have it," he announced, sitting forward excitedly and slopping half a mugful of coffee down his front, "how about a staff pantomime? I don't mind putting pen to paper to knock a script together."

"And let me guess," offered May Brennan caustically, "*you* of course will assume the role of Prince Charming no doubt?"

"Well if the slipper fits darling…" being Malcolm's coy riposte.

"Of course costumes wouldn't be a problem," Mrs. Picamole continued enthusiastically, "don't forget I've had an old horse's head for years now."

This was the point at which no one dared breathe, nor were we able to make eye contact with any colleague, especially not with Malcolm but then surely he wouldn't risk one of his earthy ripostes, not with The Head Teacher present? For what seemed like an age a strained silence reigned in the room, just the faint sound of Malcolm Molyneux nibbling away at the inside of his cheek in a valiant attempt at self-restraint until finally, no longer able to contain himself, the bubble burst:

"Well to be honest Mrs. P, the rest of you has never been all that special!"

Eventually The Boss did manage to regain a sense of order once more and after thanking Malcolm for his suggestion, attempted to steer the ensuing discussion along rather more conservative avenues. Finally it was decided that we would see the year out with *Carols by Candlelight* interspersed with extracts from the Christmas story read aloud by staff – all very tasteful too as it turned out.

- - o O o - -

Before that however, as I said there was our mammoth production to contend with. Assembly morning dawned cold & frosty and for once there was a discernible buzz of excitement about the place as the children checked their props and climbed into their outfits. Mrs. Picamole had actually come up trumps here as her sister's cousin just happened to be the proprietor of a fancy dress outfitters locally, (which did explain the earlier horse's head reference)

224

and so costumes were absolutely not a problem. Consequently the place was awash with serfs and nobility, we were waist-deep in chain-mail clad knights and there was even a jester capering about in cap and bells. Some children looked slightly nervous and sat apart from the others to better practise their lines and there was a constant stream of villagers in and out to the toilets, although this may have had more to do with checking their make-up in the mirrors than attending to any particularly urgent need.

It was certainly a hive of activity with both classes crammed into my room and as excitement and noise levels continued to build, I was quite relieved to see DT appear in the doorway once more, returned from the kitchens and therefore able to offer assistance should it be required, to help quell a potential peasant's revolt.

"All done?" I enquired anxiously.

"All sorted, Mrs. P is doling out cupfuls to the audience as they arrive while the Boss is still busy in her room with you-know-who."

We'd taken the decision, given the chilly weather of late, to offer the parents a warming drink on arrival and so had got together to concoct a wassail pot of fruit punch, cinnamon sticks and sliced apple with which to welcome our guests. This had been bubbling away in the cook's biggest saucepan for some time and was now apparently, being ladled out into paper cups for audience consumption.

"I've stuck some of this in too for extra kick,' DT announced ominously, indicating the empty *Ringmaster Sherry* bottle concealed in the carrier bag he was carrying.

The you-know-who being referred to, was in fact the recently appointed Director of Education, invited along to our little performance as guest of honour. David had assured me that it would do our career prospects no end of good to be seen strutting our stuff in front of the man, but I wasn't entirely convinced about this to be honest as I'd met the guy recently and just didn't like the look of him. Mr. Mountford was a portly little man from Stoke-on-Trent, blessed with an oily complexion and personality to match. Attempts to disguise rapidly advancing baldness with a strategic comb-over using several strands of lank, greasy hair were only partially successful, and even then only on days when it wasn't windy. His overall greasiness brought to mind an unfortunate and long-suffering colleague from class 3B at Grammar school who had been blessed with the wickedly unkind nickname *chipfat* for the majority of his school career. In education terms the new incumbent might well be in possession of skills to rival those of Maria Montessori or even Plato himself for all I knew, but as usual, I was finding considerable difficulty in overcoming my initial impressions and so for me, he would remain until proven otherwise, merely an unpleasant little slimeball.

An expectant hush descended as we led the throng down the corridor to the doors of the hall, there to listen out for the opening bars of *Greensleeves* with lute accompaniment, which was to be our cue for a grand entrance.

I felt a tug at my sleeve and looked down to see Alastair McManus aka *Peter, loyal squire to Sir John*, empty-handed and dismayed:

"Mr. Critchley, I can't find my cudgel."

"Well I'm sorry Alastair, but there's no time to make another, you'll just have to mime instead."

*"Mime*? I can't *mime* brandishing a cudgel. How am I supposed to beat the vagabond into submission using just thin air?"

He did have a point.

"OK look, sneak into the PE stockroom on the way past and pick up a rounders bat, but for heaven's sake, be careful what you do with it."

The music started and we inched forward into a packed hall, squeezing past the back row of seated parents, several of whom were now on their feet, cheerfully waving cameras to record the event for posterity. The School Hall at Briar Field was a fairly miniscule space even when unoccupied, wholly inadequate for the teaching of Physical Education for example, especially so for the older, larger classes and my preamble to PE lessons had by necessity been amended. For years now I'd always instructed classes to:

"Walk into the hall sensibly please everyone, find a space, and sit down."

Now this had been revised to the simple command:

"Walk in sensibly please everyone and sit down."

A small but essential alteration intended to prevent entire lessons going to waste as participants hunted in vain for the valuable but non-existent commodity that was *space*.

A combination of super efficient oil fired central heating teamed with hundreds of assorted bodies crammed into a confined space, made for what can best be described as a *close* atmosphere within. Among the adults present, there were several flushed and ruddy complexions apparent, including that of Mr. Mountford, his florid expression a rather disturbing smile / leer as he repeatedly shuffled his chair in increasing proximity to the Head Teacher's.

Bella Appleton's mum had arrived prematurely this morning in order to secure a prime spot, front row centre. Being so early also ensured there had been ample opportunity to have her wassail cup replenished two or three times and it was her uncontrollable attack of hiccups which resounded around the hall during the quieter moments, much to everyone's extreme amusement and Bella's absolute mortification and embarrassment.

These things apart however, the event was an unqualified success, DT and myself sat close by, clutching scripts and ready to offer prompts but this service wasn't actually needed, as the entire cast were absolutely word perfect. There was poetry and dancing and there were gags from the jester at which everyone chuckled. We held aloft artwork in the form of illuminated manuscripts and we guided our guests through the architectural innovations of improvements in castle design while the mummers presented mimes that were received to enthusiastic applause – in short, it was a triumph. An enormous amount of time had been invested in preparing for today, but I had to admit that this was clearly the way to bring history to life, as opposed to having children pore over pages of uninteresting text.

As the applause died down, Mrs. Richardson – eager no doubt to escape the continuing, unwelcome attentions of Mr. Mountford, who had been pawing at her person throughout the performance and who also appeared to have left a trail of dribble down her sleeve – stood to speak in glowing terms about her pride in the efforts shown by the children and also their hard-working teachers. Yet more clapping welcomed this praise and as our new Director of Education smiled across disturbingly at us, I tried hard not to focus on his sweaty face and those plump lips which glistened with saliva as he leaned closer to The Head once again. It would appear then that everyone was happy. We took the children back down to class where they began changing back into the twentieth century once more while DT and myself watched through the window as the last remaining mums who, having stayed behind to help shift chairs and avail themselves of the dregs of wassail, giggled off unsteadily up the school path.

# CHAPTER SEVENTEEN – 'I Know That my Redeemer Liveth.'

I was confused it's true. Whilst Christmas may not have warranted a great deal in terms of beating the annual drum of feasting and merriment, Easter apparently was a completely different beast.

Top dog event was of course the school Spring Bingo. To be honest I've never really understood the lure of this game, and whilst sitting in a silent hall *sweating on a line* or holding your breath awaiting the announcement of the magical remaining digits to guarantee a *full house* undoubtedly has its army of fans, it's not something that has ever really held any major appeal for me whatsoever. Love it or loathe it though, The *Easter Egg Bingo* was an absolute triumph of marketing, bringing guaranteed returns to swell the coffers of school fund and requiring precious little in terms of effort or outlay. Yes indeed, whoever came up with the idea in the first place was a total genius, just consider the set up for a moment:

Step 1. Ask the children to bring in a chocolate egg or box of chocs, which will then become prizes for this prestigious event.

(Ah I hear you say, isn't there a flaw here, I mean just suppose the children don't show sufficient interest in the whole project and the *prizes* don't in fact materialise? Well, should such an unlikely situation arise, then this is indeed simply remedied by announcing a Non-uniform Day - *often erroneously referred to by the children instead as "No Clothes Day."* In order to enjoy the undoubted novelty of being allowed to turn up for lessons wearing their own outfits, the children must *pay* for the privilege with...? correct, a pile of chocolate. This is guaranteed to ensure classrooms are soon absolutely stuffed to bursting with the very finest seasonal products by Cadbury's, Fry's, Nestle's etc)

Step 2. Purchase several hundred books of bingo tickets from the local Cash 'n Carry for the equivalent of a few coppers. At the same time, pick up some orange cordial and crates of crisps to be sold at profit during the intervals, of which there will be several.

Step 3. Set out tables and chairs in the hall one evening.

Step 4. Open the doors to school and stand back out of the way as the crowds swarm in impatiently.

Step 5. Sit back and enjoy the sound of mountains of filthy lucre being handed over.

So then, just to recap: mums & dads go out and purchase rafts of edible prizes which are brought freely into school on a given day by their casually attired offspring. Families then spend considerably more of their hard-earned cash on admission, plus the purchase of refreshments and multiple books of bingo tickets in excited attempts to win back prizes which actually belonged to themselves in the first place – simply brilliant. Thankfully too, these were the days before the launch of any well-meaning Healthy Schools' Initiative, thereby enabling a conscience-free attitude to such goings-on. Indeed any nagging concerns about the potentially detrimental effects to children's well-being such as rampant dental cavities or enhanced levels of obesity were surely outweighed by the undoubted benefits to the general school community brought about by considerable financial returns?

- - o O o - -

There was of course just the very faintest possibility that there may yet be some pupils requiring even more of a sugar fix and if so, then their needs would be attended to by The Easter Bunny. This was a new one on me to be fair, Father

Christmas, Guy Fawkes or Hallowe'en goblins and ghouls I didn't have much of a problem with, but the acknowledgement of Easter Bunny as an actual entity was definitely way off my radar of experience. Not so with the Mrs. Richardson however, she was a huge fan of this annual springtime visitor. To this end then, she arrived in school at the crack of dawn one morning, (ie even before my own car featured on the car park) to don an apron before mixing up a large pot of brown paint. Thus armed, she toured the school, daubing rabbitty footprints along the floors of all the corridors and into each room where a sack of tiny chocolate eggs would be left on the teacher's desk.

When the children arrived later to discover the pawprints – the paint on these now well and truly dry thanks to the thermostat being set between *sizzle & torrid* for a couple of hours - their confectionery-fuelled excitement knew no bounds.

They soon calmed down once back in class though after being reminded that it would be myself, rather than Easter Bunny who would be distributing this bounty at the day's end. Out came the RE books then in order that we might continue our study of the events of Holy week. Admittedly it is asking a great deal of Primary aged children to engage with some of these weighty matters including the concept of the necessary faith required to accept alien notions such as resurrection from the dead or transubstantiation.

"So one minute it's a cup of wine and then – SHAZAM! - the next it's God's blood, is that what you're saying?"

"Well yes, I suppose so if you want to put it that way…"

"Cool. And could he do other stuff too Mr. Critchley?"

"Such as, Simon?"

"I mean, could he hover if he wanted to?"

'Hover? How do you mean could he *hover* for heaven's sake?"

"*Hover*, you know – levitate, 'cos if you ask me," the lad argued with flawless logic, "levitation has to be a whole load easier than dying and coming back to life again a couple of days later, don't you think?"

Cue a somewhat unsuccessful discussion as I attempted to distinguish between a *miracle* and the sort of entertaining conjuring trick that might be performed by the likes of David Nixon, everyone's favourite Saturday evening TV magician.

Much interest continued to centre on certain elements of Christ's passion, in particular the Scourging at the Pillar and the Crucifixion for example.

"You'd never get away with that these days would you Mr. Critchley?"

"What's that Becky?"

"I mean forcing a crown of thorns onto someone's head must really hurt, did nobody get *done* over that?"

"Yeah," someone else chipped in, "why didn't he take them to court or summat?"

Oh dear God, maybe I'm just not cut out for ecclesiastical interrogation. As a distraction I played them *Herod's Song* from Jesus Christ Superstar - which they all seemed to enjoy.

I felt on much safer ground as we continued exploring the concept of loyalty, taking as our starting point the actions of Judas and also Peter's denial of Jesus following his arrest. Thankfully we'd moved on now from the embarrassing opening skirmishes of last week, which had at the time, prompted a good deal of sniggering around the room:

"He said **cock** then, did you hear him?"

"I know, I know, he doesn't get it does he?"

"Naw, listen, he said it again, that's three times now!"

Today the children were actually making some valid points in their consideration of Peter's predicament, speaking with unexpected maturity about issues including self-preservation, survival strategies and peer pressure.

"I think Peter really wanted to stand by his friend but didn't want to get himself killed either so it was really difficult for him."

"Good comment Alison and what do you think you would have done had you been in his shoes?"

Before she was able to answer however, there was a knock at the door and Easter Bunny walked in unannounced. In his left hand was a cassette player and the play button was pushed immediately on arrival, thus enabling Flanagan & Allen to begin crooning *Run Rabbit Run*. This was Easter Bunny's cue to begin scampering about the room, hopping over tables and shaking his fluffy little tush. The children were at an absolute loss for words. Only a moment ago they had been wrestling with Judas Iscariot in the Garden of Gethsemane and now here was an adult in a grey rabbit outfit, complete with two-foot ears and oversize plastic incisors bouncing about in their midst. The fact that no-one had actually pre-warned me of this visitation only served to fuel the total surrealism of the moment, I mean for all I knew, this person could actually be some psychopath fruitcake who's simply bobbed in from the streets on the off-chance of havoc and mayhem. Indeed there was a moment when I had considered wrestling the rabbit to the ground before sending a mature and trustworthy child off to fetch some backup, but then the music stopped suddenly with a *click* and my fears began to subside.

As fantasy rabbit costumes go, there's no denying this was top drawer quality, and I wondered whether it had been Mrs. Picamole who'd supplied the outfit on this occasion. Possibly maybe a size too small however, the only thing that let down the whole ensemble were the legs which were lodged firmly at half-mast revealing a pair of scruffy black work shoes - now where had I seen similar footwear before I wondered. Once the prosthetic teeth had been removed I thought there may also have been something vaguely familiar about those bits of face still visible behind the whiskers...but then he began to sing and that unmistakable Scouse accent meant that I had it in an instant:

'If you're happy and you know it…

… shake your bum,

…if you're happy and you know it…"

Now this was a side to the school caretaker - Liverpudlian Lionel - that I had certainly never encountered before. Normally he was quite a taciturn character with whom folks would really struggle to even pass the time of day let alone engage in conversation, and now here he was, cavorting about in a wholly inappropriate manner in my opinion – wearing a furry costume. The mask and whiskers made it rather difficult to judge his mood and feelings about being required to carry out these additional duties, which, I'm guessing, probably didn't feature in his original contract of employment or conditions of service. Chances are he won't have been impressed. He was probably hopping around the classroom now whilst inwardly bemoaning the negative impact that rabbit mimicry was having on his working day, doubtless having thoughts along the lines of:

'Well this isn't getting the hall floor stripped & sealed and heaven knows when I'll get time now to put that new fluorescent tube in the ladies' toilet.'

Or maybe I'm completely mistaken – possibly this is how he likes to spend his free time? Maybe in his CV – if indeed there had been such things in the late seventies – under the section: Pastimes and Hobbies, he may have entered: Impersonating woodland mammals and assorted small, cuddly vertebrates of the British Isles & Europe - who knows? Whatever, I'll certainly look at the man in a different light next time he's sweeping the playground or putting up shelves.

After a single verse of his cheery little ditty during which he waggled his cottontail relentlessly, Lionel hopped back over to the open door and disappeared back into the corridor with just a cursory, backward wave of goodbye over his shoulder. The door closed behind him and to the relief of one and all, sanity made a welcome return.

"So then children, let's make a list of all the emotions that Peter and the rest of the disciples may have been experiencing on that fateful night. Now who's going to start us off?"

- - o O o - -

And there was yet more still. All visitors to school would receive a timely reminder about the underlying message of the season as they opened the door and stepped into the entrance hall. Across the notice board, positioned just above the pamphlets offering helpful and oft-requested advice on the home treatment of nits, was tacked a simple backcloth showing a faraway hill with three crucified figures in tasteful silhouette. Below this was a full-size freestanding tomb made from scrunched up sugar paper that had been artistically enhanced by children from the top class to represent stonework. Obviously the entrance boulder had been rolled away, thus facilitating a view within, to where a discarded sheet lay untidily at the foot of an altar table bearing a lone candle. It was never a good idea of course to place flammable objects in close proximity to paper sepulchres and so understandably, the candle remained unlit at all times. Nevertheless though, this powerful symbolism representing the light of the world being rekindled at Easter time, surely can't have failed to strike a seasonal chord with whoever crossed the threshold.

As the entrance hall was also a space shared each day by the bronchial, the lame and the unruly – ie those children unable for whatever reason to participate in outdoor playtime – it really wasn't uncommon to find the occasional discarded Twix wrapper or several empty Quavers packets littering the floor of the tomb from time to time. This did give the unfortunate impression that The Saviour of the World had been snacking away heavily in advance of his big resurrection moment.

Beside this was a sign reading PLEASE TAKE ONE, which referred to the nearby stack of prayer cards entitled: *A Thought for Easter*. Each of these depicted an image of *La Pieta* by Michelangelo, the iconic sculpture which showed the Virgin Mary cradling the crucified body of Jesus in her lap, and included also a neatly printed verse taken from The King James Bible:

*I am the resurrection, and the life: he that believeth in me, though he were dead, yet shall he live: And whosoever liveth and believeth in me shall never die. (John 11:25-26)*

All this of course was The Head's way of reminding one and all of the real purpose and driving force behind the season's celebrations, sentiments which were, I thought, nothing short of commendable. In my opinion however, the poster taped to the door of the secretary's office did appear somewhat at odds with the general mood and message. This showed a cheerful cartoon duckling in luminous yellow, with a speech balloon issuing from its beak bearing the reminder:
HAPPY EASTER EVERYBODY!!

Don't forget Juniors -
next week's Decorated Egg Competition
has prizes for every class!

Ah yes – the decorated egg contest – and therein lies another tale.

- - o O o - -

I had been elected to judge this prestigious event, even though I hadn't even been aware that the role was up for grabs. Malcolm Molyneux had been my unexpected sponsor in this, announcing his endorsement of my suitability one rainy lunchtime, his mouth heavy with undigested morsels of hot-cross bun:

"Oh come on now everybody," he announced, spraying crumbs in every direction, "we've all enjoyed our turn at this, so let's give David a chance this year as it's his first Easter at Briar Field, it'll be awfully good..."

I shot him a threatening look at this point, half-expecting the next word to be "experience" but instead he ended the sentence with "fun." This I suppose ought to have provided reassurance, but there was something about those grinning faces around the staffroom, which left me with feelings of acute unease.

The initial heats were judged in class, with each teacher sending forward three entrants to the grand final in the school hall on the last day of term. Eight junior classes, three eggs from each, it's piece of cake thought I, how hard can it be to pick a winner from two dozen entries - surely this would be nothing short of child's play?

The hall was packed once again, two smiling rows of parents belonging to the lucky finalists seated on *guest chairs* behind the junior department who were crammed onto the floor in front. During the morning session there had been a similar scenario as the Infants had cranked up the *cute* factor by parading around school in their Easter Bonnets with May Brennan presiding over the judging of this, and now it was about to be my turn to do the honours. The Head was leading an awards assembly, giving out certificates, prizes etc whilst I repeatedly circled the table that had been set up behind her back frantically scanning the assembled prize-winning entries in search of an overall champion. Consequently there were at least twenty-four pairs of children's eyes - plus those of their associated parents - focused directly on my actions rather than on whatever the Head Teacher was doing. Lingering over an egg for closer inspection provoked tremors of agitation from its owner and as I picked one up in order to better assess its overall quality I became aware of excited murmurings from a couple of parents close by:

"He's got hold of yours Gerry look," exclaimed one of the mums.

"Yessss – get in there," hissed the husband, "go on sir, you know that's a winner."

And therein lay the problem. Sitting in the palm of my hand was an incredibly detailed eggy caricature of local rugby league legend Billy Boston, resplendent in his cherry & white-hooped Wigan jersey. It was really a quite amazing piece of work - apart that is from a tiny hairline crack across his domed skull, possibly the result of a hand of sabotage from another competitor or indeed by an irate Saints fan who had taken exception to this representation of their rival team. The thing is, Billy Boston had hung up his playing boots, long before any child in the room will have been born, meaning the only contact this egg will have had with junior hands will have been when one of the children carried his dad's master work into school for judging. It was a similar picture with almost all the other entries too.

These included the unmistakable portly form of *Boss Hogg* from that popular Saturday teatime TV show - *The Dukes of Hazzard* - complete with his egg-shaped white suit, matching stetson and cigar. Telly Savalas was there too, in easily recognisable *Kojak* guise, sucking on his trademark lollipop behind a speech bubble proclaiming 'Who loves ya baby?' Meanwhile the wings on the Boeing 747 taxiing away from its egg-box hangar were an absolute triumph of miniature engineering and look, there's even a tiny pilot waving out from the flight deck too. Next to this came an egg that was predominantly blue in colour, topped with well coiffed nylon locks and clutching a teensy handbag – Mrs. T to a T. They were all quite, quite brilliant but without a shadow of doubt, the majority were the result of very many hours' painstaking adult involvement. Turning to face the audience, I was greeted with several warm smiles and thumbs-up-type gestures of encouragement from mums & dads desperate as they seemingly were to secure the victors' spoils and thereby guarantee honour & celebrity status for the entire family.

Malcolm Molyneux's face, grinning out at me as it was from beside the wall bars certainly did nothing to help my predicament, he knew just what he was letting me in for when my name had been put forward for this unenviable task. I certainly hadn't expected that the parental desire to win at all costs would have been quite so intense. Time was running out, the pile of certificates in the Head's hand was almost exhausted and any minute now she would be looking for me to close the proceedings. What ever I did, there would be some disappointed, disgruntled customers out there and that's for sure.

"And so now everyone," Mrs. Richardson announced cheerily, "we turn to Mr. Critchley, our judge for the afternoon to announce this Easter's junior winner who will step forward to collect this three pound book token as their special prize – Mr. Critchley, everyone."

Appreciative applause was followed by anticipatory silence as I walked to the front of the hall, still without the faintest clue who I was going to choose. I stalled for a little while, blathering on with a handful of the usual platitudes:

"...very difficult task...such talented children...you are all winners really...let's have a round of applause for all who have taken part...blah, blah..."

But the children were now restless and totally disinterested whilst the parents were literally on the edge of their seats, unwrapping cameras with which to record their offspring's moment of glory and mentally willing me to choose *their* egg. I had to do something.

"And the winner is..."

as I turned back to face the entries set out on the table behind me once more, I swear I still hadn't made up my mind, but then suddenly, clear as day, I heard my dad's words of advice which had been repeated to me many times over the years:

"Never forget David, whatever you do in life, whenever you're faced with difficult decisions, you should always be true to yourself."

".... Jennifer Dawson from Junior One."

There were some puzzled expressions among the parents it's true, with Billy Boston's creator for one, looking alternately perplexed and deeply irritated, but surely no-one looked quite so surprised as Jennifer herself, scrambling to her feet to bask in the sporadic applause that greeted my announcement. Beaming broadly, Jenny gratefully accepted her prize before returning to her place where classmates congratulated her warmly and leaned forward to take a closer look at her handiwork, an Easter chick egg with ill-matched pipe cleaner legs, wings made from a cereal packet and a biscuit wrapper bonnet.

"Well done David," Mrs. Richardson whispered in my ear, "a brave decision and the right one of course."

# CHAPTER EIGHTEEN – Up the Creek Without a Paddle.

The hangover really started to gain serious momentum in the middle of the river. This was a first for me, as across all my years attempting to manage the aftermath of alcoholic excess, I'd never before been called upon to do this whilst simultaneously paddling a canoe-full of excited children with Native North American Indian war paint daubed across their faces. Surely though, the extravagant stripes of vibrant colour slashed across my own nose and forehead would distract attention from an otherwise ghastly, green pallour, or at least that's what I hoped. As had always been the case in such situations, it had all seemed such a good idea at the time.

We were in deepest Shropshire, at an *Activity Centre* for a weekend of 'Thrills & Adventure' along with children from top Juniors. DT and myself were convinced that this place may well in fact have been the actual location at which the phrases: '*absolute middle of nowhere*' or quite possibly: '*the back of beyond*' were indeed first coined by an early traveller. In fact the remoteness of the location was probably, a major contributory factor to my current somewhat parlous state of health. Yesterday's instalment of Thrills & Adventure had been billed as an afternoon of pony trekking, which, to be honest, sounded innocuous enough on paper:

"Enjoy a relaxing afternoon taking in the majestic Shropshire countryside from the saddle of one of our well-schooled ponies."

But the reality turned out to be anything but relaxing, and I for one had found the whole experience extremely stressful. I've always been slightly nervous around horses or indeed for that matter, any mobile contraption without free and ready access to a clutch or handbrake, and the events of yesterday did nothing to ease my worries on that front. Of course I was at great pains not to transmit any such misgivings to the children in my group, putting on the very bravest of faces and adopting my best cheery manner as we made our way down through the woods to the stables.

"Oh I'm so looking forward to this children, aren't you?" I lied, "it will be just like being aboard *Champion* himself as we gallop off towards adventure and excitement."

This prompted looks of puzzlement from those around me, while a request for further clarification came from Sally Pennington:

"What on Earth is *Champion* Mr. Critchley? I've never heard of it and I don't think anyone else here has."

Never heard of Champion? This was indeed a startling piece of news, which left me reeling in disbelief – didn't they know what they were missing? In a trice, the years fell away and I was six years old again, sitting on the living room carpet at home, nursing an after-school bowl of Sugar Puffs and a glass of Dandelion & Burdock, my eyes glued to the tiny, black-and-white TV set standing in the corner. Bursting out from this was the unmistakable sound of Frankie Laine, his voice signalling the start of my weekly escape on horseback across the monochrome plains of the mid-west:

*"Champion the wonder horse*

*Champion the wonder horse*

*Like a streak of lightnin' flashing 'cross the sky*
*Like the swiftest arrow whizzing from a bow*
*Like a mighty cannonball he seems to fly*
*You'll hear about him everywhere you go*
*The time will come when everyone will know*
*The name of.....Champion the wonder horse*

*Champion the wonder horse."*

Suddenly I came to my senses and realised that I'd been belting out this theme tune at maximum volume, meaning the expressions on the faces of my group now suggested a growing concern with my mental well-being. Time to move on.

Standing beside the rail of the stable block, I, for one was most definitely all ears as our instructor issued directions about basic riding techniques while his minions doled out protective headgear. A perennially active inner pessimism gene convinced me that only mayhem and disaster lay in wait, and so I invested much time in ensuring the chin strap of my riding helmet was fastened tight. Indeed so successful was I in this that my neck was pushed forward to a quite unnatural angle and my gaze forced into a permanent, downward trajectory. One by one the children were beckoned forward and introduced to what were to be their mounts for the next couple of hours, each of these ambling out sweetly with a mouthful of warm hay to nuzzle the hand of their little riders. The ponies were gentle, pot-bellied, good-natured beasts, and the whole scene bore an uncanny likeness to a Norman Thelwell gymkhana cartoon.

The children were soon all mounted and, finding myself alone at the rail, I began to harbour selfish hopes that the stalls would now be empty, meaning I would be required instead to wait behind after waving the children off for their trip. However, listening to the instructor call across to the stable lad, the realisation dawned that such dreams were, on this occasion, not to be:

"Sally, bring out *Trojan* would you please, for the teacher here."

The mighty creature's ears easily brushed against the underside of the door lintel, as it clopped skittishly out into the yard to shoot me a sneering, dismissive, glance of disdain. From all sides the children cooed in awe and obvious appreciation of my waiting challenge and, against all expectations, I managed to find yet another notch on my chinstrap.

True, it was only after a monumental effort that I succeeded in hauling myself into a position from where I was able to make a frantic scramble into the saddle, but following an hour or so spent dawdling along at an idle pace, I began to relax and settle into a considerably easier frame of mind about the entire horse-oriented undertaking. I pictured myself this time as a latter-day Roy Rogers-type figure, sashaying across the prairies aboard my ever-faithful golden palomino – *Trigger* - whilst strumming on a guitar to serenade the sagebrush with the comfortable chords of *Home on the Range* and *A Four-legged Friend*. Wisely perhaps, on this occasion I chose not to share these images with the rest of the group. The children too though were enjoying the afternoon, with only the occasional, anxious squeal to disturb the tranquility of the forest:

"I CAN'T STOP IT EATING!"

Echoed about the pine trees for example, as a pony would halt in order to munch a tasty wayside morsel. There was also the regularly repeated announcement:

"MY HORSE IS HAVING A WEE AGAIN!"

"Well don't forget to stand up in the stirrups Jason until it's finished," I advised, surprising even myself with this newly discovered understanding of equine matters.

The boy was right though, his pony: *Triple–X* did appear to be suffering from some sort of bladder incontinence disorder as every hundred yards or so, she would pause to puddle the woodland trail with a prolonged and extremely noisy bout of peeing. It was on the fifth or sixth such occasion that I suddenly realised Jason Armitage, myself, *Triple–X* and *Trojan*, did appear to be spending a disproportionate amount of time in one another's company, the reason for this being explained by one of the passing stable-girl chaperones.

"Oh those two ponies are never too far apart from each other, wherever she goes, he's bound to follow. Yes they're definitely an *item* that's for sure."

Ah, then that would explain why my pony's nose had never for a moment been too distantly removed from the hind quarters of Jason's steed and indeed, whenever his animal had come to a halt, then so too had mine. Who would have expected such open displays of affection from two romantically inclined animals? – aw quite sweet really, I thought.

A further half hour passed in similarly pleasant fashion before we left the shade of the trees and woodland behind and emerged onto an open tract of sunshine-stained meadow beside the river. Here our instructor ordered everyone to halt for a little while and dismount in order to stretch the legs and allow the ponies a few moments' rest. It was as I sat to ponder the logistics of this, and consider the most appropriate means by which I might attempt a descent from a saddle currently perched at Himalayan altitude, that the uproar began. Rather than pausing to contentedly nibble the grass alongside the rest of his colleagues, and wholly oblivious to my repeated requests for restraint, Trojan continued instead with the relentlessly amorous pursuit of his stable mate. Meanwhile, Triple–X who had obviously endured quite enough of a salivating stallion hungrily snuffling her chuff all afternoon, opted to register her displeasure by setting off from the group at a quite fearsome canter across the pasture.

Now then, remind me again, how does it go? Ah yes:

"...*wherever she goes, he's bound to follow,*"

and indeed that was exactly what he did, at quite terrifying speed. Yanking at the reins to no avail, as the countryside suddenly began hurtling by at a really quite alarming rate and clouds of assorted insect-life arrived to pebble-dash my face, I ran through with considerable haste my entire repertoire of pony-calming strategies. To be honest, these were actually somewhat limited in number, consisting mainly as they did of yet more repeatedly forceful yanking at the reins whilst simultaneously calling out "WHOA BOY, WHOA!" at the top of my voice – well it always seemed to work for John Wayne.

In a matter of moments, I was no longer *cool dude cowboy troubadour*, but more inclined instead towards *hapless slapstick character from an early episode of Dad's Army* as my feet left the stirrups and progress across the hummocky grass immediately became anything but elegant. I narrowly avoided capsize by managing to cling onto anything I could, (apart from my dignity of course, obviously) and despite my previous determined efforts with the securing strap, I was greatly disappointed to discover the bright orange riding helmet had now slipped across one eye to partially obscure any forward view, which, all things considered, was possibly not a bad thing. Unable at such short notice to master the *rising canter*, I found myself instead required to accept a situation in which Trojan's saddle arrived to batter my testicles from beneath several times each second. Bizarrely in the midst of this chaos I suddenly began to wonder just what the children were making of it all? For obvious reasons relating to personal well-being, I was unable to turn around to check on this and anyway, even if this had been possible, such action would have been fairly pointless as the helmet had now slipped yet further to the point at which it covered my face completely.

And then he stopped.

Wasting no time at all, I slipped to the ground and snatched off the riding hat, mistaken in the belief that I may still be in possession of some shred of self-respect, only to then experience grave concerns about the ringing sensation in my ears. It was a great relief to discover this was merely the sound of distant rapturous applause as the group of children from which I had departed so abruptly, began noisily celebrating their teacher's display of horsemanship and bravado. With a trembling hand I gave them a cheerily nonchalant wave whilst at the same time making myself the promise – 'never again.'

--oOo--

And so it was that I felt the need to turn so readily to drink in a possibly over-exuberant manner yesterday evening. After tea, the children had been encouraged to charge energetically to all corners of the estate as eager participants in something called a *wide game*, the principal purpose of this being to blot up any remaining dregs of energy, thereby ensuring immediate and unanimous sleep the moment their collective head struck the pillow. This had been followed by a *Bonfire Singalong & Sausage Sizzle*, to which all the school groups had been invited. As our children had been positioned downwind of the evening's blaze, it was a row of blinking, sooty faces that peered out from their sleeping bags at bedtime, in a dormitory now imbued with the aroma of a kipper-smoking facility. David and myself popped in briefly to bid them all good night before slipping out again into the evening air, secure in the knowledge that from this point on, a team of eager *Groupies* would assume responsibility for the children's nighttime well being. This we agreed was an extremely civilised arrangement, thus enabling weary teachers to escape for a bout of well-earned rest & rehabilitation.

Standing as it does at the end of a lonely, two-mile footpath through thick woodland, a visit to the *Bridge Inn* is not an undertaking for those of faint heart. I for one however, was not about to let the combined minor distractions of pitchy blackness, hooting owls or eerily rustling undergrowth deter me from a much needed pint at day's end. Eagerly pushing open the door to the taproom, I was returned once again to the world of 1950's black & white Western movies. You know the scene I'm sure – the swing doors open on creaky hinges and the honky-tonk piano falls silent as every stetson turns to face the newly arrived cowboy framed in the doorway.

"Say mister," growls the bar-tender, absent-mindedly polishing a whisky glass, "you're new in town in't ya? Polly, find this hombre a chair…and get him a drink."

Polly, the head dancer from the saloon's burlesque troupe, past the first flush of youth it's true, and outwardly hard as nails but with a brittle heart of gold beneath, does as she's asked, sauntering across to the newcomer with a bottle of hooch in her hand:

"You got business in these parts stranger?" she purrs in velvet tones, "here let me pour you a shot of red-eye, ya look like ya could use it."

It took a Welsh voice from the corner of the pub to break the spell:

"Now *there's* a man who I know for sure is in definite need of beer."

At this, the clatter of dominoes resumed, conversations picked up where they'd left off and the ageing terrier sitting under a bench by the door stopped growling and lowered its scruffy head to the flagstones once more. The comment had come from *Idris*, one of the stable lads that had been present during my earlier ill-fated four-legged exploits and we were invited to sit and join his group. He and his fellows were all students apparently, taking a premature break from their studies to earn some cash by caring for school groups during the summer. The rate of pay wasn't that wonderful they kept reminding us, which is presumably why they were more than happy to allow DT and myself to buy additional rounds of drinks from time to time, and caring for ponies and youngsters it would appear from their insatiable appetite for the local brewery's offerings, is particularly thirsty work.

The Bridge Inn was a somewhat unconventional pub that was for sure, with a surprise or two becoming evident over the course of the evening, including for example a rather easy-going attitude towards the deployment of its serving staff. Looking up from my wallet at the question:

"Yes sir and what can I get you?"

I was much taken aback to discover a ten-year old barman smiling across at me. Whilst his Junior Four contemporaries were tucked up and dreaming of adventures yet to come back at the big house, this lad was busy earning money in his dad's boozer, standing on a beer crate in order to reach the pumps as he filled yet another tray with foaming glasses – truly amazing. But there was yet more still to demonstrate rural middle-England's defiantly casual engagement with several key pillars of UK licensing laws. Remember this was 1980 when rules governing our inflexible opening hours were rigidly enforced. Not for us the giddy, unimaginable luxury of all-day access to alcohol and bonhomie signalling Britain's half-hearted attempts to embrace café-style society - oh dear me no. Instead, partaking of an evening beer was then still a traditionally hectic process during which drinkers would keep conversation to an absolute minimum in order to better focus on jamming down several pints of bitter before an inconsiderate landlord rang the bell for last orders at eleven 'o clock.

At 11:15 the door to the Bridge Inn opened once more and the night staff clocked on, taking their place behind the bar and releasing the youngster from his place on top of the crate. A chorus from around the bar bade the lad farewell as he turned to head off upstairs:

"G'night Billy."

"See you tomorrow Bill, get me the usual ready at about six o'clock eh?"

"Sleep tight young Bill."

And even dad took time out from his noisy game of darts to offer a reminder:

"Just make sure your homework's finished before you turn in Billy, d'you hear me now?"

The beer continued to flow and the boys continued to regale us with all manner of tales and behind-the-scenes snippets from the estate, including the scary revelation that my horse *Trojan* actually had quite a history of disorderly conduct.

"You should count yourself fortunate David," Idris went on, wiping a crescent of froth from his upper lip with the back of his hand, "only last week the big daft bugger threw a teacher from Weston-Super-Mare and we had to stand around half the morning waiting for an ambulance crew. Turned out he'd fractured his pelvis, but he should be up and about again in a month or two. Time we got rid of that horse if you ask me, more trouble than it's worth - probably send it for glue at the end of the season. Anyway *Cheers* to the pair of you and well done to yourself for hanging on today – good man."

At a quarter to midnight a horn sounded outside on the car park and there was a sudden mad scramble to be first in line at the waiting Fish & Chip van. This provided but a momentary distraction from the drinking however, as bags of chips, battered fish and deep-fried sausage were brought back indoors to be consumed alongside the freely flowing ale. It was indeed a long night.

- - o O o - -

And that was why I found myself paddling a canoe through meadows and open countryside, wearing a rictus grin and feeling for all the world as if I'd been recently run over. Teaching is in part a performance art of course, and I'd like to think that my crew was unable to see through the thin veneer of jollity, which had been hastily applied after breakfast. A set of desperately gritted teeth was the means by which I attempted to cope with tribes of mini-squaws and braves singing along to *Row, Row, Row Your Boat* at maximum volume.

On entering a broader stretch of the river, we brought the canoes together in close formation as directed, and a raft was formed by holding on tight to the boats either side. This afforded me a welcome opportunity for recuperation as individuals from the four boat crews were called upon to perform - standing up gingerly as they did to deliver *Heads, Shoulders, Knees and Toes* and enjoy other similarly wobbly mid-river antics. The peace was however, only short-lived and I was soon shaken from my reverie by Robbie our instructor:

"Now then sir, no falling asleep in your boat, because I think it may be your turn to join in very soon now."

I'd had a feeling all morning that such unwelcome attention might well be on the cards at some point during the day, but that didn't make the situation any more welcome. Whilst my carefree grin might have been saying – *no problem, just bring it on*, my eyes were actually pleading - *Dear God Robbie, no, no for pity's sake, no, - just leave me here to fester.*

"What do you say kids? D'you think we should get your teachers taking part as well eh?"

Cue loud cheers of affirmation and encouragement - there would be no way out.

'Ok then," continued Robbie, warming to his task, "first thing then young sirs, is for you two to change places."

David grinned over at me from his place four boats away and the pair of us rose warily to our feet to begin the short but perilous journey. The children were loving every minute of this, immediately starting a chorus of rhythmic clapping to accompany us on our way whilst a pair of Friesian cows on the riverbank displayed only mild curiosity. They'd seen it all before presumably and I'm guessing they also knew just how it would all end. For a little while at least, it was all going so well - after an initial stumble I managed to regain my composure, landing heavily in the neighbouring canoe but steadying myself with an outstretched hand on top of Alexandra Considine's head. Meeting up with my colleague at the mid-point, DT and myself exchanged a brief handshake before continuing with the second leg of our journey. By this time I'd discovered my sea legs and so strode out with misplaced confidence towards the safe berth, which awaited my arrival in the furthermost canoe. Sanctuary was indeed within inches of my grasp for sure, but as I raised one leg to step forward and clamber aboard, Geraldine Pickles let go her grasp on the gunwales of the canoe and pushed it quite deliberately away from the others.

Such wilful, peevish action of course could lead to only one inevitable conclusion and the last thing I saw before hitting the water were the two cows on the bank exchanging a *told you so* shrug before returning disinterested to chewing the cud. The turgid, brown waters immediately blotted out the raucous cheering all around and as my feet settled into the mud of the river bed I felt certain that once again, my previously immaculate Dunlop Green Flash pumps might no longer be fit for purpose.

Things came to a head shortly after this. I waded to the riverbank, there to await the whooping, laughing party paddling across to join me for our midday picnic. Sitting there in the sunshine, I mused that at least the day couldn't possibly get any worse, and then to my amazement I discovered that actually it could. As the lunchtime sandwiches were unpacked from their clingfilm packaging, the conflicting twin aromas of Marmite and peanut butter obviously caught my stomach at a particularly vulnerable moment and left me with no option but to squelch away surreptitiously into the Shropshire undergrowth and vomit silently over a patch of nettles.

- - o O o - -

A hospital visit is obviously an unwelcome addition to any weekend schedule, but to be honest, and without wishing to play down the undoubted distress caused to the individual concerned, one injured child out of a party of twenty-seven isn't all that bad a ratio in my opinion. Given the nature of our few days away I suppose a trip to A&E was always going to be a distinct possibility, especially as the promised *thrills & adventures* had come along pretty thick and fast. Over the course of three exhausting days we'd been required to face up to all manner of potentially hazardous and often quite fearsome engagements, these including: pony trekking – enough said on that one I feel, archery, two types of canoeing, abseiling, liver casserole, raft construction, roller skating and zipwire to name but a few. Oh and not forgetting sailing of course, how could we ever forget sailing?

The morning we were introduced to those cheery little, bright yellow *Optimist* dinghies beside the sailing lake had been particularly windy. This had made it very difficult to catch much of what our instructor was explaining at length about centre boards, starboard tacking, handling sheets, close hauling, gybing or for that matter, how to *come about* without serious incident. Not that the children were paying even the slightest attention anyway as they sat on the grass playing with the straps of one another's life jackets. Eventually they were released onto the waters, one pair of clueless sailors assigned to each boat, as a howling gale wafted them all briskly away from the jetty then skimmed them across the lake only to deposit each hapless vessel around the shoreline like so much abandoned flotsam. Being forcefully run aground without the faintest idea of how to get afloat again caused considerable upset, and to a man the group decided to sit and cry for a few minutes before then taking a unanimous decision to abandon ship. My abiding memory of our sailing session to this day, is the sight of a purple-faced instructor standing up in his boat to scream into the teeth of the wind:

"GET BACK IN YOUR BOATS YOU WHINGEING LITTLE *****!"

His words, scattered as they were across the wilds of Shropshire, went completely unheeded, and a string of whimpering children set off back up to the house where they would spend the remainder of the morning in their dormitories reading comics and eating chocolate.

Our trip to Shrewsbury Infirmary however was not as a result of someone being pierced by a wayward arrow nor thankfully, was it a follow-up to a calamitous fall from the top of the abseiling cliff. Unbelievably, after all we'd gone through, it was an evening's fly-fishing, which had caused the one and only injury of any real significance.

Surely it would have been only the world's most incompetent trout that managed to get itself caught at the hands of Briar Field's band of fishermen after tea. The children obviously hadn't quite grasped the need to exhibit the wily skills of the canny huntsman as they threw stones into the fishing pond and charged around its fringes in their bright orange waterproof jackets, screaming for the Groupies to come and help them disentangle their lines from where the majority were fastened securely amongst the overhanging trees. Jason Armitage was the exception to this pattern, being seemingly the only child to have paid any real attention to the demonstration that had begun the session. His face was a study in concentration and focus as he displayed a real mastery of the rolling cast, dropping his lure with pin-point accuracy at various points across the pond time after time. Whilst he may have avoided lassooing the upper branches of the surrounding elms, neither was he successful in landing a fish, however what he did manage to do after half an hour standing patiently at the water's edge, was to effortlessly bury the fish hook deep into the ball of his thumb – ouch!

Having foreseen the possibility of similar eventualities, it had been decided to bring along my car too for the weekend and so it fell to me to ferry the two boys to the Infirmary. '*Two* boys?' I hear you ask. Ah yes indeed, even though only one child was actually injured, in such situations there would always be two children present – a safeguarding lesson which had been drummed into me by my Teaching Practice Tutor several years earlier:

"Never allow yourself to be placed in a situation which means you will be alone with a child David, as your reasons for doing so may easily be misinterpreted. Always remember," his solemn warning continued, "that the Primary School environment can be an absolute minefield for the unwary male teacher."

So then, there would always be two children present - in the back seat of course. An exception to this rule being if a sick child was being driven home, in which case you would set off from school with three children on the back seat - one of whom would obviously have been issued with an appropriately capacious paper bag and a damp paper towel. This would ensure that on the return leg you still weren't left in a potentially compromising situation.

Only five minutes of our three-hour stay at the Infirmary was actually spent within the confines of a cubicle having Jason's predicament attended to; the remainder of the time passing by painfully slowly for everyone concerned, and not just the lad with the punctured thumb either. An extensive line of locals was queued ahead of us, the majority of whom seemed to require the removal of pitchforks and a host of other assorted agricultural implements from various parts of their anatomy. This meant the boys and myself were required to spend what seemed like days, sitting on sagging canvas chairs in the world's most depressing waiting room. The place was painted in post-war National Health green, its sole concession towards entertainment being a pile of dog-eared magazines from around the same period; top of which I noticed, was a copy of *Practical Householder*, open at an article by Barry Bucknell in which he set about modernising a Victorian bedroom door using a sheet of plywood and a replacement Bakelite door handle.

The only other attraction in the place was a nearby poster pinned to one wall, (Blu Tack obviously hadn't yet made its debut here in rural Shropshire) advertising handy hints to avoid the contraction of Venereal Disease. I really hoped the boys wouldn't pick up on this one and so tried my best to distract them with endless rounds of simple word games – the sort of thing that might be played with mum and dad during long holiday car journeys. They joined in the spirit of this well enough I'm pleased to say, but throughout the time we were playing I half-expected to hear at any moment:

"I spy with my little eye, something beginning with *V... and then D!*"

It was a great relief then when Jason's name was finally called out and the three of us trooped off behind the screen to the waiting nurse.

"And are you the boy's father?"

prompted guffaws of laughter from Jason and his pal before we settled down to business and Nurse Hackett, (I mean come on, to be honest, in her profession you'd just change your name wouldn't you?) examined his hand.

"Ah yes, you've got a fish hook stuck in your thumb young man," being her considered verdict.

Well obviously those years at Nursing College hadn't all been wasted then.

"We'll just numb things up a little," and at this point she emptied the contents of a hypodermic into the top of Jason's thumb to freeze it, "and then you just sit there quietly for a moment while that takes effect."

After a couple of minutes, the lad appeared quite taken by the sensation of having all sense of feeling removed from his hand, as he waved the offending digit about in the air while shouting:

"Heh heh – can't feel my thumb! Can't feel my thumb! Can't feel it at all Mr. Critchley. Go on, pinch it, squeeze it really hard… harder - I can't feel anything look – heh heh!"

This was the cue for Nurse Hackett to make a return appearance, pushing back in briskly through the curtains, before pointing to a space somewhere behind Jason's head to exclaim:

"Look – there's a squirrel at the window."

The lad turned round to look to where she pointed, and was immediately disappointed to discover that not only was there no squirrel to be seen peering in to the cubicle, but neither in fact was there even a window through which the creature might have looked. This distraction, brief though it may have been, was all the time that was needed for Nurse Hackett to stride across the floor, seize hold of the fish hook, and snatch it out of Jason's thumb with a deft and practised ease. A bandage was quickly taped in place and before we knew it, our party was being ushered outside once again, the entire procedure having been completed in the blink of an eye.

- - o O o -

Some time after our return from hospital we all came together as a group once more, this time in a huddle on the lawns outside the big house as David counted heads again for the umpteenth time and reported "all present and correct." We were awaiting the arrival of the Fire Brigade to give the place the *all clear* before being allowed a return to our beds following what was undoubtedly - given the complete absence of smoke and conflagration – a false alarm. As *Blue Watch* would be required to negotiate the winding 'B' roads in the dark all the way from Wem, heaven knows when they'd finally show up. The fire alarm had frightened us all awake and after shepherding the children out onto the dewy grass we'd realised immediately that we were actually one body short of our required total. I'd dashed straight back inside to search for our absentee, showing incredible fortitude I thought, slithering across the tiled floor of the entrance hall towards the staircase whilst mentally composing the banner headline for the front page of tomorrow's *Much Wenlock Gazette* - GALLANT TEACHER BRAVES STATELY HOME INFERNO should do the trick nicely I thought. A strangely repetitive *clumping* sound drew me towards the missing child and rounding the stairs onto the second floor landing I discovered Abigail Potter dragging the world's biggest suitcase down from step to step.

"Abbi what on Earth are you doing, didn't you hear the fire alarm? We need to get out of here as quickly as we can."

"Yes I heard it Mr. Critchley, but this is my Auntie Marian's new luggage and she's off to Tenerife next weekend, so I'd be in big trouble if it got burned. I'm coming as quick as I can."

"Oh I see, and I notice you took the time to pack before setting off!"

"Well I've got some new tops in here as well," was the best the child could offer by means of an explanation, so I grabbed her by the wrist and we hurried off to join the rest.

Doesn't time pass slowly when you're straining to hear the sound of approaching sirens carried on the night air? Reaching to the discreet little button beneath the winder of my brand new Casio digital timepiece, I watched with my usual sense of awe and wonder as the magical, luminous green display came to life and confirmed the time to be 02:47. Liquid Crystal Displays eh, *Tomorrow's World* technology sitting right here on my wrist – truly amazing, whatever will they think of next I wonder? It had been a very, very long day, I was exhausted, the children were exhausted and now already it was Monday.

## CHAPTER NINETEEN – Back to the Future.

"And so what of the future David, any specific thoughts forming on your personal horizon at the moment?"

It was a rainy 1970 lunchtime back in sixth-form days, and I'd wandered into the Careers Room at The Grammar School. As this was at the height of my Led Zeppelin appreciation period, the visit's sole purpose had been to prevent my Rapunzel hairstyle from becoming all lank and unreasonable in the continuing drizzle of the yard. I really hadn't expected to be ambushed by the Careers Master, and being quizzed with regard to my long-term aspirations was certainly not something for which I was in the slightest prepared, having consistently given the wholly troubling notion of *a future* an extremely wide berth.

*Careers Room* was actually a rather tongue-in-cheek soubriquet for a claustrophobic little airless cupboard tucked away behind the library, originally designed as an annexe for silent study away from the main body of the reading area. It still proudly displayed that famous quote by renowned scholar and philosopher Francis Bacon, neatly painted across the door lintel, and which some adolescent wag had recently modified with a felt tip:

*'Reading maketh a full man, conference a ready man, and writing an exact man' – Bacon* ...maketh a fat man!

The tables were scattered with yellowing prospectuses from solid, dependable Universities and... well... nothing else really, that was about it, certainly not the most inspiring of spaces it's true. There was nowhere to sit for example, as all the chairs had been pillaged long ago, carried off to areas of greater need such as the nearby Language Lab or the Sixth Form Common Room. Small wonder then that no one ever lingered long in the place, indeed I was much taken aback to find a member of staff skulking in there during his lunch break, the poor sod must have been bored witless – which is presumably why he pounced so readily on my arrival.

You see, there I've done it again, describing this person as a *Careers Master*, as if it was his saintly vocation in life to leave no stone unturned in a quest to guide bewildered boys towards the much-longed-for destination of *Happy Ever After*. The reality was that over the course of a term, there would be a dozen or more different faces come along to reluctantly shoulder this role. Mind you it won't have been easy for any of them, exchanging the comfortable, nicotine-rich, Gentleman's Club atmosphere of the staffroom for a lonely hour spent in a windowless beige box. I had a vision of them, standing around the teapot as they drew lots each morning to determine who would be forced to endure that day's bout of midday purgatory. There would be hoots of derision as some poor, leather-elbowed old unfortunate shuffled resentfully out of the door clutching a short straw, while his much relieved colleagues settled back down again with copies of *The Sporting Life* and a celebratory packet of Woodbines.

Today's unfortunate incumbent was Mister Masterson, known to one and all of course as *Master Misterson* – oh come on now, loosen up, regress a little, allow yourself to be fifteen again – there, doesn't that deserve a chuckle or two? It probably belongs in the same genre of juvenile wit as the imaginary introduction of Joseph Bates and his parents on arrival in school:

"Good morning Head Teacher, this is Mr. & Mrs. Bates and their son Master Bates."

"Oh really? Well we all need a bit of sport from time to time I always say."

Joseph was actually a lovely lad from Ditton in Widnes, who was required to put up with this mildly humorous routine played out daily by a tireless cast of untidily blazered, acne-ridden comedians during his seven year journey through school. It must have been very difficult to endure similar repeat performances with the good natured stoicism that he always managed to display, so maybe a career in the priesthood would have suited Joe? Anyway, I digress.

Not content with the deep-shouldered shrug that had been my response to his opening question, Mr. Masterson continued to probe more deeply:

"Well have you considered teaching perhaps?"

Whoa, whoa, whoa, wait a minute now, haven't we missed a stage here? I mean just what happened to talk of successful University application and the whole UCAS scenario? Who's been talking behind the staffroom door eh? OK it was true that in future months my 'A' Levels would come and go, much as my GCE's and Eleven Plus had done in years previous, ie with reasonable but limited success, but hey, let's not be presumptuous here Mr. M – give a lad a break eh?

Up until that moment the truthful answer to what he'd just asked would have been most definitely a resounding:

"No."

In much the same way that my response would also have been in the negative had he enquired of me:

"Have you considered a future as a pastry chef?"

or indeed for that matter, any occupation he cared to name – as I simply hadn't given any of this one single moment's thought.

Standing there, in that shabby little room, I rolled his suggestion around my head for all of several seconds before then gratefully adopting the notion as my very own – and so yes… I was indeed going to be a teacher.

OK so that's my future planned out, now what's for lunch?

- - o O o - -

My 'career interview' then, had lasted approximately six minutes in total, and included within this, were several periods of silent confusion as I mentally cast around for an appropriate response of some sort with which to silence my persistent inquisitor. Memories of this less than momentous occasion would return to torment me on an increasingly regular basis, haunting my dreams or keeping me awake and restless during the wee small hours to fuel the troubling doubts which never seemed too far away over my early years of employment. Indeed as we now approached the close of another school year, the self-questioning about the appropriateness and validity of what I was doing seemed to grow yet further still in intensity.

Q. Should I have taken the whole *Careers thing* more seriously all those years ago? – A. Undoubtedly.

Q. Should I have considered other avenues to explore? – A. Probably.

Q. Would I have been good at doing other things? – A. Quite possibly.

Q. Do I really want to morph over the years into a cynical, embittered old fart like Malcolm Molyneux, holding court in a lunchtime staffroom wearing scuffed brogues and a tea-stained tie or worse still, become a dried up prune like May Brennan, actively searching out daily opportunities to humiliate children? – A. Dear God no.

After initially stumbling into this whole teaching business I had now begun to question my desire to spend the next thirty years sitting at a desk each evening like some modern day Sisyphus, marking interminable sets of books - a notion that sparked a bizarre mental calculation to determine the total number of red biros that might be required to complete such a task.

It didn't help my self-belief or sense of purpose either; that friends and family appeared only too ready to suggest that genuine success in life, was only ever really measured against the yardstick of material gain:

"Well Stuart's done well for himself – he's a qualified solicitor you know, now there's a licence to print money if ever I saw one  – solicitors and undertakers - never be out of work I allus say – got himself a new colour telly and wall-to-wall fitted carpets all through - very nice. "

Or even:

"And what about that Lucy over the road – married a dentist – absolutely rolling in it they are - he drives a Daimler, she has a little Mini – not a new one you know but, very nice all the same - they're off to the Greek Islands this summer - Corfu I think – on a plane."

Not once did anyone ever pass a similarly awe-struck comment about members of my profession, and indeed I would wait long and in vain for a comparable gasp of admiration:

"Look across there, it's David - teaches Standard Three you know - by 'eck he's doing well for himself - used to be covered in chalk dust but not any more – got his own wipe-clean board markers now – two of them - sets off each morning carrying his own plastic lunchbox – *Tupperware* too, none of your rubbish."

Small wonder that I would regularly be filled with misgivings about the value of my chosen pathway.

Mind you it's not just the man in the street refusing to graciously acknowledge the worth of the profession that continually unsettled me, it was the fact that even *the great and the good* had never seemed able to resist having a pop at us when the mood suited.

"Those who *can*, do. Those who *can't*, teach."

Oh my word, just hearing this has always been enough to bring my blood effortlessly to the boil. God how I hate that grubby, little head-up-the-arse wholly affected, pretentious piece of claptrap. I can only assume that its author was very badly startled by a stick of chalk during his infancy. One of my favourite middle-of-the-night-fantasies has always been about coming face-to-face with the man in a dark alley some time. In this scenario, I'd grab him by his perfectly groomed snowy white facial hair, (the short bits you know, right above the sideburns beneath the temples where it hurts like hell, just the way Brother Ignatius would do when encouraging my deeper love of Latin conjugation during First Form) and I'd treat him to a thoroughly severe, close-up tongue-lashing. There'd be nothing particularly erudite or overly witty in this instance you understand, instead just a good, old-fashioned, no holds barred, earthy piece of prose, delivered with spitting venom:

"You know what George Bernard Shaw? – You make me really quite bilious with your smug, pious, self-satisfied, cheap-shot little sound bites. How dearly I'd love to take each and every one of your tawdry one-liners, roll them into a ball and push them right up your Pygmailion until those little reptile eyes of yours go *pop*."

Or maybe it's me that's got it wrong after all? Maybe it is a worthless profession, mostly populated by poisonous harpies like May Brennan? Perhaps I should begin looking for other means of employment, but what else would I do?

- - o O o - -

The welcome moment during which I began successfully to dismiss these periods of doubt and despondency once and for all, arrived totally out of the blue – well out of the grey at least - one day at the start of the summer holiday – a new dawn that was heralded in part by PG Tips and Tony Blackburn. I had been spade in hand for an hour or more, attacking the unruly space behind the house that we laughingly referred to as 'the garden.' Plants continued to display considerable reluctance to perform there due presumably to this still being an expanse of impenetrably dense, brown clay, liberally sprinkled throughout with assorted builder's debris and I had already spent countless hours in several fruitless attempts to coax elegance from this sorry swamp. Digging away today however, provided a welcome distraction from pondering the thorny issue of whether or not I actually wanted to return to school when September arrived. From a transistor radio on the back door step, Boney M were warbling away cheerily about the attractions of a "*Holi – holi – day…*" so really I should have been in pretty good spirits, but instead I could feel the dark clouds of melancholy begin to gather once more, and so went off indoors to put the kettle on.

As I'd come to expect, the inner questioning resumed the moment I sat back with my cup of tea, but unusually, for once, this took a rather unexpected tack, which I actually found quite heartening.

Q. Have I been happy in what I've been doing so far? – A. Yes.

Q. Would I change much from the past six years? – A. Well…actually…no I don't think I would as it happens.

Goodness me, positive responses for once, well whoever would have imagined that? As I reached into the biscuit tin for a second, and then a third celebratory Jammie Dodger, Boney M finally stopped singing, ("*hooray… hooray*") and the Nation's favourite, perennially chirpy DJ managed to inadvertently tune in to my increasingly agreeable frame of mind by playing Ian Dury's *Reasons to be Cheerful Part 3*, which I took as a cue to start a *good things* list of my very own. So what's been *good* so far then?

Well – I've established several lasting friendships, which can't be a bad thing.

I've gained the respect of many colleagues and also the two Head Teachers under which I've served.

I had also earned the respect of *most* of the children with whom I'd worked, and had hopefully improved the prospects of many of those children through my teaching.

Perhaps most important of all though, I'd had a great deal of fun in doing all these things.

This wasn't an exhaustive list by any means but just beginning its compilation had left me in a far better frame of mind all of a sudden, and already I was looking forward to making additions to the list from the start of next term. It was really quite pleasing to feel this clarity of understanding re the value of what I was doing, eventually seep through the fibres of the snug-fitting hairshirt of despair, which I'd insisted on wearing on far too many occasions. Finally I was sufficiently confident to believe that whilst the financial reward and conspicuous material acquisition flaunted by some of my peers, will often be accepted by many as the chief indicators of success, these must actually come some way down the list behind the essentially more important considerations of *being happy* and *feeling fulfilled* in what you do. In short then - although this phrase wasn't actually around in the seventies and eighties - I needed to be *happy in my own skin*, and at long last, I had finally begun to feel that I was.

- - o O o - -

So the summer of 1980 proved to be something of a watershed, as perennial self-doubts were dismissed and I took stock of my life, and with the ghosts of inadequacy having successfully been laid, it was time to consider the way forward from this point on. This I realised with some dismay, would require a plan of some sort – a notion with which I wasn't entirely comfortable as it would obviously require me to look to the future, a process at which I was only marginally better now than I had been in the long-ago days of spotty adolescence.

If indeed these early years had truly been the commencement of something resembling a *career*, then there had to be a good deal more to what I did than merely turning up each day to deliver lessons in a reasonably engaging manner. My switching schools had clearly demonstrated just how quickly the daily situation can change and move on, and in years to come the job too would surely have altered beyond all recognition - and hopefully for the better. Amazingly, I found the more I began to look ahead, the more I began to take heart from the whole process.

For example I started to have utopian dreams of a far brighter future, (good lord I was turning into Martin Luther King) in which a teacher's contribution to society would be valued and applauded by all. The workload of teachers everywhere would be manageable and realistic, enabling them to relax in the classroom and enjoy their time there. Children would be happier because of this, and also because they would be freed to develop at their own pace, rather than being hindered by unrealistic targets or bowed under from the burdensome pressure of repeated and unnecessary testing. The opinion of those in schools would be valued to the point at which Head Teachers are left free to make appropriate decisions about what is best for their schools and their children, unencumbered by the poorly-informed intervention of clueless, meddlesome politicians. Funding would never be a problem, as successive governments would surely earmark appropriately generous financial provision right across the education sector, to be spent simply as institutions saw fit.

The result of openly cherishing our young people in this heroically common-sense manner would be the emergence of Great Britain once again as a serious contender on the world stage. Our school leavers would be well-balanced, well-informed, thoroughly able citizens, brilliantly communicative and eager to make their mark in a positive way as key stakeholders in a society that would surely be the envy of every other nation. There would be other advantages too which shouldn't be overlooked. An undoubted windfall benefit of this shift in perception being that as we teachers would therefore in future be recognised as the drivers of this newly successful society, then generous financial reward would surely soon be heading our way. This would enable us to emerge from a life of near-penury, being required instead to adjust to circumstances wherein we too would be able to enjoy the trappings of wealth. The future then, both for the profession and for me as an individual looked decidedly brighter as we prepared to tread a rosy path, lined either side with Daimlers, Mediterranean holidays and top of the range household devices.

I would come over all emotional whenever these Arcadian visions of a much better world arrived to pay one of its regular visits and I also became fiercely determined to ensure I played an active role in the establishment of just such an educational promised land. No longer merely content to be a hard-working foot soldier among the *Poor Bloody Infantry* of the classroom, I looked ahead to the greater challenges of senior management and eventual leadership.

In the medium term, I reckoned I would need new experiences, new mentors and also new pastures as already, even after a relatively short time in post, the walls of Briar Field felt too limited and enclosing, with several of my colleagues and staffroom acquaintances appearing dull and uninspiring to say the least. DT had recognised this too apparently and he was off elsewhere again at the start of next term, leaving me behind in his wake once more. It was too soon for me to start looking at vacant posts for myself, but I decided to let the boss know at the earliest autumnal opportunity that I was in the market for increased responsibility as part of my career development.

All through that summer break then, I rehearsed what I was going to say and in my mind it would be a stirring and impassioned piece of oratory that I would lay before the Head Teacher, leaving her dewy-eyed and emotional; swept away by the all-consuming fire and yearning of my longing for personal betterment. I considered the inclusion of Churchillian elements in this as I promised her "blood, toil, tears and sweat" or possibly even some bits of The Bard as I launched into my Henry V moment.

- - o O o - -

Monday September 1 1980 then, saw me sitting outside The Head's room eagerly awaiting the opportunity to share my vision of the future. A certain Mr. Molyneux managed to interrupt my thought train as he sashayed by along the corridor carrying a tottering pile of as yet unopened exercise books in a range of colours, a new pack of glue spatulas and two cartons of pencils.

"My, my – it hasn't taken you long to finish up on the naughty chair has it sweetcheeks? Tut-tut, indeed, and what was it this time eh, spotted having a quick fag behind the bins were you, or did Miss catch you trying to sneak a peek down the front of her cardie again?"

Oh yes, I thought, definitely time to move on. He wasn't finished either:

"Oh come on flower, there's obviously something troubling your good self, so let it out, share your pain, unburden yourself to Uncle Malcolm why don't you?"

There was of course no way that *Uncle Malcolm*, with his steadfast refusal ever to volunteer for any extra duty or task, no matter how small or seemingly insignificant, together with a regularly-expressed personal motto of "never let the buggers grind you down" would be in any way capable of empathising with my desire for personal betterment. I could just imagine the scenario were I to try and outline the blueprint for development on which I'd been working all summer long. With a wry smile of resignation and a pitying shake of the head, he would lean in close to gently pat the back of my hand before offering advice illustrated with homespun nuggets from the Malcolm Molyneux pamphlet of survival. Like some wily old Fagin encouraging an impressionable young Oliver Twist back into the fold, I would be dissuaded from considering a life of decency and contentment with kindly old Mr. Brownlow, and directed instead, back onto the streets to continue relieving the innocent of silk handkerchiefs and pocket watches.

Thankfully at that moment the office door opened and Mrs. Richardson's arrival spared me any further torment from the man. Her harassed expression however, did suggest that in all honesty, I could probably have chosen a better time for launching this discussion than eight-fifteen on the opening morning of a new school year. She was preceded into the corridor by a character of rather eccentric appearance – apparently a supply teacher - newly arrived in response to a frantic early morning phone call. This woman's somewhat timid expression was teamed with a faded, ankle length floral print dress and a pair of down-at-heel espadrilles. A wide brimmed straw hat hung from the fingers of one hand and in the other she carried a battered guitar case – an unusual vision that was of course guaranteed to prompt a response of some sort from Malcolm:

"Oh my – how very *Laura Ashley*. Looks as if the agency has loaned us Maria Von Trapp for the day."

This resulted in the sort of threatening glare from The Boss that soon had him scurrying away in the direction of his classroom to continue sharpening pencils.

The door closed behind me and I took to the corner seat in readiness for my big moment, however before I could launch into my well-rehearsed oration, the phone rang and The Head's attention was taken elsewhere, thus providing opportunity for a further fine-tune of what I was about to present. The intention was to begin with a general overview, setting my goals and aspirations into context before moving on to indicate how this level of ambition would surely benefit school in the short-term. I would be upfront about my desire to move on to new surroundings when an appropriate opportunity arose, but would also be at pains to offer reassurance of absolute and complete loyalty to my current situation until that point in time. I would ask for her considered opinion and advice regarding the best way to further my career choices and we'd probably finish the meeting off with tea and biscuits as we chatted away together casually, rather in the manner of fellow professionals kicking around issues from the world of education.

"Bloody hell – what a day this is turning out to be,"

was the surprising comment as the receiver was replaced rather more forcefully than was usual. It was the first time I'd heard The Head use an expletive of any sort and I was encouraged by this – obviously she was already beginning to see me as a peer and equal - two fellow educators sharing a moment of professional intimacy.

"That was the Local Authority auditors, they're coming in later to check on the accounts and run an eye over our procedures for managing school fund. The children haven't even set foot in their new classes yet and all hell's breaking loose."

Looking ahead to the time when I would be Head Teacher myself, I knew already that such visits would hold no fear. My faultlessly completed double entry book keeping system would be ready and waiting for even the most diligent of inspections, every last penny of the public purse entrusted into my care being meticulously accounted for in a set of immaculate ledgers on the office bookshelf.

"I noticed a supply teacher earlier," I began, looking to share the burden of management, "is there an absence…"

"Yes," she interrupted, "we needed someone to cover Class Two. Jeanette Pumphrey was on her way in this morning when her waters broke as she changed gear on the roundabout beside the Co-op. She's a month early so let's hope that woman we've been sent is up to the job, as you know what a handful Class Two can be."

"Indeed," I offered, "isn't that the class with Kieran Palmer?"

"That's right – *Klepto Kieran*, the thieving little sod. I've told his mother I'm having no more of his light-fingered antics this term. Last year he'd siphoned off enough pencils and stationery to undermine the future of W.H. Smith. He was even taking advance orders and helping himself to the contents of the stock room during wet playtimes. Anyway, time's getting on, what was it you needed to speak to me about David?"

This was it, my moment was arrived at last. There were no nerves apparent on my part, just a quiet confidence about the quality of my presentation, borne out of extensive, regular rehearsals in front of anyone who could be persuaded to listen throughout August. Here goes:

"Well I was actually looking to perhaps take on some extra responsibility this year, because you see…"

"Oh that's brilliant news," she cut in immediately, "couldn't have come at a better time either with the other David having just left us."

Whilst being grateful that she seemed receptive to the notion of my increased involvement, I couldn't help but think this meeting wasn't really progressing entirely in the manner I'd foreseen over recent weeks. In fact as I felt a guiding hand in the small of my back begin to propel me back towards the door once again, the realisation began to dawn that I was in fact experiencing yet another Mister Masterson moment.

"I'll announce in tonight's staff meeting that you'll be taking over responsibility for PE then, and when Mr. Lawrence is in later today I'll send him over for a little chat. Now then, I really must get on – exciting times ahead eh David?"

The door closed behind me with a *click* and my sense of the surreal was compounded as Malcolm approached once more, this time carrying a new roll of Fablon. *The Sound of Music* was obviously still on his mind as he waltzed along the corridor, treating everyone within earshot to extracts from the show. Drawing level with myself, he paused to tuck the roll under one arm, joined his hands together as if in prayer and offered me an expression of mock piety before launching into his interpretation of the Mother Abbess classic: *Climb Ev'ry Mountain.* There was a knowing look and a smile whilst lingering over the lines about *following rainbows until I might be able to find my dream,* before he was gone once more, loudly humming the refrain and deftly twirling his roll of sticky-backed plastic in mid-air.

What a lovely singing voice he has, I thought to myself, watching him skip away in the direction of the staff room. Anyway, enough of this hanging around, onwards and upwards as they say, onwards and upwards

Printed in Poland
by Amazon Fulfillment
Poland Sp. z o.o., Wrocław